REV. CHARLES NERINCKX, Founder.

LORETTO

ANNALS OF THE CENTURY

BY

ANNA C. MINOGUE

Author of CARDOME : A ROMANCE OF KENTUCKY

BORROWED FROM THE NIGHT

THE WATERS OF CONTRADICTION

With an Introduction by the

MOST REV. JOHN J. GLENNON, D. D.

ARCHBISHOP OF ST. LOUIS

NEW YORK

THE AMERICA PRESS

1912

NIHIL OBSTAT

REMIGIUS LAFORT, S.T.L.,

Censor Deputatus

IMPRIMATUR

✠ JOHN CARDINAL FARLEY

Archbishop of New York

March 12, 1912

IMPRIMATUR

✠ CAMILLUS PAULUS MAES

Ep'us Covintonen.

Die 26a Februarii, 1912

TO
THE REVEREND CHARLES NERINCKX,
WHOSE APOSTOLIC LABORS IN
KENTUCKY
WERE CROWNED BY THE ESTABLISHMENT
OF THE LORETTINE SOCIETY;
TO THE FOUNDERS,
MARY RHODES, CHRISTINA STUART, NANCY HAVERN
AND THEIR COMPANIONS;
TO THE EQUALLY VALIANT WOMEN WHO,
IN THE YEARS SUCCEEDING,
HAVE FED, BY THE CONSECRATION OF THEIR LIVES,
LORETTO'S HOLY FLAME,
THIS BOOK
IS DEDICATED
BY
THE AUTHOR.

INTRODUCTION.

A word is asked of me to serve as a prelude to the story beautiful which follows. This should be an easy task; for, as a prelude introducing a song that is to be sung adopts from the song itself its spirit and its motif, so in our case it will be only necessary to point the way to "Old Kentucky," and tell you that there one hundred years ago the order of the Sisters of Loretto was founded.

There, by the running brooks, amid forest trees, with the cedars and the stars as sentinels of their vigils, they set up the symbol of sacrifice, rude and crude as became the frontier; but, for those who stood beneath it, henceforth the Holy Rood. There was formed the Society of the "Sisters of Loretto at the Foot of the Cross."

These were pioneer days: not as yet, though Boone had blazed the way westward, had the fires died by the wigwams of the savage: not as yet were hushed the wild voices of the forest. The log cabin was the castle where lived the hunter's wife, while the master himself went forth to the freedom of the forest and the limitless savannah.

And yet the scene and times were not without their inspiration. It was typically American, with the flavor of the frontier. They who came together there to chant their Song of Faith, to form with God's benediction the first American Sisterhood, had undoubtedly all that splendid enthusiasm, that self-sacrifice, that high resolve, which the faith at the frontier is sure to inspire in noble souls. There were united the pure Catholic strain with the generous American spirit, which has ever since distinguished the Order of Loretto. We of the West know what this American Catholicity means; we know that it stands for hatred of sham, purity of heart, gentleness of manners, loyalty to Church, consecration of life.

v

INTRODUCTION.

We owe much to the Catholicity of Kentucky, and we hold the brightest blossoming of it began when Father Nerinckx summoned his spiritual daughters to dedicate their lives to Jesus and His Sorrowing Mother.

We see in their wondrous development since then an evidence of their zeal then, of that vital faith and passion for sacrifice which distinguished the founders, and which remains with all the daughters of Loretto, at once their heritage and their protection.

In every western diocese to-day there are Catholics proud to claim Kentucky as their mother State, and the Kentucky Catholic, wherever he may go, yields to none in his tenaciously holding and loyally defending the Faith of his Fathers. And equally so, practically every western diocese boasts of one or more houses of the Loretto Sisterhood, which it undoubtedly cherishes as among its most helpful Sisterhoods.

A teaching Order in the beginning, it has remained true to its first love—its primary purpose. It is still at the frontier, where the battle of Christ is being fought—that greatest battle of modern times, where the prizes are the souls of children. The future of civilization and humanity is largely dependent on the outcome.

On your centennial our greetings go to you, the Sisters of Loretto. We gave back to you from Missouri the ashes of your Founder, but we want to retain his spirit and yours.

✠ JOHN J. GLENNON,
Archbishop of St. Louis.

St. Louis, Mo.,
   March 7, 1912.

INTRODUCTION.

The Institution of the Sisters of Loretto at the Foot of the Cross was founded in Kentucky one hundred years ago by the pioneer missionary, Father Nerinckx. The history of his life and labors is known, and his good judgment and prophetic eye are seen in the result of his work. He left his footprints wherever he walked, and they have not been blotted out. He was long alone in this great State with the exception of a single companion, Father Badin, who labored with him in the wilderness in the battle for souls. The heroes sleep; their work endures. The volume here presented gives an account of the work of Father Nerinckx, particularly as regards the foundation of the community of the Sisters of Loretto. The early records of this Institution are a treasured memory of which little is left but the twilight. Who could then have imagined that Loretto ever would become what it is now? Tradition mainly tells the story of its humble beginning; the historian tells what the Institution has accomplished. One hundred years have passed, and the Institution has grown from the grain of mustard seed into a great tree, whose branches now extend far beyond the spot where the corner-stone was laid. The ashes of the Founder rest in the shadow of the convent he established, and the heart of Father Badin, his companion in labor, privation, and toil, watches near by, where a relic is enshrined in the monument which pious hands have erected to his memory. Those who read this centenary volume will learn much of the history of Loretto from the story that its pages tell.

✠ D. O'DONAGHUE,
Bishop of Louisville.

vii

FOREWORD.

IN offering this history of the centenary of their Society
to the Sisters of Loretto I should be ungrateful indeed
if I failed to acknowledge my great debt to their Superior-
General, the Reverend Mother Praxedes Carty, who placed
at my disposal such records as were necessary, aided me by
her advice and encouragement, spared herself no pains, in
short, that I might perform my allotted task with ease.

It may appear singular to these spiritual daughters of
hers that the glorious part performed by their present
Mother-General is all but missing from this volume. If
the last chapters lack the interest that inheres to the story
during the closing years of Loretto's century, the cause is
not attributable to inappreciation or want of knowledge of
it on my part, but to the humility of her who has achieved
so much for her beloved Society. If, however, in the
proper place I was denied the privilege of paying just
tribute to her worth, I claim the right to say here on a
page she shall not see until the printed book is in her hands;
and in claiming it I know every Sister of Loretto sanctions
my act, that, beginning with that memorable December day
in 1812 when Mother Ann Rhodes laid down her briefly
held rein of authority in the cabin-convent of Hardin's
Creek, the glory that illumines each radiant figure in that
long line of great, loyal and self-sacrificing women finds
its brightest culmination in her who now rules the destinies
of her beloved Loretto.

In New Mexico, where her noviceship and first years of
professed religious life were spent, her name is held in
benediction; Florissant knew her as a prudent Superior,
and Loretto Heights rightly regards her as her savior.
Called to the office of Mother-General at a solemn hour of
the Society's existence, she proved anew the wisdom of

FOREWORD.

Loretto's God-directed choice, in providing it with a Superior capable of leading it out of every difficulty and bringing it to this auspicious day, crowned with richest blessing. What her hand found to do, she did; and lowly the task or mighty, one purpose ran through all: God's honor and glory, the salvation of souls!

I also gratefully acknowledge the kind assistance rendered by the Reverend Edwin Drury, Chaplain of the Mother House; likewise by Sister Mary Antonella, whose tireless research rescued many an interesting fragment of history and whose loving interest in the progress of the work never flagged.

As all must who write of Kentucky of the days of the pioneers, I am indebted to the admirable "Life of Reverend Charles Nerinckx," by the Right Reverend Camillus Paul Maes, D.D., Bishop of Covington; "Sketches of the Early Catholic Missions in Kentucky," by the Most Reverend Martin John Spalding, D.D.; "The Centenary of Catholicity in Kentucky," by the Honorable Benjamin J. Webb; also to "Soldiers of the Cross," by Most Reverend J. B. Salpointe, D.D.; "The Catholic School System of the United States," by the Reverend J. A. Burns, C.S.C., Ph.D., and to the Sister annalists of the various houses of the Society.

That this history of Loretto's century of existence falls far below what its readers, from the theme and the occasion, have a right to expect, I am most painfully aware. There are circumstances which might be offered in excuse; but I prefer not to renew old acquaintances and begin new ones with an apology for my word of greeting. To temper a too severe criticism, however, I would plead that had my time and my ability been the equal of my love and veneration, then should I have laid at Loretto's feet on this day of her centennial a gift worthy even of her acceptance.

ANNA C. MINOGUE.

Dinmore Park, Latonia, Kentucky.

ILLUSTRATIONS.

TABLE OF CONTENTS.

xi

TABLE OF CONTENTS.

CHAPTER I.

EARLY MISSIONS OF KENTUCKY.

THE lure of the West has been felt by man in all ages. It matters not what the object of his quest may be, the land of the setting sun draws on, nor is any danger deemed too great, any obstacle insurmountable, when he goes forth to answer that unaccountable call. Whether it is true or not, as legend has it, that the Redeemer on the Cross faced to the west, from time to time adventurous spirits providentially directed have led the race into undreamed of possessions, bearing aloft the torch of Faith as they followed the sun in its course. A trivial event may sometimes point the way to great achievements, or causes that shake empires and bar the progress of civilization may contribute to form characters destined for new fields and greater enterprises. When the French Revolution forbade religion, it awakened apostles to the divine call to spend their lives and be spent in moulding the destiny of the western world.

Because he could not forswear his conscience and promise allegiance to the government Napoleon had set up in place of the throne, a Belgian priest, no longer in the first flush of manhood, found himself deprived of his office and his livelihood, his liberty dependent upon his ability to find cover, his very life imperiled. The experience was soul-harrowing, but it brought the enlargement required to transform the simple parish priest into an apostle lifted up to the desire for the world-wide establishment of the Kingdom of Christ. The contentment that had marked his days as he passed among his people, guarding their faith, and cultivating the truths of religion in the minds of their children, was gone. In his ears had sounded the call of the

1

loftier emprise, which all who hear must obey or be thereafter the most wretched of men. From the realm of the West it came, and the response was swift and royal. Without thought of self or fear of the future, Father Charles Nerinckx sailed for the American shore.

Before proceeding farther in a narrative which a poet might weave into an epic let us acquaint ourselves with the earlier history of this remarkable man. Like many who have accomplished the great works of the world, Father Nerinckx was sprung from the middle class of people. His father, Sebastian Nerinckx, belonged to a respectable family, and was a physician by profession; his mother, Petronilla Langendries, possessed the virtues and qualifications that distinguish true Christian womanhood. Of their union, Father Nerinckx was born on October 2, 1761, at Herffelingen, in Brabant, Belgium, being the eldest of fourteen children. With the parental generosity that has made Belgium the nursery of religion, they gave three sons and three daughters to the service of God.

In 1762 Dr. Nerinckx, with the view of enlarging his field of practice and giving his children more educational advantages, moved to Ninove, province of East Flanders, and there Charles began his primary studies at the age of six years; later he passed to the College of Enghien, to Gheel in 1774, and completed his course of Philosophy at the Catholic University of Louvain. Having then determined to study for the priesthood, he entered the Seminary of Mechlin in 1781. He was ordained priest, November 4, 1785.

Divine grace had not been impeded in its workings in this chosen soul, and he appeared before his superiors as one to whom could be entrusted duties that ordinarily call for the test of experience. He was appointed vicar of the Metropolitan parish of St. Rumold, Mechlin, and in the discharge of his office early proved himself the ideal pastor of souls. The needs of the poor made special appeal to his priestly zeal, and they, recognizing his understanding love, were quick to respond to his efforts for their spiritual advancement. He possessed a well-balanced character, and if he gave himself completely to his pastoral work while it engaged him, he never forgot that to be able to aid others one must have strength oneself. His own advancement was never neglected, and he grew daily in piety and knowledge.

His worth was not unappreciated by the Archbishop of Mechlin, and when the important parish of Everberg-Meerbeke became vacant by the death of its pastor, Father Nerinckx, although then but thirty-three years of age, was promoted to its charge. He found difficulties awaiting him in his new field of endeavor, the most obstinate being the apathy of the people toward their religious duties. To one so greatly in earnest, so deeply imbued with a sense of the gravity of life, and the necessity of making every moment of it count for eternity, such a condition brings the most painful anxiety, especially when to those sentiments is added, as was the case of Father Nerinckx, an acute realization of his responsibility as shepherd of his flock. But the Divine Guidance soon brought him to the mastership of the unhappy situation. A little child shall lead them, it has been promised, and Father Nerinckx saw its fulfilment in Everberg-Meerbeke, as afterward on the Kentucky frontier.

He sought out the children, and, winning their love and obedience, it was not long until their elders followed them to the good priest's side. In the brief period of three years he had wrought so complete a change that the mighty wave of irreligion which had swept northward with the victorious armies of the French Revolutionists was ineffectual in its attempts to engulf the inhabitants of that town. They opposed a barrier to the devastations of the Prince of this world, and his emissaries, knowing well the source from which they drew their power of resistance, directed their

3

efforts against Father Nerinckx. Their opportunity came when, refusing to take the oath demanded by the Government, and which would have been a violation of his conscience, he continued to officiate in his office of pastor. His arrest was ordered, but, by the vigilance of his people, he was able to make his escape.

Disguised as a peasant, Father Nerinckx left his parish and, reaching Dendermonde, August 6, 1797, was received at the Hospital of St. Blase, of which institution his aunt, Mother Constantia Langendries, was superior. But his continued safety depended solely on his caution. For months he lived in the attic of the hospital, not daring to stir abroad until the darkness of night had set in. Yet amid such conditions he found God's work to be done. The Sisters and their hospital had been spared because their services were required by the Government, and to these devoted women, deprived of their chaplain by the same enmity which had made their guest a fugitive, the presence of Father Nerinckx was as an assurance from on high that they were not utterly forsaken. There were also the patients to be ministered to, and the prisoners condemned to death for defending their country. These the heroic priest visited in the dead of night, consoling them with religious rites, preparing them for their last end.

Thus passed four years. In the meantime, in the heart of the hunted priest a change was going on. The conditions imposed on the clergy by the French Government were to him, and many other pious priests, impossible. He was offered again his parish at Everberg-Meerbeke, but he declined it, feeling that in the existing state of affairs all effort of his would be useless. His zealous activity called for free scope, nor could he endure seeing God's work hedged in and trammelled by its enemies. In another portion of the world there were souls to be saved, yea, crying for salvation, and they now became the objects of his solicitous thoughts. The Western world called for him, and if his response was generous in his ignorance of what life meant there for the missionary, it never was regretted when knowledge, the fullest and the bitterest, was his measure. He applied to Bishop Carroll for admission to the Diocese of Baltimore, and when he came and that sorely burdened prelate assigned him to the Kentucky mission, he accepted the charge in holy joy.

There is not any record left us of what the word Kentucky meant to the Belgian stranger as he received his appointment from the lips of his bishop, and as he set forth for the hospitable Jesuit college in Georgetown, in the District of Columbia, to perfect himself in the English tongue, he little dreamed what a light his coming was to spread over that fair land, how precious a heritage he was destined to leave to it, how inseparably entwined was to be his name with its history. He learned to love it well, too. His brave old heart, that could sever freely the ties that bound him to the land of his nativity, broke when he was driven from Kentucky, to find, as had poor Daniel Boone before him, a refuge for his hoary head in generous Missouri, and we are fain to believe that both gallant pioneers slept better when kindly hands gave back their ashes to their adopted mother's keeping.

At the time Father Nerinckx reached the American shore (1804) some thirty-five years had elapsed since Boone had left his "peaceable habitation" on the Yadkin, as he has handed the description of his North Carolina home down to us, to take up his dwelling in Kentucky. The way he blazed through the forests had been widened by the civilization that had poured after him, and the beautiful land that none of the Indian tribes had ever been able to lay claim to, and over which all had fiercely contested from earliest traditional days, became the possession of the white man. Kentucky kept herself for the superior race, and it is the generally accepted opinion that that portion of it inhabiting her is in some indefinable way the superior of the

5

remainder. Boone's immediate followers, hailing largely from Virginia, established themselves in the rich Bluegrass Belt; they were the settlers who fought the Indians in their last battles for their favorite hunting ground, and coming out victorious, began to build the foundations of the State. It was not until 1785 that the Maryland Colonists began to arrive, and they took up their abode in what is now Nelson, Washington and Marion Counties. Webb, in his "Centenary of Catholicity in Kentucky," questioning why these Maryland Catholics should pass by the fertile level lands for the less favored district, suggests that Divine Providence withheld the material wealth the more worldly wise Virginian gained that they might seek and obtain the higher spiritual good, and, as if to illustrate the contention, afterward relates the sad fate that befell the little Catholic colony which abandoned its journey to Pottinger's Creek for a more promising home in Scott County. We must also remember that the Reformation ploughed a bloody line between Englishmen, and the mutual hatred of Catholic and Protestant was carried by them across the sea; and we can readily believe that the descendants of the followers of Lord Baltimore would find themselves ranging as far as they prudently could on the frontier from the descendants of the founders of Jamestown.

Through many perils and hardships, and attended by we know not what weariness of body and loneliness of soul, the Maryland colonists drove on until their new home on Pottinger's Creek was reached. Then began a life of which not the most fervid imagination can form an accurate conception. No child of Kentucky but is familiar with the history of the days of the pioneers. We know of the lordly trees felled for the construction of the cabin, the chimney built of mud and wattles, the earthern floor, and the loopholes for its defense against the wild beast and the Indian; of the stockades; of the perilous labors in the field, where the musket was carried along with the hoe; of the rude fare

6

so hardly gained; of the rough apparel secured by such toil: all this and more we have been taught of the struggle made by those heroic men and women to plant civilization on the Western frontier. But only outlines has the most industrious historian given us of that period of travail, out of which a great and glorious Commonwealth was born. Some figures stand out splendidly on the canvas of that time; some incidents are revealed that shall command love and veneration while valorous deeds and acts of honor shall appeal to the souls of men. But who shall ever know of the hidden heroes who shall unfold from the silence of the past the lost stories of their lives? Who shall tell us of the toil of the men, the suffering of the women, the repression of pathetic childhood, experienced by the dwellers of those first rude habitations of Kentucky, whether amid her mountain fastness, the ample reaches of her Bluegrass Belt, or the picturesque hills and long, sequestered valleys of her Maryland District! Sacred for us should be the spot that held one of those poor cabins, and more beautiful in our eyes than the shafts of marble that mark the last resting-place of our latest born to fame, should be some poor slab, crumbling to decay, that points to us where one of those unknown heroes sleeps.

The Maryland pioneer brought with him something that but few of his brothers of the Bluegrass Belt possessed, that Faith which, reaching back unbroken through the centuries, bound him by cords of gold to the Manger in the stable of Bethlehem where the Lord of the world first opened His eyes upon the earth He had come to redeem. The treasured knowledge of that poverty made this easier to bear, the loneliness of that Heart, cast out by His own, made more endurable the austere solitude with which Nature enfolded them. The practice of a religion handed down through the generations gave them an invincible armor, and in a conflict where others, perchance, had ultimately been routed, they held out valiantly, until home and church and school were permanently established in this portion of Kentucky.

It is not at all surprising that the first priest in Kentucky was an Irishman, and the Franciscan, Father Charles Whelan, in penetrating the wilderness in 1787 to minister to the Colonists of Pottinger's Creek, was but exemplifying the apostolic spirit of his native land. Another Irishman, Father William de Rohan, his immediate successor, built the first Catholic church within the confines of the State. It was dedicated to the Holy Cross, and, like the home surroundings, it was of logs, covered with rough clapboards, and a block of wood served for an altar. But shortly after the erection of their church, the faithful settlers were again deprived of the services of a priest, Father Whelan having retired from the field and Father de Rohan discontinuing his ministrations by the order of Bishop Carroll.

For some three years this sad condition remained, though the number of colonists was increasing; then came a priest whose name leads all others in the missions of the frontier, and whose right is unquestioned to the title of the Apostle of Kentucky. Father Theodore Badin was another of the priceless gifts which the French Revolution bestowed upon the Church in the New World. Coming to America as a cleric, he was ordained by Bishop Carroll, May 25, 1793, being the first priest to receive ordination within the limits of the first thirteen of the United States. In the autumn of the same year he was sent, with the Rev. Father Barrières, a French exile like himself, to take charge of the scattered Catholics of Kentucky. They entered the State at the point where now stands the flourishing city of Maysville; and among the owners of the few log cabins they found several Irish Catholics. Thence they journeyed to Lexington, which they reached on Sunday. After celebrating Mass, they continued their way to White Sulphur, and on the same day broke the Bread of Life for the Catholics of that settlement. Then the two missionaries separated, Father Barrières going to Pottinger's Creek and Father Badin remaining at White Sulphur. The conditions confronting him being so unlike those to which he had been accustomed, and feeling, perhaps, he was too advanced in years to hope to accommodate himself to them, Father Barrières after four months abandoned Kentucky for New Orleans, leaving Father Badin alone in a field that embraced almost the entire Middle West. He foresaw the labors his mission as a priest must demand of him in this sparsely settled country, and if he measured his human strength and endurance against it, he would have followed his compatriot to a work not seemingly so impossible. But that was not the pitch of Father Badin's faith. With God he could accomplish an apparently superhuman task, and he continued alone in his ministry. He took up his residence near Holy Cross, and from that point set forth on his visitation of the various settlements and isolated Catholic families.

After some three years he was joined by the zealous and indefatigable Father Fournier, and a little later their number was increased by the coming of Rev. Anthony Salmon, whose brief ministry in Kentucky, beginning in February, 1799, ended tragically on November 9 of the same year, when he met his death by being thrown from his horse while on his way to keep an appointment with a Protestant whom he was instructing and preparing for baptism. Father Badin's next assistant was the Rev. John Thayer, a convert from Congregationalism, of which creed he had been a minister. He was the first native American priest to work in Kentucky, where he remained until 1803. This year found Father Badin again alone, for in the little churchyard at Holy Cross brave and valiant Father Fournier slept by the side of Father Salmon. Like the latter, his death was accidental, he having been crushed by the falling of a log which he was cutting with a whipsaw. The death of his two companions pierced the heart of Father Badin. The loneliness of his life began to weigh heavily upon him, while the immensity of his labors filled him with poignant concern. The population was increasing. On the tide of immigration sweeping into the new country were many Catholics who would be lost to the Church, and the same destiny might reasonably be predicted for the offspring of the earlier settler, since in the vast territory of the Middle West there were but two priests besides himself, Rev. Donatien Olivier, at Prairie du Rocher, in Illinois, and Rev. Gabriel Richard, at Detroit, Michigan. The cry of his distressed soul was borne to his spiritual father, and added to the misery of that most apostolic bishop. But in this crucial hour for the harassed Prelate and the lonely priest Divine Providence intervened and gave Father Nerinckx to the American Mission.

CHAPTER II.

FATHER NERINCKX' LABORS.

THE bishop's relegation of him to the Jesuit college at
Georgetown, for the purpose of studying the English
language, was obediently accepted by Father Nerinckx; but
as time passed, and an opportunity of traveling companions
in a community of Trappist monks who had decided to locate in Kentucky presented itself, he importuned Dr. Carroll to be allowed to depart for his mission. The request
was granted, and Father Nerinckx started for Kentucky.
As the Trappists traveled too leisurely for him, he parted
company with them, and alone traversed Ohio and Kentucky, reaching St. Stephen's, Marion County, on the 18th
of July, 1805. Father Badin welcomed him with open arms
and bade him to consider St. Stephen's Farm as his home.
For seven blessed years their companionship lasted, and
when Father Badin, also an exile from the land that he
loved, lay down to die, his will was that his heart, encased
in a crystal, should be carried to Loretto and buried by the
side of his well-loved Father Nerinckx.

That Father Nerinckx was a man far in advance of his
time, the works that he accomplished and those in which he
failed amply prove. Hardly could an ordinary mind have
grown familiar with the situation which he found in Kentucky when he was grasping conditions of a distant future
and planning to meet them. He would establish here a
missionary centre, and from it would go forth priests to
scatter far and near the seeds of the Gospel, and the nucleus
of that band would be men of his own nationality, who, denied their calling at home, were eager to follow him to
the New World. He knew their zeal, their learning, their

11

spirit of self-sacrifice, and the love it had thus early aroused in him, made him ardently desire to secure these ministers for Kentucky. Well may we lament the frustration of that magnificent scheme. We find to-day the descendants of those Catholic pioneers and later immigrants, whose forefathers bedewed English and Irish soil with martyr blood, we find them filling the pulpits of Protestant churches, for congregations many of whose members share a like lineage of Catholicism. We see the mountainous district still in a condition of ignorance and irreligion that is a disgrace to a civilized State, and in a population of about two million three hundred thousand count but some one hundred and fifty thousand of our Faith. How differently would the history of Kentucky, and especially that part referring to the growth of religion and the progress of education, read had Father Nerinckx been able to accomplish his broad design!

A seer he was, but no visionary . He realized on what an ample foundation the Church here should be laid, but he did not stand in idleness awaiting its beginning, nor expend his energy in seeking that inauguration. He laid his plan before his superior, and then turned himself to the work at hand. While he dreamed of the splendid structure religion might see raised to her service in this fair country, he felled trees and hewed logs for her first temples, and praised God when he had one of these rude places of worship for his people. While he pictured the regeneration that was to come to this neglected land when priests with his own zeal should be scattered plentifully among its inhabitants, he rode from settlement to settlement, teaching, preaching, administering the Sacraments, celebrating the august Sacrifice, and rejoicing in the spiritual fruits he was garnering. While he reveled in imagination on the comfort and happiness that would be his to meet and dwell among those cherished friends of happier times, he cheerfully shared the log hut with a poor parishioner when on his missions,

OLD LORETTO (engraved in Belgium, 1816).

(A) The Monastery and Chapel. (B) School for Orphans. (C) Kitchen and Refectory. (D) Garden. (E) Servants' and Smoke House. (F) House for Guests and the Sick. (G) Confessor's House. (H) Kitchen. (J) Stables. (K) Gate to the Road.

or dwelt contentedly in the scarcely better appointed parochial residence at St. Stephen's.

A year after his coming, Father Badin gave Father Nerinckx the property which had been purchased by Father Fournier on Rolling Fork. Here Father Nerinckx began the erection of his first church, which he placed under the protection of the Blessed Virgin Mary. The cornerstone of the church was laid by him November 15, 1805, and in a letter to his parents he announces his intention of building three rooms to the church for those "good Flemish priests" he was expecting. In this church he placed the statue of Our Lady which he had brought with him from Belgium, and he relates that the appearance of the new shrine made such an appeal to a young lady convert, who gained her living by her handiwork, that she gave a fine linen alb, the material of which she had bought for a new dress. Thus was the first altar society established in Kentucky, and its foundation stone was sacrifice and personal service.

In the following year, 1806, he built the church of St. Charles. It was of logs and had attached to it a room for himself during his visits. His manner of securing material for these and the other churches he erected was unique. He obtained from the members of the congregation the donation of the logs, and when these had been all delivered the men assembled and, assisted by Father Nerinckx, whose physical strength was a marvel even among those hardy pioneers, set them in place. The work of "house raising" required about two days. To the missionary there came about this time a small donation of money from Belgium. Part of this he invested in a bell for his church of St. Charles. It was probably the first church bell in Kentucky, and is now carefully treasured among his other relics at Loretto. His love for the adornment of the house of God was pronounced. Accustomed from his infancy to the richness and beauty of the venerable shrines of his native

13

land, the utter want of attractiveness in his poor churches in Kentucky was one of the many crosses he had to bear. But where another would have yielded to seemingly inexorable conditions, Father Nerinckx sought a remedy. With the aid of the children, he fashioned an altar and a pulpit, using the various native woods for the purpose. At Loretto this altar also is preserved, and its design and workmanship continue to awaken admiration.

Up to the year 1812 Father Nerinckx had built seven churches and exercised his ministry wherever it was known to him a Catholic was to be found. Mounted on his good horse, Printer, he soon grew familiar with the long trails, and fashioned new ones as from far portions of the State came the call for ministrations of the priest. Fayette, Bourbon, Scott and Woodford Counties we know were visited by him, as were Louisville and other settlements in the western part. Writing of his work and endurance, Archbishop Spalding, in his "Sketches of Kentucky," says:

"Father Nerinckx' courage was unequaled. He feared no difficulties and was appalled by no dangers. Through rain and storms; through snow and ice; over roads rendered almost impassable by the mud; over streams swollen by the rains, or frozen by the cold; by day and by night, in winter and summer, he might be seen traversing all parts of Kentucky in the discharge of his laborious duties. Far from shunning, he seemed even to seek hardships and dangers.

"He crossed wilderness districts, swam rivers, slept in the woods among the wild beasts, and, while undergoing all this, he was in the habit of fasting and of voluntarily mortifying himself in many other ways. His courage and vigor seemed to increase with the labors and privations he had to endure. As his courage, so neither did his cheerfulness ever abandon his. He seldom laughed, or even smiled; but there was withal an air of contentment and cheerfulness about him which greatly qualified the natural austerity of his countenance and manners. He could, like the great

14

Apostle, make himself 'all to all, to gain all to Christ.' He appeared even more at home in the cabin of the humblest citizen, or in the hut of the poor negro, than in the more pretentious mansions of the wealthy.

"He was averse to giving trouble to others, especially to the poor. Often, when he arrived at a house in the night, he attended to his own horse, and took brief repose in the stable or in some outhouse; and when the inmates of the house arose next morning they frequently perceived him already up and saying his office, or making his meditation. He made it an invariable rule never to miss an appointment whenever it was at all possible to keep it. He often arrived at a distant station early in the morning, after having ridden all the previous night. On these occasions he heard confessions, gave instructions, and said Mass for the people generally after noon; and he seldom broke his fast until three or four o'clock in the evening.

"In swimming rivers he was often exposed to great danger. Once, in going to visit a sick person, he came to a stream which his companion knew to be impassable. Mr. Nerinckx took the saddle of his friend, who refused to venture, placed it on his own, and then remounting the horse, placed himself on his knees on the top of the two saddles, and thus crossed the flood, which flowed over his horse's back. On another occasion he made a still more narrow escape. He was swept from his horse, which lost its footing and was carried away by the current; and the rider barely saved himself and reached the other shore by clinging firmly to the horse's tail.

"On one of his missionary tours he narrowly escaped being devoured by the wolves, which then greatly infested those portions of Kentucky which were not densely settled. While traveling to visit a distant station, in what is now Grayson County, but what was then almost an unreclaimed wilderness, he lost his way in the night. It was the dead of winter, and the darkness was so great that he could not

15

hope to extricate himself from his painful situation. Meantime, while he was seeking a sheltered place where he could take some repose, the famished wolves scented him and came in hundreds, fiercely howling around him. With great presence of mind, he immediately remounted his horse, knowing they would scarcely attack him while on horseback. He hallooed at the top of his voice, and temporarily frightened them off; but soon they returned to the charge, and kept him at bay during the whole night. Once or twice they seemed on the point of seizing his horse, and Mr. Nerinckx made the sign of the Cross and prepared himself for death; but a mysterious Providence watched over him, and he escaped, after sitting on his horse the whole night. With the dawn the wolves disappeared.

"He had charge of six congregations, besides a much greater number of stations, scattered over the whole extent of Kentucky. Wherever he could learn that there were a few Catholic settlers, there he established a station or erected a church. The labor which he thus voluntarily took on himself is almost incredible. To visit all his churches and stations generally required the space of at least six weeks. . . .

"God blessed his labors with fruits so abundant and permanent as to console him for all his toils and privations. He witnessed a flourishing Church growing up around him, in what had recently been a wilderness, inhabited only by wild beasts and untamable savages. He saw, in the virtues of his scattered flock, a revival of those which had rendered so illustrious the Christians of the first ages of the Church. . . . The results of his labors prove how much one good man, with the blessing of God, can achieve by his single efforts, prompted by the lofty motive of the Divine glory, and directed with simplicity of heart to one noble end."

The following is a list of the churches built by Father Nerinckx in Kentucky: Holy Mary, Calvary, 1805; St.

FATHER NERINCKX' LABORS.

Charles, 1806; St. Clara's, 1808; St. Bernard's, Casey
Creek, 1810; St. Romoldus (now St. Romuald), Hardinsburg, Breckenridge County, 1810-1816; St. Paul's, Grayson County, 1811; St. Augustine's, Grayson Springs, Grayson County, 1811; St. John's, Rude's Creek, Hardin County,
1812; St. John Baptist, Bullitt County, 1812; St. Anthony's,
Long Lick, Breckenridge County, 1812; St. Benedict's,
Spencer County, 1815; St. Augustine's, Lebanon, 1817,
finished by Father Deparcq in 1820; St. Vincent's, New
Hope, 1819; Holy Cross, 1823. The last named, of brick,
is still in a good state of preservation. He did not merely
inspire the erection of these churches; some of them were
literally built with his own hands; indeed, he did some
manual work on all of them. Upon those hills, and within
those peaceful valleys, he set up the standard of the Cross,
and if an ever increasing and devout people gather around
the altars it surmounts, it is largely due to the careful training their ancestors received from the zealous missionary
who so truly spent himself for Christ on the Kentucky frontier.

Naturally, such a priest could not remain unknown to
his bishop, even though so widely separated, and it is not
surprising that when upon Archbishop Carroll was laid the
additional burden of caring for the distracted See of New
Orleans he should remember Father Nerinckx. With him
in charge of the new territory which the purchase of Lousi-
ana by the United States had added to the diocese of Baltimore, Archbishop Carroll felt the danger threatening the
Church in the South would be averted. The memorable
year of 1808 saw the erection of the new Sees of Boston,
Philadelphia, New York, and, to the joy of Father Nerinckx, who more than three years ago had advised it, of
Bardstown. With the Bulls for the four new bishops was
issued the Brief from Rome appointing Father Nerinckx
Administrator of New Orleans.

Hitherto revealing a submission to his superior that essentially marks the servant of God, Father Nerinckx now refused, but he did it as one who refuses to attempt what, in his humility, seems to him utterly impossible. The entreaties and expostulations of the bishop he withstood, and fearful that they might become a command, he appealed to friends to save him. Father Badin and the Dominican Fathers who had, in 1806, settled at St. Rose, in Washington County, were petitioned to add their voices to his, which they did, knowing his usefulness to Kentucky. Reluctantly, at length, the prayer of the humble priest was granted, and then, believing the southern territory had greater need of him than Kentucky, he announced his willingness to Archbishop Carroll to labor as a missionary priest in Louisiana, where no inducement could obtain his consent to rule as a bishop. Against this Father Badin, unsolicited now, made protest, and Father Nerinckx, ever thrusting self into the background when duty demanded, cast aside this one of many desires, and continued his work in Kentucky. It was plainly God's will for him to remain there, and in conformity with that, he well knew, lies the path to peace.

In the meanwhile the diocese of Bardstown, the first established in the West, had received its new bishop in the person of the Right Reverend Benedict Joseph Flaget. His consecration took place in Baltimore, November 4, 1810, but for want of money to defray the traveling expenses he did not reach his See until six months afterward. In a letter to his brother the new bishop, who had been met and welcomed by Father Nerinckx in Louisville, thus describes his entrance into his episcopal city:

"At a distance of half a league (a mile and a half) from town an ecclesiastic of my diocese, accompanied by the principal inhabitants, came out to meet me. So soon as they perceived us they dismounted to receive my benediction. I gave it to them, but with how trembling a hand, and with what heaviness of heart! Mutual compliments were now

18

exchanged, and then we all together proceeded towards the town. This cortege, though simple and modest in itself, is something new and very extraordinary in this country. It was the first time a bishop was ever seen in these parts, and it was I, the very last of the tribe, who was to have this honor!"

This arrival at Bardstown, where was then no church, took place June 9th, and two days later he reached St. Stephen's now to be the episcopal residence. Father Badin has thus described his installation:

"The bishop there found the faithful kneeling on the grass and singing canticles in English; the country women were nearly all dressed in white, and many of them were still fasting, though it was then four o'clock in the evening, they having entertained a hope to be able on that day to assist at his Mass, and to receive the holy communion from his hands. An altar had been prepared at the entrance to the first court, under a bower composed of four small trees, which overshadowed it with their foliage. Here the bishop put on his pontifical robes. After the aspersion of the holy water, he was conducted to the chapel in procession, with the singing of the litany of the Blessed Virgin; and the whole function closed with the prayers and ceremonies prescribed for the occasion in the Roman Pontifical."

It is probable that Bishop Flaget's first Mass in Kentucky was offered at St. Stephen's, there being no church at Bardstown, and it is interesting to note that on the spot where the reception of the bishop took place is now erected a life-sized statue of Father Nerinckx. The new home of the bishop has thus been described by Father Badin:

"Mr. Badin had for his own lodging but one poor log house, and in consequence of the expenses he had lately incurred in building a house for a monastery, which was burned down ere it was completed, it was with great difficulty that he was enabled to build and prepare, for the residence of his illustrious friend and the ecclesiastics who ac-

19

companied him, two miserable log cabins sixteen feet square. One of the missionaries was compelled to sleep on a mattress in the garret of this strange episcopal palace, which was whitewashed with lime, and contained no other furniture than a bed, six chairs, two tables, and a few planks for a library. Here the bishop resided for a year, esteeming himself happy to live thus in the midst of apostolic poverty."

Thus was St. Stephen's Farm, the present Loretto Convent and Mother House of the Lorettine Sisters, the cradle of Catholicity in Kentucky. Here the first missionaries lived, here the first bishop had his residence, and here was established the first seminary for the education of ecclesiastical students in the West. It is a hallowed spot, and with tender reverence every tradition concerning it has been preserved by those into whose hands, through the providence of God, it has fallen.

CHAPTER III.

THE SCHOOL AT HARDIN'S CREEK.

IN the beginning of his priestly life Father Nerinckx, when he sought to win a people back to God, had used as his instrument the children; in Kentucky his hope to preserve the Faith and bring about its increase rested greatly on the little ones. Moreover, he loved them. In simplicity and guilelessness he was their close kin. They had no fear of him. The religious exercises he held for them they never found wearisome. He had a fund of wholesome stories as interludes in the course of instruction and prayer, and little gifts as rewards for the industrious pupil. We can readily believe that by none were the visits of the good priest more eagerly anticipated than by those first children of Kentucky.

But well did Father Nerinckx realize the limitations of his work with this portion of his flock. The advancing mind of youth required more of the truths of religion, the knowledge of science, than he could impart on his occasional visit, and he realized that unless these were supplied but barren would be his labors for the coming generation. The appalling figure of Ignorance loomed darkly against the canvas of that period, and seemed to obscure his vision of the future. Education, he knew, would come but gradually to the country districts, and an education without religion it must be when it did come. The destiny of these little ones always disquieted him. A product of Catholic countries, the remedy of religious orders naturally suggested itself to him, and the September after his arrival he wrote to his parents of his intention to establish a Sisterhood to assist him in his work. Failure attended his first effort, and, with the humility of a great soul, he attributed the

21

cause to himself, and called upon Father Badin to undertake the foundation. Father Badin entered into the project with the energy that characterized him . A farm owned by James Dent, consisting of four hundred acres, was offered the priests for the proposed foundation, and when the plans were laid before Bishop Carroll, in 1807, by Father Badin, that prelate graciously accorded his assent to the undertaking.

On the return of Father Badin from Baltimore the building of the new convent was begun and carried speedily to completion. It stood on the road to Holy Cross, about one-half a mile from St. Stephen's, on a tract of one hundred acres, donated for the purpose by a brother of James Dent. It was intended to be a school for the instruction of girls, and another house for orphans was later to be erected. On February 23, 1808, Father Nerinckx was able to write his parents, whom he filially kept in close touch with his work, that the foundation had been laid, and in another letter, written the second day after Pentecost, informs them that the building is now under roof, and adds:

"It is seventy feet long, and will have a chapel about as long and wide as the house, surmounted with a turret. Some outbuildings will be added. It is situated one mile from Father Badin's house. Six or seven of our young ladies have applied to be the first religious, but it seems there are many more who are anxiously watching how the undertaking will succeed, and who will join the community as soon as it is an accomplished fact. May God bless what has been begun for His honor and glory; His providence is our only reliance."

But until God's hour has come our efforts fall unripened fruit from the tree of time. Other souls had he selected for the carrying to fulfilment of this great work, and the holocaust of Father Badin's labors was required to prepare the way of their destiny. The convent was completed, the little company of expectant Sisters ready to take possession

22

of it, when fire broke out and reduced the house to ashes. Father Badin's disappointment was as deep as his hope had been high. Kentucky became a place of sorrow and affliction, and he sought relief among his more distant missions, leaving the work at home to the equally crushed Father Nerinckx.

Of this first convent in Kentucky and the West the two chimneys were spared, and, perchance, as the edge of his cruel disappointment wore off, those fire-scarred objects became for Father Nerinckx prophetic of future success. Certain it is that as those two blackened chimneys stood over the ashes of the poor convent hope lived on in his soul, a hope nourished by faith in God's providence, by his love for the salvation of his people.

We may read also into the failure of these first two attempts the design of God for the instruction of the daughters of Loretto to depend upon Him alone. Of their own volition the founders of the Society turned to their destiny. While ever under the guidance of their spiritual father, their history shows them to have been self-reliant from the beginning, and when it came to a question touching the integrity of their congregation we find them not hesitating to take an independent stand, albeit their counsellor was Father Nerinckx himself. God out of stones could raise up voices to proclaim His hidden majesty and, had all that history relates of early Catholicism in Kentucky been different, we doubt not that Mary Rhodes, Christina Stuart and Nancy Havern would have begun their work of Christian education, and we should see their log convent school growing into the wonder their Society reveals at this close of a century of existence.

Like many another whose life-work has changed the course of affairs, we know comparatively little of the history of the founders of the Sisters of Loretto, the first purely American Congregation in the United States. We know that Mary Rhodes was born in Maryland, and had

23

received a convent education, presumably with the Pious Ladies who established themselves at Georgetown, D. C., in 1799, and adopted the Visitation Rule in 1816. A brother, Bennet Rhodes, and a sister, Nancy Rhodes, had earlier emigrated to Kentucky with the Maryland colonists. Bennet Rhodes was married, and lived with his family on Hardin's Creek, in Washington County, while his sister was a guest of their cousin, Mr. James Dent, who, it will be recalled, had offered Father Badin and Father Nerinckx a tract of four hundred acres for the establishment of the convent when it was first proposed. Going to Maryland on a visit, Mr. Dent on his return was accompanied by Miss Mary Rhodes, who remained under his hospitable roof for several months before taking up her residence with her brother on Hardin's Creek. The traditions that have come down to their spiritual daughters proclaim these sisters to have been the possessors of culture and refinement, and it is easily understood that when Mary Rhodes became a member of her brother's household the condition confronting him in regard to the education of his children called forth a responsive apprehension in her own breast. What she could do to remedy it she did, and she gave the children daily instruction.

From her brother's home she looked abroad upon the ever-increasing community, and beheld everywhere the same necessity. In those many homes was a young generation, heirs, like her own brother's children, of education and religion, and denied every opportunity of coming into their inheritance of the former, while the latter they stood every chance of losing. Her generous heart yearned over them, and through we know not what hours of solicitous thought and fervent prayer, she conceived the idea of extending her labors, and giving to all the children of the neighborhood the advantages her own relatives were receiving. While Bennet Rhodes may naturally have shrunk from seeing his young sister assuming the hardships of a teacher's

24

profession, he was in full accord with her desire to make her life beneficial to the youth of the new country, henceforth their home, and Father Nerinckx, before whom she laid her project, was gladdened to find his dear concern shared by this young and generous soul. With his consent and blessing, Mary Rhodes opened her school in a cabin which, from neglect and a long-uninhabited condition, was in a sorry state of decay. It had no floor, its roof let in the rain and snow, and the chinks between the logs, while conducive to health in admitting fresh air in abundance, did not promote the comfort of the inmates when the chilling blasts of winter swept over the land. It is doubtful, however, if Miss Rhodes felt the commiseration for her lot a more supine generation bestows upon her. We are inclined to think that, with the Psalmist, she cried out that her lines had fallen into pleasant places, that the joy of one who was coming into her own made the little cabin school a veritable heaven to her, and her dreams of what the future held for her caused her to be oblivious to the discomforts of the present.

The children came fast enough to the little school on the hill above Hardin's Creek, and the progress they made rejoiced the heart of Father Nerinckx. He perceived, however, that her tasks were growing beyond her, and he offered her an assistant in Miss Christina Stuart, who, like Miss Rhodes, was desirous of employing herself in this great work. Gladly did Mary Rhodes accept the proffered assistance, and when Miss Stuart took up her residence at Mr. Rhodes' hospitable home the regard of the teachers for each other grew into the deep affection of friends. They could reveal to each other what before they had wisely hidden from the uncomprehending, that the prospects to which the other girls of their acquaintance turned gladly were repellent to them. The higher thought that had led one on was now known to be also the lodestar of the other; and thus drawn together by the ardent desire of the soul, they unconsciously advanced toward the hour decreed for them since the beginning. The social demands which the neighborhood made upon them distracted them from their spiritual progress and interfered with their work in the school; and possessed now of the passion for perfection, they determined to set themselves apart from their family and friends. Adjoining the school was another cabin, in an equally dilapidated condition. Here the two young women concluded to take up their abode, relying on Providence for their maintenance.

Had the community decided that a sudden madness had seized upon the two and restrained them from executing their project, the action could scarcely have been more condemned; for assuredly nothing seemed less in harmony with good sense than this abandonment of a fairly comfortable home and the protection of relatives for a deserted and unfit cabin, with only an equally deluded woman for a companion. But likely the people held that the best cure for folly was to allow it to run its course, and felt convinced that within a short time they would see the young women returning to the society they had foresworn. But the spirit of enterprise that so strongly filled the land found unimpeded way in the bosom of the two teachers. They were bent upon planting Christian education on the frontier, and accepting the condition of sacrifice as the necessary ground for a great work, they, in saying good-bye to the life they had known, knew their departure was forever.

They made the cabin as nearly habitable as possible, and with sublime trust entered upon their new world of endeavor. Scarcely was it begun when a third young lady came to offer herself, and Miss Nancy Havern was accorded the welcome her courageous act merited.

We may allow our fancy to play around that little cabin on the hill, and question which of the three intrepid ones suggested that step, the taking of which thousands of consecrated virgins shall bless as they follow in the glorious train of the Lamb throughout the eternal day. That has not been recorded by any human pen, but her words found an echo in the hearts of her two companions, and they turned to Father Nerinckx and offered themselves to him, and through him to the Church and to God. The joy that filled the good priest's heart was tempered by the spirit of prudence and obedience. Long tried in the school of experience, he knew and pitied the ignorance of the young women before him, and warned them that the life they elected to follow demanded sacrifices of which they could form no conception. They dutifully acquiesced in his statements, but, remaining in the mind to continue as they had begun, they besought him to give them some rule by which to govern themselves. He yielded to their importunity, and wrote a few directions on a slip of paper, then he set forth to inform Bishop Flaget of the pious project of the three young women, and of his own action in their regard. No restraining motive was experienced by the bishop, who knew Christ does not fail His Church, and in the wilds of Kentucky He could produce her necessary religious orders as well as in the populous places of the Old World. He gave the undertaking his warmest approval, and placed it under the care of Father Nerinckx. God's way of answering prayer for him was a royal way. He had honestly and steadfastly tried to bring about the realization of this, his dearest wish, and twice had met failure; then, at an unexpected time and place, God handed him his heart's desire. The convent was founded, the religious community was established, he had only to undertake its direction.

Father Nerinckx lost no time in acquainting the young women with the decree of the bishop, and angels surely sang the tidings of great joy on the hill overlooking Hardin's Creek on that day. The three aspirants immediately asked Father Nerinckx to appoint a superior, and then he established a precedent to which strict adherence would have been well in this Society as in others: he bade them

27

choose their own superior, until they should number five or six members, when they could hold a regular election. They selected Mary Rhodes, and thus the first religious Institute of the West was practically established.

Straightway the voice of Divine Love began to be heard from His new abode among the Kentucky hills. It did not fall on world-deafened ears, and let it be set down to the glory of the people of this State that still it is heeded; still youth and beauty, wealth and position, are forgotten, and throughout the round of the year the doors of Loretto, and other convents, swing open to admit these swift-footed daughters of Sion bringing the offering of their lives to the King. In the vicinity of Holy Mary's church a Miss Nellie Morgan was teaching a few children in the home of her widowed mother, and she counted among her friends Miss Nancy Rhodes, sister of Mary Rhodes. To them first came the call, and their applications were favorably considered; Miss Morgan, however, was not free to remain until her term as teacher should have expired. A fifth applicant in the person of Miss Sally Havern, a sister of Nancy Havern, soon gladdened the dwellers in the little cabin.

By this time the new project had been the subject of much comment, and when Father Nerinckx announced to the congregation of St. Charles that the veil was to be given to the three young ladies who formed the nucleus of the new Institute a large gathering from the surrounding country assembled for the occasion. The date fixed was April 25, 1812, and in the little log church of St. Charles, in the presence of an audience that failed to grasp the full significance of the act, Father Nerinckx performed the ceremony of religious reception for Mary Rhodes, Christina Stuart and Anne Havern, and the cornerstone of Loretto's foundation was laid.

On the same day they formally admitted Ann Rhodes and Sally Havern as postulants, and on June 29 of the same year these received the veil from Father Nerinckx with ap-

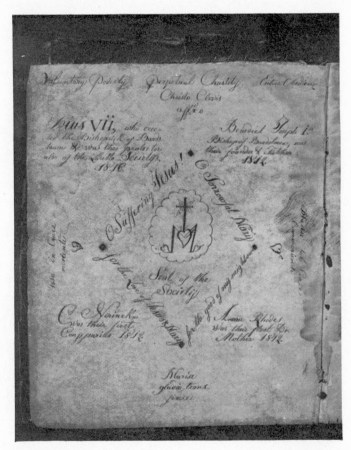

TITLE PAGE OF RULE IN WRITING OF FATHER NERINCKX

propriate ceremony in St. Charles' Church, at which time Miss Nellie Morgan became a postulant, and on August 12th she received the habit and the name of Sister Clare, in honor of the saint whose feast it is, while the others retained their baptismal names.

The school, meanwhile, was growing beyond the fondest expectations. Children living at a distance were entered as boarders, and the strain on the small community was consequently increased. The domestic arrangement of that convent academy, unique in the annals of religious communities, proved that necessity is the mother of invention. During the day the room served as kitchen, dining-room and living-room; at night it became a dormitory for the girls, when the beds, which had been laid on the "upper shelf," as the attic where the Sisters slept was termed, were handed down and spread on the floor for the boarding pupils. And no feeling that hardship was their lot disturbed the minds of those children, daughters, some of them, of Maryland's best families, and who afterwards took their places in the highest social ranks of the young State, and whose daughters and grand-daughters have helped maintain the fame of the women of Kentucky for beauty, grace and intellect, a fame these first pupils of Loretto had their part in establishing. They were happy and contented, and their progress in their studies was satisfactory.

This happiness and contentment in the school had its fountain head in the spirit of holy joy that permeated the little community, and the condition must have rejoiced the heart of Father Nerinckx. His great humility, however, seems to have brought him unnecessary anxiety concerning the new Sisterhood. It made him doubtful of his ability to guide its young destiny, and, perhaps, as he contrasted it in this formative period with the remembered olden communities of his native land the great difference of their advantages added to his solicitude. That there was a contrast we can readily believe, for what were they but half a dozen young girls, only one of whom, as far as we have been informed, knew, and that but from schoolday experience, what conventual life was? What training had they for the stupendous work before them, and how could they impart spiritual instruction to others who had received none themselves? His fears impelled him to make a provision for this, but before he attempted to carry it into execution he laid it before the little community. He opened his heart to them, and told them that in his opinion it were better for them to be placed under the guidance of souls long schooled in the spiritual life, and for that purpose he would invite some nuns from Europe to give them the necessary training.

Then the indestructible spirit that had upheld their forefathers in the moulding of the young Republic, as it was now aiding their descendants in shaping the destiny of the young State, revealed itself in these founders of Loretto, into whose willing hands had been entrusted a work equal in holiness and loftiness to that of their fathers. They wanted no other spiritual guide than himself, they answered. The way he led to spiritual perfection lay as a shining path before their young feet, and humbly they would follow in his footsteps.

Father Nerinckx had not spent these long years in Kentucky without having become acquainted with the spirit that made that declaration by the lips of his obedient and dutiful children; and while he might, had he been of a narrower nature, have found in their answer incontrovertible proof that they lacked discipline, he must in any case have admired their independence. They were not ignorant of what it would mean for themselves to be taken under the protection of an old and well-established religious house, and fully realized the burden of responsibility of which they would be relieved; but the temptation was set aside, and to the steadfast faith and spotless courage of six young Kentucky women the American Church owes the first flawless gem

30

on her brow, the Society of Sisters of Loretto, or the Friends of Mary at the Foot of the Cross.

Father Nerinckx did not press the matter upon them, and neither could he rest satisfied until he had laid it before his bishop. Again the good bishop ranged himself on the side of the Sisters, and, approving of the decision of the young women, entrusted the care of the Society entirely to Father Nerinckx. If Father Nerinckx' great humility at times seemed to endanger the success of his undertakings, his ready and complete obedience to the voice of authority redeemed every apparent loss, and we always see him taking up with renewed vigor the work his modest opinion of himself was on the point of causing him to relinquish. The bishop's decision swept away every lingering uncertainty, every foolish fear, and from the depths of his humility he lifted up his eyes to see the hand of God pointing him to his lofty work. Out of his most fervent, constant and longest prayer this religious body had been born, and now he was to form it into what he had dreamed it might become. He had not held himself to be worthy or equal; but the voice of God, speaking by his bishop, had denied that opinion and bade him to complete the work he had begun. Perhaps the veil was momentarily lifted and Charles Nerinckx beheld why he had been driven from his native land to the untamed hills of Kentucky; why his ardent desire to join the Trappists or devote himself to the whites and Indians of Upper Louisiana had been frustrated; why he had had the strength to deafen his ears against the voice of his superior calling him to the honors as well as the burdens of the episcopate; perhaps, too, one fleeting glimpse of the future was vouchsafed him, and he saw the long train of Loretto's black-robed daughters carrying religion and education to lands where these were unknown, and patiently cultivating them in lands into which they had been introduced; perhaps he saw, their tasks below completed, that never-swerving line moving on into the City of God to join in the glorious throng that are taught the new Canticle and follow the Lamb wheresoever He goeth.

On his return to the convent Father Nerinckx acquainted the Sisters with the order of the bishop, and, receiving anew their avowal that they had no other wish than to continue in the life they had chosen, he bade them to consider themselves as aspirants to the religious state. He exhorted them to have great confidence in Providence, Who never forsakes those who piously trust in Him, and stated that as religious they should have for their characteristic name: The Friends of Mary at the Foot of the Cross. He then read to them the following instruction:

In their silent hours, in their labors and their devotions, the members of the community shall try to keep their minds in a state of contemplation of the sufferings of Jesus and the sorrows of Mary, His Blessed Mother. The grand object of the Society will be the "glory of God, the sanctification of their own souls, and the salvation of their neighbors, by educating and instructing females." These three intentions are to be in all cases the leading motives in all their labors, teachings, mortifications, and meritorious works. They shall call each other Sister, and by name. A religious dress or uniform shall be adopted, and its color, form and quality determined upon; for the present, owing to their poverty, the Sisters can only wear whatever dresses they already have. Silence shall be kept all the day, except during the recreation following the three meals, and prayers shall be said in common at fixed times during the day. He also exhorted them to have great vigilance in the tuition and government of their pupils, a great zeal in teaching them their prayers and catechism, and a motherly care in forming their manners and morals.

That he might more completely give himself to his duties as spiritual director of the new Society, Father Nerinckx abandoned his home with Father Badin at St. Stephen's Farm and took up his residence in the little room adjoining the church of St. Charles. A poor old woman carried his meals to him, and when he was at home he daily celebrated Mass in the convent for the Sisters and their pupils.

With the reception of the postulants on June 29 the community became established, and Father Nerinckx called upon the members for a regular election of a superior. They went to their cabin, seated themselves on the earthen floor, and the eldest voting first, the first regular election of the Society of Loretto was held. It was a brief meeting; their choice fell upon Nancy Rhodes. "You have chosen the youngest among you," was Father Nerinckx' comment. "If she is the youngest she is also the most virtuous," they rejoined, and their answer and the spiritual and material advance made by the pioneer Sisterhood during the brief span of time Mother Ann Rhodes governed them showed they had acted under the direction of the Holy Spirit. So we find that not only was the Lorettine Society founded in the year 1812, but it was formally established as a self-governing body, invested with the rights and powers of such an organization, and entered at once upon its career. Their founder then presented them with their Rule. Afterward he amplified it, and as it came from his hand was on its presentation commended by the Holy See in 1816. Organized in 1812 under a Rule drawn especially for them by their founder, all the first members, natives of the country, recognized and approved in 1816 by the Holy See, Loretto has the distinction of being the first religious Congregation founded in America without affiliation or connection with any other.

Mother Ann's first act was to purchase the tract of land on which the cabins stood. For this she paid seventy-five dollars. The money she obtained from the sale of her negro slave, for whom she received two hundred dollars. The bill of sale of this slave, together with the other personal property of Nancy Rhodes, has been handed down to us, and for the sake of its historic value it is herewith given:

"Know all men by these presents that I, Ann Rhodes, of the County of Washington & State of Kentucky, for divers good causes & valuable considerations me hereunto moving & for & in consideration of the sum of one dollar to me in hand paid, the receipt whereof is hereby acknowledged and also the sum of two hundred dollars procured to be paid on the first day of November ensuing the date hereof by the Revd. Charles Nerinckx of the aforesaid County and State have bargained sold and delivered & by these presents do bargain sell and deliver possession to the said Charles Nerinckx a negro man slave named Tom to him his heirs &c forever - - And the said Ann Rhodes also for & in consideration of the sum of fifty dollars in hand paid to me by the said Revd. Charles Nerinckx do bargain sell deliver the following personal property, to wit, one bedstead bed and furniture; two spinning wheels, all her wearing apparel together with her household & kitchen furniture. And the said Ann Rhodes for herself her heirs, &c, warrants to defend the right and title of the said negro Tom & personal estate to the said Charles Nerinckx & his heirs against the claim & claims of all and every person or persons whatsoever claiming the same by through or under her heirs in any manner whatever.

"IN WITNESS WHEREOF the said Ann Rhodes hath hereto set her hand & seal the 27th day of August 1812.

"Ann Rhodes   . . . .
: L S :
. . . .

"Teste:
    "James Flanagan
    "Austin Flanagan."

They were now landowners. They had driven down the stake of their Society's first home, and they set to work to build its foundation. They made the roof secure against the rain, and fashioned a second story by laying planks across the joists, this attic becoming their sleeping apartment. A portion of the lower room was transformed into a kitchen, and on the stump of the tree which, as was the case in many pioneer cabins, had been left standing in the center of the floor they nailed a board for a table. They built a rail fence around the yard and improved one outhouse for their meat, and another for the chickens. All this labor they performed themselves, and yet departed not from womanly dignity and refinement; and the noble example they left has during the century of their Society's existence inspired every daughter of Loretto with reverence for lowly occupations.

Father Nerinckx, having given the Sisters the Rule by which they were to fashion their spiritual life, began to provide for their material well-being. He now was convinced of his life-work, and it must be laid on a substantial foundation. Though he performed his missionary work with the same zeal, though he traveled far and wide in the service of the Gospel, and strove as manfully to form congregations and erect churches, we find that through the remainder of his life the Daughters of Loretto were his dearest care. And well they merited that solicitude, faithfully have they preserved his saintly memory and have continued until this day his labor for the salvation of souls. Still is that heroic and dauntless spirit an inspiration when difficulties crowd around their steps; still does his humility remain the pattern after which they weave this fair mantle of the soul; and his burning love for God and man, handed down like a torch, enkindles that deathless flame in their own hearts. Still before their hundred altars cluster the Sisters of Loretto, keeping, as he was wont to do, faithful tryst with the Dweller of the Tabernacle; still does the Morning Manna, his last legacy to them, strengthen his children; still does his Rule, the priceless heritage restored to them by the hand of Rome, guide them up the steep of perfection. Long have the log churches he built fallen to decay, and their site passed from the recollection of men; but treasured as a jewel in the crown of beautiful structures that the Society owns is the rudely fashioned cabin he built for himself at the first convent on Hardin's Creek.

With the passing of the generation that knew him his name would have become but a memory for the Catholics of Kentucky, revered, indeed, along with those of Flaget and Badin; but until the last Sister of Loretto shall have lain down for the everlasting sleep, Father Nerinckx shall be remembered, his heroic life extolled. The humblest, perhaps, of the little company of men whose names in the history of the American Church are like stars in a winter sky, he builded himself a monument whose beauty and greatness command attention, and whose completion lies in the unmeasured years. Fame he would have fled from as from the Evil One; but coming to him in the guise of love, love for God, for man, for State, for Church, she drew near, and sweetly wreathed for him an immortal crown.

CHAPTER IV.

FATHER NERINCKX began to impress upon the people of Hardin's Creek the fact that the convent and school were to be permanent organizations; the former to be supplied and perpetuated by the fairest blossoms of their homes; the latter to confer Christian education on the rising generation and the generations to follow. He made them realize that they owed a duty to these institutions only second, if indeed not equal, to that which they owed their parish church, and the congregation began to build a comfortable home for the Sisters and the children.

The admirable Life of Father Nerinckx written by the Right Rev. Camillus P. Maes, Bishop of Covington, gives a description of that first group of conventual buildings in the West, and we need make no apology for inserting it in full.

"Father Nerinckx," writes Bishop Maes, "now called upon St. Charles' congregation for assistance in the good work. It had become not only advisable, but strictly necessary, to erect more suitable buildings. Untiring in his efforts for the temporal as well as for the spiritual welfare of his little community, which was in the most destitute circumstances, he started a subscription that realized a few hundred dollars, mostly in trade, and he requested those who could do no better to assist in getting out logs for the erection of a new convent. On that same memorable day, June 29, 1812, the first log was cut; and notwithstanding the greatest difficulties and hardships, the common share of every pious undertaking, the work progressed most satisfactorily. The trees around the two little cabins were felled and hewed for house-logs, thus at the same time

37

clearing the ground on which the two rows of buildings were to be erected, and having between them an extensive square yard. The Sisters themselves subsequently cleared this yard of stumps by chipping them away and burning them down into the ground. Father Nerinckx made the plan of the buildings and staked out the place where each one was to be erected. Nor did he spare his strength. Many a log which the united efforts of three men could not move was lifted by his powerful arms and thrown out of the way. He labored with his own hands, and put his shoulder to the timbers when they were raised up. The foundation timbers, or sills, having been placed in position, stone hauled from Hardin's Creek was built up under them as support or underpinning, and afterward the crevices were filled in with mud and straw. Through reverence for the One who was to dwell therein the logs intended for the walls of the chapel and house connected with it were hewed. The different buildings were erected at a small distance from each other, forming two rows of houses on two opposite sides of the square yard. The first house to the right of the entrance of the yard was the school, and the one opposite in the left-hand row of houses was Father Nerinckx' dwelling. Like the school, it was a double cabin of one story, with its wooden chimney outside; the space between the rooms formed a little entry protected by weather-boarding. He built most of his own dwelling-house himself, and the entire work done on it by others only cost him six dollars and fifty cents!

"His kitchen, the second building in the left-hand row, being smaller, was soon finished, and his old cook, who was living in the neighborhood, came to take possession of it, carrying the priest's meals to St. Charles' sacristy, where he was still living. The poor woman also made herself very useful to the Sisters, carrying their messages and doing their errands to the neighbors when necessary. Whenever home, Father Nerinckx came over and assisted at the building, lifting and raising logs, preparing mortar and plastering the walls in the very primitive fashion of the day, viz., filling up the empty spaces between the logs with handfuls of clay mortar, which displayed for years afterward the imprint of his fingers. Having finished his own house, he left his sacristy residence at St. Charles', and moved to Loretto. One room of his house served him for sitting-room, study, bedroom and refectory, the other one being reserved for the accommodation of the bishop or of any priests who might visit him. This was the unpretending palace of Father Nerinckx, whom popular instinct, which is scarcely ever at fault, spoke of as 'the saintly priest,' and it was his home for the last twelve years of his life.

"The building next to the school on the right-hand side of the entrance to the grounds was the church and convent. It was two stories high, and consisted of two square cabins with upper rooms; the space between the cabins was weatherboarded in, and thus formed a rather neat looking chapel. When finished it was blessed and received the name of Little Loretto, in honor of Our Lady of Loretto, in Italy, for whom Father Nerinckx had a most tender devotion. The two rooms at the sides of the chapel were intended for the use of the community, but they were not finished till about two years later.

"The schoolhouse was soon occupied by the boarders and day-scholars. A similar double cabin next to the convent was used for kitchen and refectory, and the church not being completed at the time, the same room was also used for dormitory, and the second one fitted up as an oratory. The altar and statue of the Blessed Virgin were transferred to it, and Mass was said in it by the Director whenever home from missionary duty. Thither also Sisters and children repaired for their daily devotions. The building fronting this one in the left-hand row, and like it in all respects, was reserved for a workroom, and was used, as necessity required, for guests' room and for infirmary.

LORETTO.

"Father Nerinckx now enclosed the buildings and yard with a rail fence, thus dividing them from the garden that extended to the summit of the hill, the opposite portion of which stretched to the brink of the creek, and its declivity was utilized as an orchard, which the holy priest set out with his own hands. The large square yard was leveled down and sowed in bluegrass, thus giving a neat and pleasant appearance to the whole. Finally, at the other side of the church he paled in a small plot of ground, which was to serve as a graveyard for the Sisters, and in the middle of it he planted a large cross surrounded by an evergreen arbor with shrubs, trees and flowers. He now tore down the two old log cabins, and with the serviceable lumber built a small double cabin at the further end of the yard, which was used for a meat-house."

This was not accomplished all at once. In the meantime a rumble of the storm that afterward was to break upon the defenceless head of the venerable priest was heard in the accusation made by some misguided persons that part of the money he had collected for church purposes had been differently employed. This brought from Father Nerinckx a letter of defense, a copy of which document, printed in 1812, is preserved in the archives of the Society. From it we learn some interesting facts concerning the convent and the school. The latter was forming fast, we are told, and of every denomination. The scholars are instructed by two Sisters of the Society, and rules are strictly observed. The common branches, needlework, etc., sound morality and Christian politeness make up the sum of instruction received from the Society. Aiming and sincerely wishing to be useful to all, without any self-seeking, the terms are uncommonly low, to wit: $5.00 a year for schooling, of which one is cash; internes or boarders are, moreover, to find themselves—that is, to provide for bedding, washing, victuals, etc. None is to be admitted for less than three months, and no distinction is to be made of religious denomination if willing to submit to the rules of the school. Needy orphans, as much as possible, will be admitted gratis.

In the communication Father Nerinckx makes a statement of his needs for the institution, and there was a generous response from the neighboring people. Gifts of corn, wheat and pork were made. The names of the donors and the amounts given are among the precious documents preserved at the Loretto Mother house, and succeeding generations of religious will read and remember in their prayers the first benefactors of their Society.

Poverty, which had always menaced him, was afflicting him in his work for the advancement of the Society, and he appealed to Bishop Flaget for permission to go to Europe and solicit alms for the church and the convent; but scarcity of priests prevented the bishop from acceding to the request. The bishop was then on the eve of his departure for Baltimore to confer with Archbishop Carroll. Before leaving his diocese he paid a visit to Loretto. This memorable event occurred on September 8, 1812, and the little community and its founder, strengthened and encouraged by the presence of their saintly superior, turned to their labors with renewed zeal. The convent was now in the course of construction, and the many privations they endured showed them to be indeed women of heroic mould. It is related that their original cabin home having been removed to make way for the new buildings, they, having no place of abode, put up the logs again with their own hands. The wood that warmed them during that winter, and many a subsequent winter for that matter, they cut and hauled home. Poverty the direst was theirs. They knew what it was to experience cold and hunger, and with the dawn of every morning met fear of the future face to face. And yet they never quailed. Never once did they look back, never did they doubt. Trust in Providence and Providence will never desert you. This was the motto their Director gave, and they inscribed it on their hearts.

41

But a greater trial than poverty and suffering that first year of its existence held for the young community. Death, at whose feet have fallen hopes as fair and fond as were sustaining those young women, battling for the existence of their Society on the sparsely settled frontier, was to come among them. Early in the summer they caught a glimpse of its forerunner, sorrow, as they looked on the face of Mother Ann Rhodes, where a color too bright for health showed at times on her cheek and a light too brilliant burned in her dark eyes. Slowly but sternly came the knowledge that the days of their superior were numbered, and well then might desolation and surrender overwhelm them. From the hour she had first come among them she had been their inspiration and their guide, and their instinctive recognition of her superiority had made them select her for their superior when, reasonably, their choice should have fallen upon her sister, or one of her two first companions.

Yet never did the spirit of Mother Ann Rhodes reveal its lofty character more clearly than now, as around her began to fall the shadows of the closing hours. She looked death in the face unafraid, and, summoning all the strength she unconsciously had been storing for this ordeal, having taught her daughters how to live, she would show them how to die. As if the great mortal change were not rapidly drawing nigh, she continued her duties, working by their side; nor did the sorrow that seemed to break their loyal hearts dim the holy joy that was animating hers. She loved them, she would have continued with them, but if one of their number must fare forth on the long journey, illumine the pathway for them to that Other Country, who should this be if not she, their Mother, who had led them up from the level lands of the flesh to the lofty mount of the spirit?

But the time came when the rapidly disintegrating human organism could no longer obey the behests of the will, and

42

Mother Ann must perforce lie quietly on her bed of straw, while around her went on the great work of building. We have looked upon the poverty of the Sisters, and we may picture that last illness of Mother Ann; yet such was the height of her sanctity that although she had known but a few months of the religious life, she accepted the sacrifice with equanimity. From her bed she continued to direct the affairs of her community and instruct both Sisters and pupils. Father Nerinckx was often with her, and broke for her the Bread of Life. Early in December he gave her the last Sacraments. She lingered until Friday, the eleventh of the month, and then, in the early dawn of that December day, Mother Ann Rhodes entered the portals of Heaven. Precious as her life had been for them, her death was more so, and the misfortune that might have meant defeat had been transmuted into victory. She seemed to call to them from the world she had entered, "Where I am you, too, shall come." The first Mother of Loretto had a right to expect that her generation of spiritual daughters would be continued on earth to form a glorious and ever-increasing train in the court of Heaven. And so it befell that when the hour came from which they had shrunk, whose outcome they feared, they found the darts of Sorrow had been blunted, while over her shoulder looked the face of Joy.

A grave in the frozen ground was dug in the little convent cemetery, and after the funeral rite celebrated in the chapel by Father Nerinckx, they consigned to earth the mortal tenement of her who had been Mother Ann Rhodes, first Superior of Loretto. The rule of disposing of the dead, which Father Nerinckx drew up and which the founders accepted, decreed that no coffin should be used; and perhaps in nothing else was the complete victory over the flesh more boldly pronounced, for howsoever highly we may philosophize, or deeply believe, primitive nature revolts at the thought of the consignment of the body to the earth, and in the vain effort to prevent it from returning into the elements of which it was compounded steel is welded into caskets and marble built into mausoleums. Wrapped only in her poor dress, with her coarse veil drawn over her face, Mother Ann was laid down for her long sleep; and, following that first burial, the custom obtained in the heroic Loretto Sisterhood until 1839, when it was changed by orders from Rome. The change, however, was not brought about by the Sisters, but by a Rev. Father Boullier, who, witnessing in 1837 the interment of a Sister in Perry County, Missouri, burst into tears and vowed that he would have the rule revoked.

The Sisters now proceeded to elect a successor to their first superior, and they chose Sister Mary Rhodes, the actual founder of the Society. The election was confirmed by Father Nerinckx, who appointed Sister Christina Stuart Sister Eldest, Sister Clare Morgan remaining as Directress of the school. For ten consecutive years Mother Mary presided over the Society, beholding its wonderful growth from the tiny mustard seed she had planted in the wilderness. From 1822, when her term of office expired, until her death, in 1853, she sought to live in obscurity, disclaiming all honors connected with the foundation of the Sisterhood, but loved and revered, as she well deserved to be, by the other members of the fast growing Society.

Death interrupted, but it brought no cessation of the activities in the home of religion and education. The poverty, however, increased with the progress of the winter. We are told that during that year, and many an after year, their breakfast consisted of bread and vegetable soup or coffee, served in tin cups; for supper they had bread and milk, or sage tea, while their dinner, eaten from tin plates, consisted of vegetables and one kind of meat, when they could procure it. For any departure from this bill of fare they were indebted to the hospitality of their neighbors. The school was well attended, but when we remember how small a sum the boarders paid, and that many of them were received free, the wonder is that the Sisters were able to provide even this coarse fare. Finally, they reached the limit of their own resources, and then they sought work among the neighboring families; and the whir of the spinning wheel, the creaking of the loom, broke the conventual silence or mingled with the prayers and songs of the toiling Sisters.

The remuneration they received from their weaving and spinning carried the community through the winter of 1813, and left them in a position to meet an additional expenditure that the year was to bring. In August their period of probation would expire, and when they approached the altar to take the vows that should bind them to the religious life an attire emblematic of their withdrawal from the world was not only desirable, but necessary. Their clever fingers wove the material for veil and habit, and the herbs of the woods, in whose virtues they, like all frontier women, were versed, gave to the articles the sombre hue their rule required. The girdle and scapular were also supplied, and when the Feast of the Assumption, August 15, 1813, dawned the countryside assembled in St. Charles' church to witness the culmination of the act of which they had seen the beginning on April 25th of the preceding year.

Headed by the happy school children, walking two and two, Mother Mary Rhodes and her four companions, Sisters Christina Stuart, Ann and Sarah Havern and Clare Morgan, clad in the religious habit, walked from their convent, half a mile away, and, passing through the silent congregation, approached the altar, where, kneeling at the feet of Father Nerinckx, they solemnly pronounced perpetual vows of poverty, chastity and obedience, and made the Society of the Friends of Mary, called Sisters of Loretto, at the Foot of the Cross, a consummated fact. The last doubt in the mind of the community at large was then dispelled, the last fear of Father Nerinckx laid at rest, and any feeling of uncertainty that might have troubled the five women themselves was banished. Come what might, their Society was established, and while life remained they were bound to it by that day's solemn compact. Every experience that could test the heart and try the spirit had been theirs during their time of probation, nor had they any reason to think that conditions would soon be altered; notwithstanding this, they would press on, and, dying, bequeath their work to those whom they doubted not God would raise to receive it from their hands. Trusting in His providence, they gave themselves entirely to Him, and turned from the altar first Spouses of Christ in the West.

The impression the service made on the assemblage was deep. In one generous young heart it was the Voice commanding, "Leave what thou hast, and come, follow Me!" Scarcely had the newly professed nuns retired to their convent, when with fawnlike fleetness their first candidate followed, and Loretto opened her door to admit Miss Monica Spalding, first of the many of her family to consecrate life and noble gifts to the service of God. Their number was increased a little later by the arrival of a Miss Hayden from Missouri. Deprived of every religious advantage, not even having made her First Communion, like the Baptist in the desert, the call of the Lord came to her, and she made haste to respond. She traversed the weary miles, and, reaching Loretto, besought Father Nerinckx to admit her into the Society. None could question that vocation, and after a course of instruction Susan Hayden made her First Communion and entered the novitiate on the same day, October 12, 1814, taking the name of Sister Mechtildes. In 1815 Loretto received her first novices from among her pupils in the persons of Agnes Hart, Ann Clarke, Esther Grundy and Ann Wathen. Miss Hart had left the Sisters' school to engage in teaching near her home in Breckenridge County; but the happiness she had experienced in the convent school life drew her back, and the pupil returned to become a novice. The other three were still in the schoolroom, and notwithstanding their youth, being but fifteen years of age, these chosen souls evinced the knowledge that is of God, and, obtaining the consent of their parents, entered the novitiate. The convent chapel had been the scene of no such ceremony until this interesting reception of Loretto's three children, August 15th of that year. All lived long and happily, and two of the three filled the highest offices in the Society.

This spirit of parental surrender did not animate every father and mother of that period, and the more worldly minded grew alarmed on beholding the fairest flowers of the community transplanted to the convent garden. Upon Father Nerinckx they fastened the blame, for the apostolic old priest in their eyes seemed to possess hypnotic power over these young maidens, by which he drew them into the cloister, there to waste their fair lives. To such a pitch did their zeal for the supposed victims of priestly influence carry them that it became necessary for Bishop Flaget to interfere. He journeyed down to St. Charles' church, and to the concourse of people assembled to hear him explained the dignity of the religious life, and bade parents to rejoice when one of their daughters had been deemed worthy of their espousals with Christ. The members of the new community were there of their own free will, he assured them, and at any time could leave if they so desired. The bishop had gained an ascendancy over the minds of the people, his words had the effect of dispelling the opposition against the convent, and the novices were permitted to continue their chosen way in peace.

CHAPTER V.

FATHER NERINCKX GOES TO ROME.

THE increase in membership opened up opportunities for the Society, but their poverty and the poverty of the people around them prevented the Sisters from taking advantage of these and accomplishing greater good for religion and education. Again, in the spring of 1814, Father Nerinckx sought permission to carry out his project of going to Europe to solicit alms. He obtained the consent of Bishop Flaget, but on reaching Baltimore he was advised by Archbishop Carroll to abandon his plans until the war with England had ceased, thereby lessening the dangers of the journey over-sea. God's time plainly had not come, and Father Nerinckx returned immediately to his Kentucky field to continue the struggle for two more years.

Divine Providence rewarded his resignation, and the great difficulty of securing labor for the cultivation of land was somewhat remedied by the offer to him of service for life of Mr. Vincent Gates, a man of irreproachable character, and whose widowed sister, Mrs. Ryan, had entered the novitiate. A gift of a horse from Bishop Flaget was another valuable acquisition, and the farm began to yield provisions for the community and school, while the flax and cotton gave wearing apparel for the nuns and dependent pupils. It was about this time, 1814, that Father Nerinckx, with money received from Belgium, bought some stoves in Pittsburg. They were the first introduced into Kentucky, and cost one hundred dollars apiece, besides freight charges.

After the war Father Nerinckx began to prepare for his trip abroad, where he hoped to secure funds and gifts for the Society and his needy churches, and obtain from Rome

the approval of his Rule for the new Sisterhood. He left
Loretto September 10, 1815, going directly to Rome, where
he arrived in time to know that at the approaching meeting
of the Cardinals of the Propaganda the Rule of the Society
would be considered. He remained in Rome about six
weeks.

"After the session," he wrote in his account of his journey, "I had the honor of an interview with one of the cardinals, who was so kind as to assure me that the Congregation of the Propaganda was well pleased with our new
Institution, the Friends of Mary at the Foot of the Cross,
and had taken it under its special protection. It conceded
to the Society all the favors and privileges attached to the
Institution of the Seven Dolors, established in the city of
Rome. He assured me that the difficulties and questions
submitted to the Congregation would be answered soon, that
my work was approved of, and that all the documents would
reach me in Belgium in time for me to set out for America
before winter. That was as much as I could wish."

On May 1, 1816, he was granted an interview with the
Holy Father, Pius VII, who assured the zealous priest that
he had read the Rules and was rejoiced and comforted by
the institution of the new Society. Father Nerinckx spent
the remainder of the time in collecting for his American
work. Equally diligent was he in striving to secure priests
for that untilled field. He obtained two Flemish priests and
eight young students. On May 16, 1817, Father Nerinckx
and his companions sailed for America. After a perilous
journey of eighty days they reached Baltimore, and then,
with one exception, Father Nerinckx' companions entered
the Society of Jesus, and the Kentucky missions were the
losers thereby. Henry Hendrickx, the one who remained
with Father Nerinckx, having been sent to the port of New
Orleans with the articles secured abroad, to avoid the long
trip with them overland, died of yellow fever within sight,
almost, of the land to which his zeal had called him.

As the result of Father Nerinckx' visit abroad Kentucky was enriched. Priceless webs of European looms, woven into vestments, became the possession of the western Church; sacred vessels of intrinsic value came to the service of her rude altars; while paintings and other works of art were secured by the untiring missionary, who sought ever the beauty of the earthly house of the Eucharistic King.

The return of Father Nerinckx after an absence of two years brought happiness to Loretto, while its progress likewise solaced his anxious fears. During this time the Society had increased to ten members, and this number had made it possible for Bishop Flaget to open a branch house at Holy Mary, under the name of Calvary. Previously a house had been prepared there as a Widows' Home, the inmates to follow a modified form of the Loretto Rule. Scarcity of applicants from this class of persons prevented the carrying out of the original plan, so the Sisters went thither and opened a school, June 10, 1816. It was presided over by Sister Christina Stuart, the second member of the Society. For eighty-four years the Sisters conducted a prosperous school, and Calvary convent could claim many a wise and holy woman among the mothers of Christian households of Kentucky and neighboring States, as well as many a devout religious who had been numbered among her pupils. As the "insatiate tooth of time" gnawed the walls and rendered extensive repairs and costly additions necessary, the academy was closed to the public in 1900, the property being used for farming purposes. Other schools of the same character having grown up with the years in the near neighborhood, the superiors decided to relinquish all idea of reopening a boarding school on the Rolling Fork.

Perhaps we now see Father Nerinckx entering upon the happiest portion of his hard missionary life. The money and goods he had secured abroad gave to the Church in his beloved Kentucky some semblance of the beauty his soul desired in the Holy of Holies; the diocese continued to be blessed with the ministrations of the saintly Bishop Flaget; there were more priests to minister to the people, while in the Seminary of St. Thomas young Levites were being prepared to continue the labors of the men who had lighted the torch of the Lord in the wilderness. An active Catholic life was being lived by the people, whose numbers were showing an increase and whose positions in the world were improving. To crown all these conditions, the Society which he had formed and on which he had centered his dearest hopes, was succeeding beyond even his expectations.

In September of 1817 Father Nerinckx gave the Sisters their first retreat. It was followed by the opening of a second branch house in Kentucky, on Pottinger's Creek, on the land Mr. James Dent had formerly offered for conventual purposes. This place had long been one of the mission stations visited by Father Nerinckx, Mass being celebrated in the Dent home. A room was reserved for this purpose wherein hung a picture of St. Barbara, which fact gave the station its name. The good couple having no children to provide for, were anxious to donate part of their property to God's service, and it was accepted by Father Nerinckx, with a view to establishing a school for girls.

In March, 1818, six Sisters of Loretto, with Sister Teresa Grundy as superior, were sent to take possession of the house vacated by Mr. and Mrs. Dent, wherein they opened school as soon as circumstances permitted. Father Nerinckx called the place Gethsemani, in memory of Our Lord's agony in the garden.

A share of the church goods which had arrived from Belgium was assigned to this convent, so the Sisters began with an oratory not quite so destitute as their first one at Little Loretto. The important adjunct of a grist mill was erected on the place by the generous efforts of their solicitous founder.

To collect pupils was the simplest of duties in these early foundations; children were almost as eager to attend school as their parents were to give them this priceless advantage. To provide them with books, food, sleeping quarters and other accommodations proved a much more difficult probley; money was scarce among the families as well as in the conventual treasury, while the articles needed were, if to be obtained at all, sold at a price which would startle us to-day. Books were almost an unknown quantity; the teachers of that date had to impart orally and gather results as best they could.

The good superior, Sister Teresa, who had conducted her co-laborers to their field of labor, earned her reward all too soon for those with whom she was associated, and Gethsemani opened a tomb almost as soon as it opened its school. Sister Teresa was called to Heaven from her garden of prayer before the end of 1818, ripe for reward as one who had in her orphaned girlhood turned from the kind attention of her father's non-Catholic relatives. A pupil of Loretto and later a member of the Society, she shed about her the fair light of solid virtues and drew others to that God for whom she gladly lived and died.

For thirty years the Sisters' school at Gethsemani continued its work of Christian education. The erection of other schools making that of Gethsemani no longer a necessity, the farm was sold to a colony of Trappist monks from France for five thousand dollars, and eight boarding pupils accompanied the Sisters to Loretto Mother House, November 5, 1848. The monks paid nine hundred dollars for movable property suitable for their work, and began at once the establishment of their Order, which under the same title has become a valuable addition to the diocese of Louisville, and still flourishes as the noted Abbey of Gethsemani.

Perceiving the good accomplished by the Sisters in their educational work among girls, Father Nerinckx desired to found a companion Society of Brothers for similar work among boys. Coinciding with the opinion, Bishop Flaget gave ready consent, and Father Nerinckx secured a tract of three hundred and eleven acres, with house and outbuildings, from Joseph Ray, for which he paid three thousand dollars, the money having been collected from the people chiefly by the Sisters. He named the place Mt. St. Mary, and the Sisters cultivated the farm for a year or more, holding the property for their founder's plan, in which they took a zealous interest. But before the end of 1819 the house was destroyed by fire; later, a violent wind storm destroyed the grist mill, an important feature at that epoch. Undaunted by these disasters, Father Nerinckx determined upon another trip to Europe to secure subjects and means for the new Brotherhood; and in the spring of 1820, being then in the fifty-ninth year of his age, the energetic priest set sail for England. He was accompanied by the Reverend Guy Ignatius Chabrat, the first priest ordained by Bishop Flaget in Kentucky, and afterward coadjutor Bishop of Bardstown. Father Nerinckx first visited London, where his brother, Father John Nerinckx, was engaged in missionary work, their sister living with him, and where he had the Rules of the Society printed by Keating and Brown, Grosvenor Square. He was, however, greatly hindered in his visit to Belgium by the persecutions religion was enduring, and his success fell below his expectations. But he brought back with him several zealous youths, some of whom entered the Society of Jesus, among whom were the renowned Fathers De Smet and Van Assche.

They arrived in America September 23, 1821. For his projected Brotherhood Father Nerinckx had secured three subjects, with whom and the aspirants in Kentucky he anticipated forming his foundation. His failure to execute his project was no fault of his. During his absence the Reverend William Byrne, who had been appointed to attend to St. Charles and Holy Mary congregations, had opened a school for boys in the Mt. St. Mary property, and was unwilling to relinquish it to Father Nerinckx upon the return of the old missionary. One of the Belgian youths died of dropsy shortly after coming to Kentucky, and the two others remained at Loretto until 1824, when Mr. Van Rysselberghe accompanied Father Nerinckx to Missouri. After the death of the priest he returned to Bardstown, where he married and settled. Mr. Gilbert, or Brother Gilbert, as he is known in the chronicles of these days, was attached to different houses of the Loretto Society, attending to the farm work, and died at Cedar Grove Academy, in Louisville, in 1867. The college thus founded by Father Byrne has been maintained as such to the present day. It was transferred from the secular clergy to the Jesuits in 1829, and abandoned by them in 1846, when the Society of Jesus left Kentucky. Reopened a year later by the secular clergy, it continued until 1869. In 1871 it passed into the hands of the Fathers of the Resurrection, who still conduct it.

The property of Mt. St. Mary belonged to the Loretto Society, and rather than disturb the school for boys which at the time of Father Nerinckx' death was in successful operation under Father Byrne, Bishop Flaget gave the Sisters St. Stephen's Farm, eight miles from St. Mary's, whither the Mother House was transferred a few months later from the original foundation. How history would have read had Father Nerinckx' project been unfrustrated offers subject for thought, contemplating the prominent part played in Catholic education in the West and South by the Society that success crowned. Although Father Byrne frustrated the birth of the first American Brotherhood, he was animated with priestly zeal, as was proved afterward by his sacrificing his life in the cause of charity. At the time of the terrible epidemic of cholera, in 1833, having prepared for death a negro woman, he contracted the disease and died, on June 6, after a few hours' illness.

But the disappointment Father Nerinckx found in Kentucky was more than compensated for in the happy surprise that had awaited him in Baltimore, where he found seven

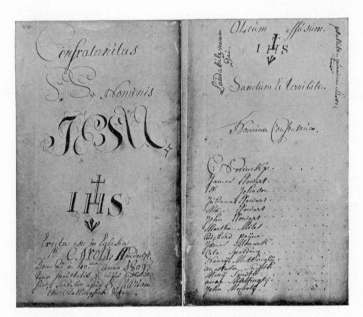

RECORD OF FIRST HOLY NAME SOCIETY IN THE
UNITED STATES.

young ladies desirous of devoting their lives to God in the Loretto Society. He was well pleased with their devotion, and accepted them, together with a Miss Mary C. Carney, who had come with him from England. The seven postulants were: Misses Mary Madden, Catherine A. Kelly, Bridget S. Kelly, Petronilla Doran, Alice Cloney, Margaret McSorley and Mary McSorley. On November 5, 1821, with Father Nerinckx and the three Belgian young men intended for the new Brotherhood, they started for their future home among the distant wooded hills of Kentucky. Soon after setting forth Father Nerinckx enjoined silence, and the conventual Rule was observed almost before the roofs of their houses had vanished from their vision. A full week passed before they reached Pittsburg; here a delay was inevitable while a flatboat was built to convey the party down the Ohio River to Louisville, which city was reached December 7, after a varied experience on the beautiful stream. A large market wagon having been procured, the young ladies mounted and sat upon their trunks for the long drive to Loretto by way of Bardstown. In the latter place they were obliged to stop for Sunday duties, and were most hospitably entertained by good Bishop David and the Sisters of Nazareth, leaving for Loretto Monday, December 10, the feast of the Translation of the Holy House.

One day later, Bishop Flaget, accompanied by the worthy Father Nerinckx, arrived at Little Loretto; then indeed was joy in the humble household; Sisters, pupils, servants came forward to greet the distinguished guests; Benediction of the Most Blessed Sacrament was given, followed by a few words of exhortation and congratulation from the saintly prelate, after which a joyful reunion took place outside the church, during which they listened to the narrative of their Father's adventures in a foreign land.

The year 1822 was utilized by the zealous founder to improve the spiritual training of the Sisters, to whom he had previously found scant time to impart instruction. He was more anxious for their interior improvement than for the increase of schools. Applications, he was sure, would never be lacking as long as the religious by the practice of true virtue brought down the blessing of Heaven upon their labors, nor was he solicitous as regards their material support, for which he ever advised them to trust to a gracious Providence. The spirit of penance and mortification was his favorite theme; even zeal without self-control is a sad delusion; but love of Jesus suffering and Mary in sympathy, near the Cross, where he wished all his spiritual children to stay, must always prove a safe one. A sort of anticipation of his own end appeared to inspire his words and make them earnest and tender, as were the great Master's at the Last Supper.

The steady increase the Society was experiencing enabled Father Nerinckx to open the new house of Bethania, near Fairfield, Nelson County. This was accomplished December 21, 1821, Sister Bibiana Elder being named superior of the community of ten Sisters. The place was well located for school purposes, but for some reason not now apparent the health of the Sisters failed in an alarming manner, eleven dying within the short space of six and a half years. In view of this great mortality, the superiors decided to close the house, and on April 6, 1828, the Sisters were recalled to Loretto. The community at Bethania had been placed under the spiritual care of Reverend Guy Chabrat, pastor of St. Michael's congregation, Fairfield, from 1812 to 1824, whose mistaken zeal and disregard of the Constitutions already approved by the Holy Father, Pius VII, and the Sacred Congregation of the Propaganda, led to disagreements and painful misunderstandings between the director and the founder. The Sisters themselves were often perplexed in mind as to the right course to pursue, so it may have been a relief to them when the summons came calling them home.

FATHER NERINCKX GOES TO ROME.

One source of regret they had, leaving the remains of their dear Sisters among strangers. Not long after the bones of the eleven Sisters were transferred to the cemetery at the Mother House, where, watched by enduring love, they rest in the company of the just, awaiting the Resurrection Morn. The Sisters did not, however, entirely abandon Fairfield, as they remained in charge of the parish school of St. Michael, which was taught by them from 1829 until 1838.

The next establishment made by Father Nerinckx was that of Mt. Carmel, fifteen miles from Hardinsburg, Breckenridge County, Kentucky. Six Sisters, with Sister Agnes Hart as superior, took possession of the convent on Ash Wednesday of 1823. It proved, however, undesirable as a location for a school, and after seven years the Community removed to a farm, the home place of Governor John L. Helm, eight miles from Elizabethtown, in Hardin County. As the removal took place near Christmas, 1830, the Sisters named their new home Bethlehem. The Helm mansion and its adjacent slave quarters, with some additions, served for the dwelling of the Sisters and their pupils for several years, until the present commodious buildings were erected, in 1845. One year after its establishment, Bishop Flaget wrote, in 1832, of this foundation: "Mr. Cissell [Reverend Charles J. Cecil] says there are twenty-six day scholars who frequent their school, and they are sighing for the moment when the boarding house [Academy] will be erected, in order to send there some boarders."

Bethlehem is the oldest surviving branch foundation established by Loretto. For more than eighty years it has contributed to preserve and propagate the Faith in that section of Kentucky. In the Sisters' quiet cemetery rest the remains of one of the founders of Loretto, Anne Havern, who received the habit with Mary Rhodes and Christina Stuart. She died at Bethlehem January 19, 1862.

Like the Mother House and other Loretto houses in

57

LORETTO.

Kentucky, Bethlehem gave a home to missionaries attending a large circuit of country in which there are now several churches with resident pastors. In the early days this meant much to the missionary and to the development of the missions. St. John's Church, near Bethlehem, was built by Father Nerinckx in 1812, and the following is a list of its pastors and those of surrounding missions who have made their home at Bethlehem Convent:

Reverend Charles J. Cecil came from St. Anthony's Church on Long Lick with the Sisters when they moved from Mount Carmel, 1830, and he died at Bethlehem, November 23, 1832;

Reverend F. Chambige, 1832-1838;

Reverend Augustin Degauquier, 1839-1870;

Reverend Charles I. Coomes, 1838-1839 and 1870-1873;

Reverend H. Mertens, 1873-1875 and 1877-1888;

Reverend Pol. Fermont, 1875-1877;

Reverend J. J. Fitzgerald, 1888-1892;

Reverend J. J. Abell, 1892, present incumbent.

One of these, Reverend A. Degauquier, rests in the Convent cemetery. The following lines from the pen of Kentucky's first native priest, Reverend Robert A. Abell, inscribed upon his tomb, indicate the veneration in which his memory is held:

"Not eloquence, but awful virtue's fame
 Sheds deathless glories 'round Degauquier's name.
 The guileless man the priestly robes adorned—
 Living, all loved him, dying, all men mourned.
 Belgium his birth, Kentucky gave his grave,
 The Catholic heart his memory shall save,
 And saving, safely point to all the road
 That led him safely to his Father, God.
 Eternal rest, eternal joys be thine,
 Thy sweet example and thy prayers be mine!"

It was given to Father Nerinckx also to witness the extension of the Society beyond the confines of the State, when, in response to the request of Bishop Dubourg of St. Louis, twelve Sisters, with Sister Joanna Miles as superior, left Loretto May 12, 1823, to open a school in Perry County, Missouri. Mother Julianna Wathen, the Mother Superior, accompanied the little band to its mission, and Father Nerinckx journeyed with the Sisters as far as Louisville. They stopped one night at Gethsemani and Bethania convents, hearing Mass and receiving the Bread of the strong before each day's journey. In Louisville they enjoyed the hospitality of Mr. James Holden, who, with Mr. Byrne, conducted them to the parish church the next morning to assist at the divine Sacrifice and communicate before embarking on the steamer Cincinnati. Here their kind entertainers bade them God-speed, and Father Nerinckx gave them his blessing.

Never did the little band of wayfarers stand more in need of the protection of God than on that perilous trip. Thrice during the voyage the boat was thought to be sinking, which fate befell it after the Sisters had disembarked. Their first night in Missouri was spent in the house of Mr. Bird, near the present St. Mary landing; the next day the little company was installed in the home of Mrs. Sarah Hayden, mother of Sister Mechtildes, who gave them hospitality for twenty-three days, the convent not yet being ready for habitation.

It was well that the Sisters had early been trained in the school of mortification and were familiar with hardships, else the conditions that confronted them might have deprived them of being the first successful pioneers of schools for all classes, especially the poor, west of the Mississippi River,—conditions that the heroic efforts of the Religious of the Sacred Heart did not surmount. Not even the founders in the first cabin convent in Kentucky endured the misery and privation known by this band of valiant souls. Their new home, erected by the good people of Perry

County, aided by the seminarians and priests of the Lazarist Foundation of the Barrens, among whom were the Reverend Father Rosati, afterward Bishop of St. Louis, and Reverend Father De Neckere, later called to the See of New Orleans, consisted of but one room, built of logs. The poverty of the structure suggested the stable of the Nativity, and they called it Bethlehem. It had no chimney, and of course the poor Sisters could not boast the luxury of a stove . For four months they cooked in an improvised kitchen composed of forked stakes driven in the ground and covered with bushes. To add to their discomfort, the summer proved dry and unhealthful, and one after another the poor Sisters were prostrated with fever and ague.

Far from home and kindred, with poverty and sickness for their companions, their bravery in supporting what was to all human seeming a forlorn hope must ever command the admiration of men, must ever be an inspiration to those who follow in their footsteps. Not only did they hold the position but, like good soldiers, went forward with their work. By September they had a room fitted up for a school, and another for a chapel, and the same year of their foundation began their duties as teachers, opening classes with six pupils. This number steadily advanced, and two years later they found themselves in a position to improve their rude convent and build a new chapel. Before this could be accomplished, however, an incendiary set fire to the lumber, destroying it and the house which had been built, after the visit of Father Nerinckx in 1824, for the reception of Indian girls. Disaster could not daunt women who had endured so much, and they recommenced work. Fortune favors the brave, and by the next year their log house was plastered, brick additions were built, and they began to enjoy some semblance of comfort.

Their sanctity equaled their heroism, and we find both Father Rosati and Bishop Dubourg writing of them words of praise. The former compares them to the strictest communities of Europe in their palmiest days, while the bishop commends the solid education they give to girls, besides providing for all the necessities of the community. In 1836 Bethlehem was again visited by fire. The loss brought the Sisters to a condition of extreme poverty. A subscription of one hundred dollars was taken up for them by Reverend J. Timon, and shortly afterward another hundred was sent them by Mr. Bryan Mullanphy. Tided over this crisis in their history, they were able in 1838 to found a branch house at Cape Girardeau, and to this more prosperous house some time after 1844, and not later than 1847, the Bethlehem foundation was removed.

Bethlehem, the eldest sister of the houses beyond Loretto's native State, and the sixth established by the Mother House, is dear to every Lorettine, though but the memory of it now remains; and while, as we have seen, the Sisters experienced here severe trials and hardships, yet their life was not without its bright side. Divine Providence raised up for them friends loyal and true in the persons of the Reverend Lazarist Fathers of St. Mary's Seminary. Had these Fathers been members of the Loretto Society they could not have been more devoted, more solicitous, more untiring in their efforts for the welfare of the Sisters; and while, also, this is true of the whole Lazarist community, it is doubly so of two: of him who was Superior of the Lazarists till 1830 and first Bishop of St. Louis, the Right Reverend Joseph Rosati, and of him who became Buffalo's first bishop, the Right Reverend John Timon.

CHAPTER VI.

FATHER NERINCKX LEAVES KENTUCKY.

GOD did not spare His own Son, we know, and the persecution of Father Nerinckx, which we are now called upon to relate, the last sad chapter of this remarkable life, shows that, like his Divine Master, he was required to tread the wine-press of sorrow, go down to death in suffering, humiliation and apparent defeat. Nor was this occasioned by an enemy from without, but by a member of his own household, a minister, like himself, of the altar; and considering it, well might Father Nerinckx cry out, with the Royal Prophet, foreshadowing the Great Betrayal: "For if my enemy had reviled me, I would verily have borne with it. And if he that hated me had spoken great things against me: I would perhaps have hidden myself from him. But thou a man of one mind, my guide and my familiar. Who didst take sweet meats together with me: in the house of God we walked with consent."

Responding to the urgent appeal of Bishop Flaget, the Reverend Guy Ignatius Chabrat had left France in 1810, when he was yet only a subdeacon, to devote himself to the missions of America. In the course of time he was made confessor of the convent at Bethania. There he found a community of women striving to reach perfection by living according to the Rule of the Society which they had voluntarily entered and vowed themselves to for life. They were well content with their Constitution, which had been commended by the Holy See, but Father Chabrat was not. The hardy piety of the Belgian priest, the rigorous pathway he had traced for his spiritual daughters to the Kingdom of Heaven, was repellent to the sensibilities of the less ascetic Frenchman.

FATHER NERINCKX LEAVES KENTUCKY.

At an earlier period the English Dominican Fathers, who had in 1806 founded their convent in Washington County, had complained of Father Nerinckx because of his extreme strictness in religious matters. So the charge of Father Chabrat against Father Nerinckx' severity in his direction of the Society seemed easily sustained. The accusation, however, only gives us another proof of the heroic virtue of this unnamed saint. Him the divested Man of Assisi would have hailed as a brother, and the self-conquering Ignatius of Loyola recognized as his kinsman. He knew the sweetness which the Lord holds for those who, leaving the things of the flesh, find the things of the spirit; and though all may not take this upward path, all can loosen the bands of earth, all can see the material is the elusive, the spiritual the abiding and the true. From the day St. Paul thundered his admonitions to the lax among the first Christians we find the same demands made by men and women of God upon the people of their times; we hear the same vehement denunciation against the supremacy of the flesh over the spirit, the things of earth over the things of heaven.

Nor can we conceive that the requirements made by Father Nerinckx of laity and religious appeared so formidable to the Kentuckian of that day, however they might impress a native of one of the most highly civilized, and consequently more enervated, countries of the Old World. The men and women of whom Father Nerinckx demanded an unflinching observance of the laws of God and the Church ought to see in that no excessive hardship, no overpowering sacrifice. If they journeyed many rugged miles to assist at Divine Service, and fasted often until three and four o'clock in the afternoon to receive from his hands the Bread of Life, their strenuous labors to subdue the wilderness, the privations they had endured in the accomplishment of this gave a robustness to their constitutions, making the trips and abstinence matters of slight moment. If they were

63

taught to believe that the Kingdom of Heaven was to be gained by violence, they found therein no startling revelation who had to use far greater violence to obtain a foothold in the earthly western kingdom they had invaded.

The women whom he had gathered into the Society of Loretto were the firstborn daughters of these hardy pioneers. If they suffered privations, endured hardships, they only sought what their mothers had accepted; and it is an historic fact that the valiant spirit of these early Religious of Kentucky had often to be restrained by their spiritual father lest their ardor to conquer nature should carry them into extremes that would be harmful to their health.

Father Chabrat was unable to appreciate the character of these early Kentucky women. Moreover, he was absolutely without experience in matters of conventual life, for he had come out to this country before he was ordained to the priesthood. He nevertheless determined to change the entire spirit of their Constitution, and asked leave of the bishop to do so. Instead of reserving the matter to himself, the bishop summoned Father Nerinckx and submitted to him Chabrat's project. Knowing the bishop's partiality for the young priest, Father Nerinckx gave up immediately, for he saw that any remonstrance would not be listened to. It simply broke his heart, but he submitted. He led his Isaac up to the mount of sacrifice, nor did any angel appear to stay his hand. He asked to leave Kentucky and his beloved Loretto, and Bishop Flaget gave his consent to the old priest's heroic act!

Loretto pleaded against the cruel sentence her well-loved founder had passed upon himself, but her cries were unavailing; and when Father Nerinckx could deafen his ears to that voice he proved his detachment was complete. And yet in nothing did he so truly show his love as in this voluntary relinquishment of his Society, this withdrawal from his own in favor of one who was not his friend, and though she stood bereft, Loretto then realized, as never before, how precious was her existence to the soul of her founder. Out of the poignancy of the hour came also the knowledge that the trials which confront men and institutions upon their material side are trivial in comparison with those that enmity or misguided zeal sends to assail the purposes of their life, rendering nugatory the accomplishments of the past and thwarting, if not destroying, the hopes of the future. The lesson was early taught and transmitted, and a future generation of Loretto's daughters were not unprepared when called upon to endure persistent persecutions as unprovoked as that which had driven Father Nerinckx from his honored place of ecclesiastical superior.

Before leaving he penned a letter of farewell to his beloved daughters, which, with filial affection, is annually read in the convents of the Society. It is as follows:

"J. M. J.

"Loretto, 29th of May, 1824.

"To the Dear Mother, Mothers and Sisters of the
   Loretto House and Society, all hail!

"Being about to start on my intended journey, which may put an end to my life, and probably to any intercourse or meddling with the Loretto House or Society, I leave as a short farewell these few lines to the Loretto House, having kept this place as a home since it was begun. It is not strange, my dear Sisters, to find in this vale of tears that mass of afflictions which holy Job affirms to be the lot of all born of woman: *multis miseriis;* of that my age and condition is to me a present and sure conviction. We are all, having been children of wrath, doomed to drink of this bitterness. Still, the Merciful Lord, the darling object and sweetness of the Loretto devotion, called, and truly so, the Man of Sorrows, by his holy passion and death, has entirely altered this unhappy condition into a state of real felicity; since he has set apart for us such a great weight of rewards and glory, for the light sufferings of a momentary life. This reflection prevents me from making any

65

remarks of an unpleasant nature, willing to bury in oblivion all that has passed.

"To leave you some knowledge of my sixty-three years of life, which are to me as many years of shame and confusion, and for which I entreat you to obtain for me by your prayers some months of true and real repentance:

"I had the happiness to be born of religious parents, being the oldest of seven brothers and seven sisters, of which the greatest number were blessed with a religious call, notwithstanding the great interruptions caused by dreadful revolutions, all directed against religion. I thank God for His mercies! and for having preserved our family from joining any of the errors and blunders, of which thousands have been the victims. I was sent to school at six years of age; to the higher studies at twelve, going through the different classes of humanity, philosophy and divinity in different places, but mostly at Louvain and Mechlin. I was made a priest at twenty-four, and that year sent as under-pastor to our cathedral, where I remained eight years. In 1794 I was sent as parish priest to a place called Meerbeke, five miles from Louvain. The French drove me from here three years after that, having given a *prise-de-corps* or order to take me, for having said Mass without taking the prescribed declaration, it being against my religion and conscience. From that I was sheltered as in a prison in the Hospital of Dendermonde, where, being requested to do so, I had for six years the spiritual direction of nuns and sick, a thing I could safely do, not being known by any one and never coming out of my shelter. In 1804, the 3d of July, having before refused another oath asked of me in order to go to my former parish, because with the advice of good and learned men I found it contrary to conscience, I started for America with letters of recommendation to the Right Rev. Bishop Carroll from the Princess Gallitzin. I had a companion, Rev. Mr. Guny, of the Order of St. Benedict, of Cambray, who intended to join the Trappist Order; and after three months of navigation at sea, amongst storms, sickness, and other miseries, having lost forty-two of our crew, we arrived at Baltimore the 14th of November.

"My intention at that time was to go to any place, even Indians, where it was thought I could do any good. The Nuncio of the Pope, Ciamberlani, had offered me to go to his missions, the Cape of Good Hope, but wanted me to have a companion of our language, which I had not. The College of the Jesuits of Georgetown harbored me for four months; there I picked up a few English words. I then went to Conewago to meet the Trappist monks, with whom I left that place for Kentucky. I arrived before them, the 2d of July, 1805, at the house of Rev. S. T. Badin, the only priest in Kentucky at that time. I staid with him seven years without any disturbance, having leave from him to act in my places and stations as I thought proper. I have, with God's help and some alms from my country, built some churches and procured some establishments for the Church. I had also at the time made an attempt to start a female school and nunnery at Holy Mary's, but met with no encouragement from laity or clergy. Rev. Mr. Badin made the second trial close by his house; the house, nearly finished, was laid in ashes, and the project disappeared.

"At the end of my seventh year, very unexpectedly, as may be seen in my advices, another attempt was made for a female school at St. Charles. It took root, and grew to what it is now, without any man having much claim to its rise. About this time I left Rev. Mr. Badin, as my presence seemed to be necessary at Loretto, being stationary priest of St. Charles' congregation. The Society began in 1812. In 1816 I went to Rome for Loretto. In 1820 I took another trip to Europe for the benefit of the Society, for some difficulties in the ministry, etc. It is now (1824) better than twelve years that I have had charge of the Society, but particularly of the Loretto House, except three years and the half of absence, not without difficulties and contradictions. As I never was fit for any charge or any part of the ministry, which, before God and men, I freely grant and agree to, I am willing to believe that the cause of all the difficulties and uneasiness originated from me, for which I beg to be pardoned by Almighty God, the congregations, and the Society.

"Being once more proscribed from my native country in 1822 by the Holland government, not, I hope, for crimes before God, and my present situation having become unpleasant and, as far as I know, unprofitable or perhaps injurious to religion, I am under the necessity of gathering, at sixty-three, my strength of forty-three years and go to a new region. I feel no less resolution of mind, but I know not whether my strength of body will hold out. However, I intend to make the trial, with God's assistance.

"You have here a short detail of the poor life of an unworthy priest who has been in this country for about nineteen years, twelve years about the Loretto Society, and in all thirty-nine in the ministry. It is unnecessary to tell you, my dear Sisters in Christ, what a hard and terrible judgment this poor wretch will shortly meet with on account of his temerity in the holy ministry, without any regard to his own corruption, knowing that it is said: *judicium durissimum his qui præsunt fiet*—very hard will the judgment be for those that are in authority. I beg of you to have pity on me!

"Should you ask me now my principal motives for leaving these parts, and what I am going to do next, although there be no real profit or necessity in the answers to those queries, I see no great impropriety in them, considering that the long knowledge you have of their nature will justify the harmless curiosity. I say then, if I know myself, that three great causes urge me to move: 1. The impossibility of holding out for want of temporals, having no help but from Europe. 2. The sake of peace, which is already somewhat interrupted, and, in my opinion, will always be tottering with the clergy and the Society. 3. The rest and tranquillity of conscience, which I cannot have here on account of difficulties in practice which are lately come or surely increased, for which, it seems, no remedy can be obtained. These are the main motives: if these could be cured, the rest might be neglected.

"As to my views and intentions, they are not yet decided or really settled. I will take Providence for guide; that *Providence* which brought me in and will carry me out, and has presided over the whole course of my life; I always find myself safe and easy with It. It was even so the case with the Apostles and numbers of their followers. Still, some of the intentions which strike my mind are the following:

"God's will at the head, and His honor.

"The propagation of the devotion to Jesus suffering and Mary sorrowing.

"The Hospital Sisters.

"The orphans' assistance.

"The conversion of Indians.

"The preservation of the Institute's zeal and purity; its propagation; its consolidation.

"The providing for its Brotherhood; out of these its directors.

"The peace with colleagues.

"The settling of conscience.

"The preparation for death . . . burial.

"Final penance.

"The Flemish mission.

"The eremitical life.

"The fixing of my writings.

"The salvation of the blacks.

"All this, or part of it, if I can suit, and God thinks fit.

"You see here a great number of intentions for old age, weak body, and poor soul, with scanty talents. The work cannot be much; yet the will may please God still. God's designs, always adorable and good, ought to be fulfilled, however opposed to our feelings and opinions or notions.

"My will I leave in the hands of Mr. Thomas Livers. I leave to the establishments what they are at present in possession of, except what I may need for my new undertakings, if any take place. This, I think, cannot be before the fall or next spring.

"If you inquire whether I know what will become of you, this I cannot tell. But from my present experience, from the nature of things and from the condition of man, without pretending to any revelation or gift of prophecy, there is not a spark of doubt in my mind but you will undergo great changes from your present state, which the far greatest number of you looks upon as happy; you must only pray that what is to come may be for the better; it was not in my power to do more or better for you. As God gave me, so did I for the poor Society.

"As to advice, for which you have so often applied, I hardly know what to say. There never was a man who stood more in need of it himself, and none who was less able to give advice. The directions which have been given by word or writing have proved to be unbecoming, too particular, and full of incorrectness, not to mention worse appellations which have been applied to them. I see no good or propriety in giving any, being sure that they would meet with opposition at the first glance. However, I can say that the whole sum of all my words and writings is nearly contained in the *Morning Manna*, read every day before Mass, which I wish you always to remember and exactly comply with.

"I wish to leave you a short paraphrase of the standard of the Society, which I beg you to say now and then for poor old

"C. Nerinckx.

FATHER NERINCKX LEAVES KENTUCKY.

> "The Suffering Jesus
> and
> The Sorrowful Mary
> Bless us all!
> Farewell!"

That to which Father Nerinckx refers in his letter as the Morning Manna is the following:

"O dear Sisters and Scholars! Love your Jesus, dying with love for you on the Cross! Love Mary, your loving Mother, sorrowing at the foot of the Cross! Love one another, have only one heart, one soul, one mind! Love the Institute, love the Rules, love Jesus' darling humility!"

The unhappy occurrence of Father Nerinckx' departure from Kentucky took place on June 16, 1824, twelve years after the foundation of the Society and nineteen since his entrance into the State. His destination was Missouri, where already there was a branch of the Society and where opportunities for his long dreamed of work among the Indians were to be found. He made the journey on horseback, and on July 2, 1824, he reached the convent at Bethlehem. The Sisters, who knew nothing of the calamity that had overtaken the Mother House and the sorrow that had been sent into the soul of their Father, were filled with joy at his unexpected appearance in their midst; when, however, they were made to understand it was an exile they were receiving, who asked them refuge for his declining days, their grief for him and their own bereft Society swept all happiness from their hearts. They gave him the tender welcome of their love and sympathy, and under their gentle care he was able, after a few days, to visit the Seminary at the Barrens, where in the company of the good Lazarist Fathers he remained a few weeks. It is significant that Bethlehem, the first establishment outside of Kentucky, should have been blessed with the last ministrations of their saintly founder. Did it forecast that the fruits of the missions Loretto has since sent out would be surpassingly rich and great, even beyond that which has blessed her at home?

On the 25th of July Father Nerinckx returned to the convent and gave the religious habit to Misses Mary Stewart and Elizabeth Tucker. He seemed to be aware that his day of life was lengthening into the shadows of death, for he assured the young novices they were the last who should be clothed by him, and spoke of his approaching departure in words that were afterward literally fulfilled. He was long that morning in separating from his spiritual daughters. He had much to say to them, knowing it was the final meeting. His counsels were repeated, as if he would stamp them indelibly on their hearts; and when he would start it was only to turn back to speak further words of admonition or advice. At last, however, he moved away and, with a blessing falling from his lips, mounted his horse and set forth for St. Louis, where he was to meet Bishop Rosati.

From St. Louis Father Nerinckx went to Florissant, where the Jesuits had been established since 1823, and in whose number were several Flemish priests known to him. He then returned to St. Louis; there meeting an Indian agent and chief, he made the arrangements for the inauguration of a long-cherished wish in having his offer of Christian education for Indian girls accepted. Twelve girls were to be sent to Bethlehem, the Government to pay for their tuition. With this income assured, the Sisters would be able to enlarge their work of educating poor children and orphans. He immediately sent the Superior at Bethlehem word to prepare for the reception of these dusky wards of the Government, along with thirty-six orphans whom he was sending her. In compliance with the order a house was built; but as Father Nerinckx' death interfered with the contract, the Indian girls were not sent to the Sisters, although the orphans came; and the care of them, with the expense of the new building, plunged the little community into deeper poverty. How they survived would be a mystery did we not believe that Divine Providence was near at hand, and that He who kept the widow's cruse replenished was not forgetful of these consecrated virgins and their orphaned charges.

Despite the misgivings with which he started, Father Nerinckx found himself returning to Bethlehem like one who had taken a new lease on life. The bishop had accepted his services for the diocese, and approved of the work which he proposed that the Sisters should do for the neglected Indians and poor orphans, and as he hastened home to Bethlehem we may picture the exaltation of that saintly soul. The step he had found so hard to take had brought him into a richer field of usefulness, and his heart grew strong within him as he lifted his eyes and saw the harvest whitening for his hands. On the homeward way he heard of a neglected Catholic colony, and true to his apostolic calling, he turned aside to bring to its people the ministrations of their holy religion. He instructed them, heard their confessions, and as this occupied the greater part of the day it was three o'clock in the afternoon of August 3d when he celebrated Mass; then, as if he had no other aim or object on earth, the old pastor began to secure funds for the new church which he urged the little congregation to build. His persuasiveness and zeal bore their usual fruit, and the subscription list was readily begun, he opening it with a gift of ten dollars. The weather was extremely warm, and he complained to Brother Van Rysselberghe, who had accompanied him from Kentucky, of feeling ill; he rallied, however, and after celebrating Mass on the third morning of his stay, Thursday, August 5, Feast of Our Lady of the Snow, felt able to go on to St. Genevieve, about twelve miles distant, where the Lazarists were stationed.

He succeeded in making the journey, but arrived in an almost dying condition. The following Sunday, August 8, he heard Mass, although remaining quite weak. His illness grew alarming on Monday, and on Tuesday three physicians were called in for consultation: they pronounced his case beyond their skill and science. On Tuesday morning the good Lazarist Father Dahmen prepared his guest for death, and at five o'clock in the evening of the same day, August 12, 1824, Father Nerinckx closed his weary eyes to the things of earth and, we trust, opened them on a glorious eternity.

Bishop Rosati had been apprised of the serious illness of Father Nerinckx, and hastened to St. Genevieve, in the hope of arriving in time to comfort the venerable priest faring forth on his last lone journey. He arrived, however, a day too late; but, giving orders that the remains should be conveyed to Bethlehem for interment, he joined in the sorrowing funeral procession. A messenger had been dispatched to apprise the Sisters of the death of Father Nerinckx and the approach of the cortege. The announcement would not have found them unprepared had they heeded the prophetic utterances of one of their members. Every Thursday night, according to Rule, the Sisters by turns kept vigil before the Blessed Sacrament from after night prayers until the end of morning prayers, and it was during one of these hours on the night of August 12 that Sister Mechtildes Hayden rose from her knees and, going to her companion, Sister Benedicta Fenwick, whispered to her: "Father Nerinckx is dead. I know he is. He is now in the presence of the Blessed Virgin whom he so tenderly loved on earth, and in a short time I shall follow." The evening of the next day, while as yet the messenger from St. Genevieve was on his way to the convent, Sister Mechtildes rose from her bed and ran through the house, crying out: "Praises to the Lord! Our dear Father Nerinckx is in Heaven! Alleluia!" As the nun was afflicted with an incurable malady, her companions concluded that her long-borne ailment had affected her mind, and no significance was attached to her prophetic utterances. A quarter of an hour later they were recalled in sorrow and awe, when the messenger arrived with the tidings of the death of Father Nerinckx.

The Sisters repaired to the chapel and there awaited the last coming of their beloved Father. At two o'clock in the morning of August 14 the episcopal escort reached the convent; the coffin was carried into the chapel and placed before the altar. There, surrounded by his daughters, Father Nerinckx kept the last of many vigils before the tabernacle. On the same day, which was Saturday, the obsequies were held. The solemn high Mass was celebrated by Reverend Father Odin of the Barrens, in the presence of Bishop Rosati, who gave the final absolution and preached the sermon. The remains were then conveyed to the convent graveyard and deposited in the grave.

The Sisters, however, not satisfied to permit these venerable relics to rest under ground, waited only until Monday morning to disinter the body and place it in the tomb which Brother James Van Rysselberghe had built. Here rested for nine years all that was mortal of Reverend Charles Nerinckx, for Bishop Rosati, though brief had been his acquaintance with the broken old missionary who had come to him for refuge from the storm that had burst upon him in the evening of his days, beheld the saint before him, and rightly prized his sacred ashes as the most precious possession of his diocese. To the pleading of Bishop Flaget and the sorrowing Superiors of Loretto's Mother House he turned for long a deaf ear; but finally prayer prevailed, and he gave back to Loretto her holy founder. On December 16, 1833, Brother Charles Gilbert reached the Sisters' new home at St. Stephen's Farm with the remains, and while the sad bells tolled across the still Kentucky hills the black-robed nuns went down the sweeping avenue of elms that Father Badin had planted, to give mournful welcome to their beloved founder. Where, twenty-eight years ago, the generous-hearted Father Badin had met him with outstretched arms and a brother's greeting,

75

his weeping children received him, and gave him what his spirit must have craved, a tomb beneath Kentucky skies, a resting-place on Loretto's hallowed grounds.

For almost eighty years he has thus held in death his still watch over Loretto from his marble tomb in the little graveyard, and there generation after generation of his daughters have resorted to pray; there they kneeled to say farewell when the voice of Duty called them far from the Mother House of their affection, and there, when their allotted task was done, they, too, laid them down for the long wait he is keeping. In this, her centennial year, Loretto has sought to honor her founder, and at the same time show her respect and reverence for the spot where Father Nerinckx and Father Badin first met when this rich country was a wilderness, where their days of holy companionship were spent, and where Kentucky's first bishop, the sainted Flaget, was welcomed to his See. Here Loretto has erected a new and appropriate tomb for her founder. It is fitting this should be. Still was something wanting from the sacred spot, the ashes of him who first planted the Cross on that height. Father Badin died out of that Kentucky which he loved, as must every evangelist the scene of his missionary labors, especially when they are so rich as were his in the harvest of souls. While not driven by persecution, as was Father Nerinckx, yet he felt, and perchance had the sad knowledge pressed in upon him, that his days of usefulness were over. Cincinnati, under the amiable Archbishop Purcell, gave him the welcome his early companion had received from Bishop Rosati, and when he died laid him beside her first bishop, Fenwick, under the crypt of her cathedral.

Kentucky had greater claim to the high and holy trust of guarding the last resting-place of her apostle, but when fifty years had passed without that claim being pressed, with commendable zeal for the honor due the proto-priest, their benefactor, whom they number among the founders of the

REV. THEODORE BADIN.

university, the Fathers of the Holy Cross Congregation, on March 17, 1904, removed his remains to an appropriate mausoleum they had erected at the University of Notre Dame, Indiana. Father Badin bequeathed his heart to Loretto, and the earnest petition of the Sisters for a relic to be enshrined at the Mother House, the home so long of Father Badin and their own venerated founder, was graciously granted by the university. With grateful hearts the precious relic was received and placed in an appropriate monument erected, at the suggestion of Reverend Edwin Drury, by the clergy of the diocese.

CHAPTER VII.

Father Chabrat Appointed Ecclesiastical Superior.

ON receiving word of the death of Father Nerinckx, Bishop Flaget repaired to Loretto with Father Chabrat and appointed him ecclesiastical superior of the Loretto Sisterhood. The distressed Sisters were ordered to turn over all the treasured writings and books of their beloved founder to the new director, who immediately consigned them to the flames. The Community was to be remodeled. But the harsh measure only served to show how very little Father Chabrat understood the nature of womankind, for when she truly and worthily loves, she loves to the end, and it were easier to separate the crimson from the rose than to thrust such an affection from her heart. The Daughters of Loretto loved their saintly founder. Under God, to him they owed in great measure their Society, by means of which they might secure their own souls' sanctification and instruct others unto righteousness, thereby continuing Christ's work among men. They knew that the Rule by which they were disciplined had been inspired as the one suited to their needs, and commended as it was by the Holy See, it were little short of desecration to attempt to tear it from their hearts. But Obedience, now a leaden hand where before it had been sweetly guiding, ruled, and the Sisters made no protest; and when Father Chabrat changed the Rule they accepted it, and strove to act as their founder would have acted under like circumstances.

But never at any time did they separate themselves from the spirit of their founder. His life was their inspiration; the strength, the holiness, the beauty of his character, were the models by which they strove to fashion theirs. His writings, reduced to a heap of ashes, had been scattered to the winds of heaven, but his words, inscribed on their hearts, could not be reached by the profaning hand. They were repeated in the convent and the chapel; in the novitiate, white-veiled novices and eager-souled postulants drank them in as they fell reverently from the lips of the mistress; in the schoolroom the children learned the lessons he had left for them, the high import of which was realized as the years brought wisdom. Father Nerinckx was dead, and even his remains were withheld from her; her new superior was obliterating every visible trace of his work in her Rule and her institutions; and yet never was Father Nerinckx more vitally a part of Loretto's life than in those days of agonizing trial.

But there is nothing more disastrous than such a duality, and Loretto experienced its effects. During the ten years Father Chabrat remained as ecclesiastical superior the Mother House knew no expansion in Kentucky. Nor was there great activity experienced in Missouri, and the three attempts at foundation during this period were unsuccessful. The first of these was at La Fourche, Louisiana, and this offers us the most pathetic page of Loretto's long story. Other foundations have failed, but with them the loss was only material, while here the Society was called upon to mourn the departure of members from it, and know the cause was largely due to the feeling of insecurity that resulted from the radical changes being wrought in the Society by the ecclesiastical superior.

Bishop Dubourg, in a letter to his brother dated March 20, 1824, states that he had received from a gentleman a small farm at La Fourche, where he desired to establish the Sisters of Loretto, of which he had at that time seventeen in the State of Missouri. In the records of the Bethlehem Convent there is found an item, dated November 14, 1825, which states that Sister Joanna Miles, Sister Rose Elder and Sister Regina Clony were sent to establish a school at Assumption, near Opelousas, Louisiana. Later on are a few lines recording that this establishment was dissolved in 1828, Sister Joanna having previously returned to the world, while Sisters Rose and Regina joined the Religious of the Sacred Heart.

From the faint outline these words give we may fill out a story of trials that finally broke the spirits even of the women who had known Loretto's poverty and Bethlehem's misery. Miles of perilous, uninhabited country separated them from the Mother House and the poor refuge the Missouri Mission could give; the language of the French among whom they dwelt was unknown to them; of spiritual aids they had but little: and yet these trials they might have borne and carried their work to a successful issue, as had and has been done, if to all these sufferings were not added the torturing fear of the instability of the Society, seeing the holy Rule they had been taught to love and revere mutilated by the one appointed to take their founder's place over them. Though one of the little band must be named among the purblind company that "turned and walked with Him no more," and though the other two separated themselves from Loretto's glorious Sisterhood, broke the tender ties that bound them to their mother, still never does word of reproach fall upon their memories, but pardon and sympathy are theirs in fullest measure.

The Religious of the Sacred Heart, coming from France, were established at Florissant, Missouri, under the Venerable Mother Duchesne, and when Father Nerinckx visited the Jesuits there shortly before his death he had excited in that truly apostolic woman sentiments of the highest admiration. His desire to labor for the conversion of the Indians appealed to her, and his example, his words and his edifying death excited to the utmost her zeal for a similar work. She had previously conceived the idea of forming a congregation of Sisters for the work for which Father Nerinckx had chiefly founded the Society of Loretto, and the faithful carrying out of which purpose has made the

80

Lorettines the pioneers of Christian education in the West. In the struggling, sadly harassed little community at La Fourche it would appear her desire was to be realized. The school had made but little progress, owing to the Sisters' lack of knowledge of French, the ordinary language of the country, and when Bishop Rosati asked the Religious of the Sacred Heart to undertake the direction of the community and school by admitting the Sisters into the Society, and the Sisters, tried to the limit of endurance and assailed by we know not what fears, were willing, Mother Duchesne appealed to Mother Barat for the necessary permission.

Her request was supported by the urgent appeal of Monsignor Dubourg, who declared that he had always regarded Mother Duchesne as a person specially guided by the Spirit of God for the spiritual good of Louisiana, and expressed the belief that Providence had assembled the little community of Lorettines at La Fourche, procured them a house and means of existence for the carrying out of her zealous desires. The pressure thus brought to bear upon Mother Barat overruled her intuitive knowledge, and she gave her consent, and allowed one of her daughters, Madame Helène Dutour, to go from St. Louis to La Fourche for the purpose of effecting the union and foundation. She was, however, very particular about specifying the nature of the new establishment. She did not intend that La Fourche should be placed on a level with the regularly conducted schools of the Sacred Heart. "It must be on a lower scale," she wrote to Madame Aude at St. Michael's, in proximity to La Fourche, "and besides religion and needlework, the teaching in that establishment ought to be limited to reading, writing and sewing. In that way it will not injure your school. If more is attempted it will be necessary to build, and then there will be debts, and both houses in consequence in difficulties for years." The wise advice was not heeded, perhaps could not be owing to the national spirit of equality. It became a crushing expense on the Society, and to Mother

LORETTO.

Duchesne's bitter sorrow had, in 1832, to be suppressed. The property was returned to the Bishop of New Orleans, who established in it another religious community which was better able to continue the work, having more means and subjects at its disposal.

Yet it must not be supposed that Loretto utterly abandoned her sorely tried Sisters at La Fourche, made no effort to hold them to her great and tender heart. At Bethlehem convent, that true Lorettine, Mother Benedicta Fenwick ruled as superior, and to her Sisters at La Fourche she sent a letter, and reading it we must believe that either the Sisters had already committed themselves or believed they were bound to abide by the wishes of the bishop regarding them, else they could not have withstood its motherly appeal. Wrote Mother Benedicta:

"Bethlehem Monastery, Missouri.

"My dear Sisters,

"Since I wrote to you by the Reverend Mr. Bonen I have been apprized that you were also about to quit this Society to join the Ladies of the Sacred Heart, or that they were to send some of their members to the Assumption, then you would become one of their Order. Is this so or not, my dear Sisters, you who were once so much attached to this Society, who have been so exact in complying with its Rules and practices, who have edified me so much in your different employments and always shown such peace and contentment since my first acquaintance with you? Alas, my dear Sisters, what has induced you to fall back from your first resolution of living and dying in the Loretto Society? Are you wearied with it, or are you afraid that if you have not members to carry on that establishment you should not be received at the Mother House, this house or any of the other houses? Be assured, my dear Sisters, that we would not only embrace you with open arms, but rejoice to see and receive Sisters once so dear to us, and at whose separation not anything but obedience or the glory of God could have induced me to be willing to see you leave Bethlehem.

"At this place we have the appearances of doing well and we stand much in need of members ourselves. Why then not come back to this place, or, if you prefer, to the Mother House? Reflect, my Sisters, on the vows and promises you have made in the Loretto Society! Certainly, it was the will of God. Our Rules and Constitutions are very much approved of by the heads of our Holy Church, and we are, as it were, only just beginning. It is true they have been changed from the first, but for the better, and that was not our wish; therefore, we shall only have the greater merit of obedience in complying with them. If you have not taken any steps yet, reflect well before you do it. You may repent. In all religious orders every one has her crosses. I do not conjecture, but I am certain from experience that you have had yours, and if the Almighty is pleased to send them why not accept them cheerfully? It is not the Society, but its members, that cause disturbances. Such members are to be pitied, and such will be found in all religious houses, even in that of the Sacred Heart. As I was told, you were doing very well since Sister Joanna left. Wait a little while, and Divine Providence may assist you. Have recourse to our dearest Mother with the greatest confidence. She will never forsake her children if they do not first forsake her, and if you cannot continue there you may be assured that you will be received at the Mother House, this house or any of the other houses. I have nothing against the Ladies of the Sacred Heart, but when once a person has made vows and promises in a particular Society let her persevere in it, and, in the little judgment that I have, she will enjoy more real happiness. I speak to you as my dearest Sisters and intimate friends, and I presume you will take it as coming from one who is sincerely attached and interested in you."

Before turning this pathetic page, it is right to add that

LORETTO.

Sisters Rose and Regina continued faithful members of the Religious of the Sacred Heart, and we hope are now enjoying the reward laid up for those who strive manfully to follow the straight, hard path of the spirit. Sister Joanna Miles was the seventeenth member of the Society, entering August 22, 1816, at the age of sixteen years. In 1822 she was elected local superior of Loretto, at the first election held under the approved Rule. She founded Bethlehem convent, Missouri, in 1823, and went with the colony to La Fourche in 1825, and, according to the records of the Mother House, left the Society May 10, 1826. Of her no more is told.

In 1831 the Sisters of Bethlehem opened St. Joseph's parochial school on Apple Creek, in Perry County. Three Sisters were in charge, with Sister Eulalia Kelly as superior. The property had been donated to the Society by a good old German Catholic, Mr. Snowbusch, but the situation was not suitable for a school, and the year following the community was transferred to St. Mary's convent, New Madrid, Missouri. After a brief existence of six years, during which the poor community struggled hard against fever and other local maladies, the Sisters were recalled to Bethlehem on June 24, 1837. The third attempt was made at Fredericktown, Mo., in 1832, with Sister Benedicta Fenwick and five other Sisters comprising the foundation. Although placed under the protection of the glorious St. Michael, health and success were denied the Sisters, and as a deed to the place could not be secured, the school was closed in 1836.

But to Father Chabrat's administration as ecclesiastical superior the present location of the Loretto Mother House stands as a lasting memorial. Be the motive what it may, the change is one for which all must rejoice, since it gave into the keeping of the first religious Society of the West the place most intimately connected with the establishment of the Church therein. A few months after assuming control of Loretto, Father Chabrat decided upon the change, and the bishop consented, giving the Sisters in exchange for their property at Mt. St. Mary's the St. Stephen's Farm, as Father Badin's place was called. The Sisters did not make the change without regret and sorrow. The old Loretto had been secured for them by their beloved founder, and by the toil of his consecrated hands much of its pleasant surroundings had been effected. Here their first struggle for life had been made, and around it some of their most sacred associations clustered. They set self aside, however, knowing obedience was meritorious, and renewing their trust in Divine Providence, they set forth for their new home. Before leaving old Loretto, however, they set fire to the log convent and school, resolved that those revered walls should suffer no desecration. The removal took place in 1824, and St. Stephen's, the cradle of Catholicism in Kentucky, thus happily passed into the watch and keeping of the Lorettines.

It was almost like beginning over again, for the few old buildings on the long neglected farm were not in good condition nor sufficiently commodious to shelter the religious and pupils of Little Loretto, even with their scant belongings, limited stock and simple implements for farm work. Again the indomitable American spirit stood the Sisters in good stead, strengthened by their lofty aims and constant reliance on Divine Providence. Buildings were begun, fences were put around special plots of ground, and brick pavements were introduced, toward which last novices and postulants contributed their share by carrying the bricks from the kiln to the locality where they were needed. It was a labor of love for all. In a short time their toil brought its reward, and the place began to blossom like a rose; the foundation was laid upon which stands the venerable Mother House of to-day, crowned with her centuried years.

In 1834 Father Chabrat became Coadjutor Bishop of the

LORETTO.

Diocese of Bardstown, and he was succeeded by the Reverend Walter Coomes as ecclesiastical superior of Loretto. The latter's occupancy of the office was brief, however, as the need of priests rendered it imperative for him to go on the missions; and from 1835 until 1846 the authority was centered in the Mother Superior, under the immediate jurisdiction of Bishop Chabrat.

CHAPTER VIII.

THE FIRST MOTHERS AND SOME ASSOCIATES.

LET us here pause in our narrative to consider the lives of those first Mothers of Loretto and some of their best known associates. In very truth were they the valiant women proclaimed above price by Holy Writ. They were called upon to meet ordeals that tried the strength of body and tested the faith of soul; yet they endured, nor lost their confidence in God and man. They saw the purpose of their Society threatened, its very existence endangered, their energies dissipated instead of being directed; they met disaster in many a guise; poverty was their close companion, and death was never far off; still they held their bark gallantly against the storm, if it prevented them from making progress toward their destined port. Great were those superiors of Loretto and her subordinate houses, and great were the Sisters who stood behind them! If in her hundred years Loretto has come victorious out of every trial it is because she could count upon loyalty from within. The superiors in whose hands the direction of the Society was placed were sustained by the knowledge that back of them were the closed ranks of their Sisterhood. We honor and pay tribute to the dauntless courage and steadfast faith of those many great, far-seeing superiors from 1812 to the present day; as worthy also of our admiration and applause are the communities, brave, loyal and true, that supported them.

The brief history of the two sisters, Ann and Mary Rhodes, first superiors of the Society, Mother Ann dying in 1812, the year of the foundation of Loretto, and Mother Mary continuing in office until 1822, has been recorded elsewhere. It is a singular and pathetic fact that of these first Mothers and their companion founders the Society possesses little knowledge. They lived, they labored, and they died; but their neighboring Trappist monks are not more unknown to the world, as far as tangible proof is concerned, than are these holy women to their daughters in Christ. Mother Ann's name signed to the document transferring her negro man and her personal belongings to Father Nerinckx is all that remains to them of their first superior; of Mother Mary, the actual founder, the following note, preserved in the family of the recipient, has at a late day come into the possession of Loretto, and is prized as the sole relic they have of her to whose courage and devotion they owe their Congregation. It is written in a neat hand, on small note paper, four by five inches, both paper and envelope having an embossed edge, the envelope being sealed with red wax:

"Calvary Convent, August 2, 1851.
"My dear Brother,
"Will you permit me to trouble you again to convey me to Loretto? If so, you will oblige by sending, if convenient, next Tuesday, the 5th instant.
"As I do not expect to be accompaniend by any Sister, you can let one of my little nieces, Benedicta or some other, come with the carriage to accompany me down. My love to *sister and to all.*
"Your grateful and affectionate sister,
"Mary Rhodes."

The envelope is addressed: "Mr. Bennet Rhodes, near St. Charles', Marion Co."

It is not difficult to believe that the first archives of the Society were not so barren, and Father Chabrat's bonfire may have been augmented by other records and papers than Father Nerinckx', while the great fire that left the Sisters homeless in 1858 swept away all that love and reverence had striven to accumulate. But ofttimes the intangible is

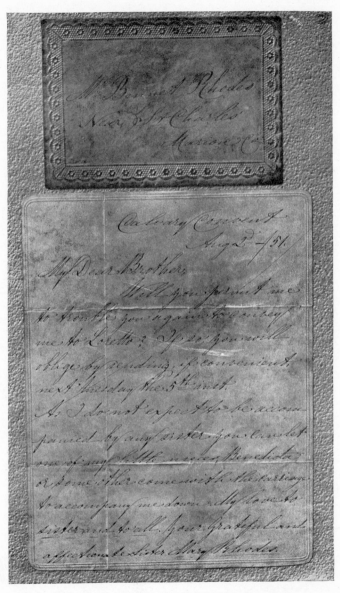

LETTER OF MOTHER MARY RHODES, Foundress.

more real to us than the things that hands may feel and eyes behold, and though no relic of them has been reverently handed down, no portrait revealing their lineaments exists, and but meagre are the facts relating to them that have been preserved, yet the lives of the little group of women who planted the tree of Loretto by the still waters of Hardin's Creek are living realities to the women who in the succeeding years have tended it, living, moulding realities, and shall so continue while it remains.

Sister Christina Stuart, the second member of the Society, was sent, as we have seen, to the first branch establishment at Calvary in 1816, as superior, and there died, in 1819, after a most exemplary life in the world and out of it, according to the testimony of Father Nerinckx. The third associate in the heroic band, Sister Anne Havern, was of a more robust constitution than her companions, and lived until January 19, 1862. Most of her later years were spent at Bethlehem Academy, Kentucky, where she applied herself assiduously to manual labor when no longer able to use her eyes at books or needlework. She was regarded as a model religious and died the death of the just.

Sister Sarah Havern, the fifth member, entered the Society at the age of twenty-four years. For ten years she lived and labored for God, giving the last years of her life to her Society as unsparingly as she had offered those of the dawn of womanhood for its inception. She departed this life at Loretto on a Friday, about the hour our Saviour expired, on the Feast of the Holy Cross, May 3, 1822. In the time-yellowed annals from which this story is gathered it is recorded that "She was made Sister Eldest a few months before her death. She was very industrious, careful, and had the interest of the Society much at heart, and it is hoped that she found mercy with the Lord."

Sometimes on a foggy morning you may have observed how a gleam of light will penetrate the mist, and, finding some object of reflection, if only a drop of water, fill the spot with sudden radiance. In some such way, out of the misty silence enfolding them, has flashed down for us the laugh of Nellie Morgan, the sixth to receive the habit of the Society, and who, on her reception, took the name of Sister Clare. We seem better acquainted with Sister Clare than with any of her companions, so truly is the gift of a merry heart a passport to enduring fame. The bits of tradition we have, like the raindrops reflecting the light, assure us she was an acquisition to the Society, on account of her gayety of disposition, the wit of her conversation, and her readiness to employ for the enjoyment of others her gift of song. We gather these fragments together and weave from them a winsome girl, who found the world a fair place, because she made it such; yet did not hesitate to leave it to answer her Saviour's call. If she found cheerfulness a help in the world, she saw it become a very staff in her hand in the poor little cabin convent she had elected to call henceforth her home; nor shall we ever know how many a cloud of gloom scurried away from that rude abode before her merriment, how often her nimble wit turned the actually tragic into the ridiculous. To think of Sister Clare is to break up the dolefulness with which we are inclined to view those first years of Little Loretto; for when the grace of God and one joyous heart are with a company, utmost misery stands at arm's length.

Sister Clare was admitted a postulant into the Society on June 29, 1812, and had the privilege of making her vows with her companions on August 15 of the following year. She had received her early training in Maryland, and after coming to Kentucky taught school, living with her widowed mother. She employed her knowledge to advantage in the classrooms of Little Loretto, and we are informed she maintained great control over the children, who were deeply attached to her. She taught them to sing, and led their young voices in the hymns which, following the custom set them by Father Nerinckx, they sang each evening on their way to the graveyard to pray for the departed. Sister Clare was a star in the forest gloom. After shining for many useful years, she went to eternal rest at Gethsemani, January 4, 1834.

Mother Mary Rhodes was succeeded in office of Mother Superior in 1822 by Mother Juliana Wathen, who, as we have seen, was one of Loretto's first pupils to become a member of the Society, which she had entered in 1815. Mother Juliana's was the first election held under the approved Constitutions. Bishop Flaget presided, signing the certificate herewith appended, the original of which, escaping many perils, is preserved in the archives at the Mother House.

"Certificate of the Election of Superiors in 1822,
"Right Reverend Bishop Flaget presiding.

"O Suffering Jesus!
"O Sorrowful Mary!

"Benedict Joseph by the grace of God, &c.,
"Bishop of Bardstown, &c.

"To all our beloved Sisters & Subjects of Loretto
Society, Greeting and blessing—

"The Election of the members for the offices in the Loretto Society of the Friends of Mary under the Cross of Jesus having been legally made, according to the Rules of said Society, we have named and do by these presents appoint the chosen Sisters as Superiors & Rulers of the houses and monasteries, belonging to the Loretto Society as follows:

"As Dear Mother & Generalissima of the Whole Society we appoint our beloved S. in the Lord Sr. Julianna (Wathen), being at present the Mother of Calvary.

"At Loretto, for Mother Sr. Joanna (Miles)
for Eldest Sr. Sara (Havern)

91

LORETTO.

At Calvary for Mother Sr. Reinildes (Hayden)
for Eldest Sr. Agnes (Hart)

" Gethsemani Mother Sr. Isabella (Clarke)
Eldest Sr. Brigitta (Flaherty)

"Bethania being recently established continues with
the present till the new Election.

"At Jericho, at Mechelen in the Netherlands we appoint as Mother of that Association, Sr. Mary
Magdalen Neefs & as Eldest, Sr. Mary De Ve-
giano.

its being our express will & command, that every one of
the members & subjects in their respectif place & station
shall have to pay due obedience, honor & respect to the appointed Superiors as to the Lord & ourselves for God's
sake, ordaining more over, that the discharged Superiors
shall perform the offices of kind assistants of the new
elected until their installation, which we fix upon the feast
of the Annunciation next being the 25 of March 1822,
two days before which time the new chosen shall repair
at the Mother house of Loretto for said ceremonies, &c.

"Done at Loretto this 8 of February 1822
"Benedict Joseph Bishop of Bardstown."

(SEAL)

Of this Jericho Branch, in Mechlin, of which mention
is made, Bishop Maes, in his "Life of Father Nerinckx,"
says that it "had most likely been aggregated to Loretto
during Reverend Nerinckx' stay in Belgium (1820-1821),
and it consisted of a kind of tertiaries, maidens who lived
in the world and observed the Loretto rule as far as practicable in that state."

The Miss Mary Neefs, or De Neff, elected Mother Superior of Jericho in 1822, was the daughter of Mr. De
Neff, who is mentioned by Bishop Maes as the friend of

RIGHT REV. BENEDICT JOSEPH FLAGET.

Father Nerinckx. He had amassed a fortune as a linen-draper, was a cultivated scholar and a man of solid piety. His wife dying, he desired to become a priest, but on being induced to abandon the intention, founded and maintained a college at Turnhout, in which young men of limited means could acquire an education preparatory to beginning their studies for the priesthood. In this college Mr. De Neff himself taught a class, and it is related that when other duty or illness compelled him to absent himself from the school, his daughter Mary took his place and "fulfilled the office of temporary professor, both with much credit to herself and with great profit to her disciples. She led the life of a pious maiden in the world, performing magnificent works of charity, and died at an advanced age a few years ago." (Bishop Maes, 1880.)

Beyond this nothing further is known of the Jericho branch. Before the next election of superior at Loretto rolled around the saintly founder had been called to his Heavenly reward, and the foreign branch of the American Sisterhood stands one of the unfinished arches in the lofty temple of life. Though uncompleted, it added a characteristic to Loretto of which we believe no other American Congregation can boast. The first American Society established in the United States, it was, and remains, the first to see a branch community established in the Old World.

As General and Local Superior, Mother Julianna lived in the chief houses of the Society, spent some years at Bethlehem, Missouri, where she died, August 20, 1835. Her loyalty and devotedness during the years of trial and difficulty have endured her name to all loyal Lorettines, who love what Rome deemed best for the welfare of the Society.

Among the early members to enter the Society was Sister Margaret Duffner, who was received in 1818 at the age of fourteen years, and in the annals of the Congregation there have been preserved some remarkable instances regarding this chosen soul. She was early associated with Calvary convent, holding the office of superior in 1839, and how long before or after is not known. In 1857 we find her in charge of the Sisters' refectory at Calvary, fulfilling her duties with accustomed fidelity in spite of her advancing years. On March 5 of that year she put the dinner on the table as usual, her last act being to bring a pail of water before she went to the choir of the church to ring the bell calling the Sisters to Examen. But the bell was not to be rung that day by Sister Margaret, for on her way to the choir she fell, dying before the altar, where the last Sacraments were administered to her. Among the blessed of Heaven we hope Sister Margaret has long been numbered.

Two others among those early members whose lives left after them a shining trail of light were Mother Benedicta and Sister Mary Dorothy Fenwick, relatives of the Right Reverend Edward Fenwick, O.P., founder of his Order in the United States at St. Rose, Kentucky, and first Bishop of Cincinnati. One of the twelve Sisters who founded Bethlehem convent, Perry County, Missouri, Mother Benedicta was for many years its superior, governing her community with the prudence of an illuminated soul. In 1838 she was sent as superior to open the convent at Cape Girardeau, where she died, July 21, 1847. A saintly woman, her life was an example to her Sisters and her memory is a benediction.

An incident is related in connection with the death of Mother Benedicta which in former times a Catholic historian might hesitate in recounting, but which the changing scientific mind of the day will not deny as impossible and label the superstition of religion. Shortly after the demise of Mother Benedicta, the Sisters at Calvary, Kentucky, convent went to the orchard to gather apples. Sister Dorothy Fenwick was one of their number. Being tired, she sat on a low rail fence to rest. The other Sisters, continuing their work, noticed that a Sister companion sat beside Sister Dorothy. When the latter came to them they inquired who was the Sister that had been with her. She replied that no one had been keeping her company. When her companions assured her that they had seen another Sister by her side, she exclaimed: "Oh! it was Mother Benedicta, then! For when I asked her to come to me after her death, she said she would not show herself to me if it should frighten me."

Like Mother Benedicta, Sister Mary Dorothy possessed a most lovable disposition, which endeared her to all. Her life was as unpretentious and holy as it was hidden in God. Of a delicate constitution, she was yet never heard to complain, and when the time of her departure drew near, with attendant sufferings, her patience and resignation seemed but to increase. She was conscious to the last, and while the Sisters were kneeling by her bedside, awaiting her last sigh, she suddenly raised herself to a sitting posture, while over her face streamed the light and the glory of one who looked upon the King and was glad. Crying out that her Saviour had come for her, she fell back upon her pillow and yielded up her pure soul. This occurred May 10, 1860, at Holy Mary Convent, Calvary, Kentucky.

The fourth Mother Superior of Loretto was Mother Isabella Clarke, who held the office for the first term from 1824 to 1826, and was again elected in 1838, serving until 1842. She was the daughter of Ignatius Clarke and Aloysia Hill, and was born near Holy Cross church, Marion, then Washington, County, Kentucky, in 1799, being the first of three sisters to belong to the Society. Entering August 15, 1815, she lived until 1875, dying, like her Divine Master, at the hour of three on Good Friday, after an exemplary religious life of nearly sixty years.

Under her first administration the Negro Sisterhood was established by Father Nerinckx. Inheritor of the best civilization of Europe, the condition of slavery was most repellant to him, while it must ever have outraged his Christian sentiments; and we find him exhibiting the tenderest solicitude for the unfortunate position in which he found the colored race in the New World. He seems to have appreciated the fact that the barrier of racial difference, being a natural one, should always be respected; and foreseeing, as every thoughtful person must have done, that the day would dawn when the young Republic would throw off from her limbs slavery's shameful shackles, he sought to provide for that trying period for the Negro by having a Congregation of Sisters of their own color ready to lead them, by Christianizing and educating them, to the right enjoyment of freedom. Forced to abandon his work, this other remarkable purpose, which was surely an inspiration of the Holy Spirit, fell to the ground, with what loss, not alone to the Church but to the nation as well, we who know the condition of the colored people to-day, after half a century of liberty, can appreciate. Truly observes Reverend Dr. Burns, C.S.C., in his able work, "The Catholic School System in the United States," that this project of Father Nerinckx "is in itself sufficient to stamp him as a man whose educational ideas ran far ahead of his time."

With her other inestimable records, the accurate and complete account of this most prophetic of the works of her holy founder perished in one of Loretto's two sad fires. It is only known that with the end of the Colored Sisterhood in view, Father Nerinckx caused a few Negro children to be adopted and educated at Loretto, and in May, 1824, shortly before his death, he wrote to Mother Bibiana at Bethania Convent: "Two days ago twelve young ladies offered themselves at Loretto for the little veil, amongst them our three blacks, who received nearly all the votes. Their dress is to be different, also their offices and employment, but they will keep the main rules of the Society; they will take the vows, but not the perpetual ones, before twelve years of profession. Their rules are set apart."

THE FIRST MOTHERS AND SOME ASSOCIATES.

The Rule which Father Nerinckx gave the Loretto Society required that: Desirants wear the Little Hearts. When they take the Little Veil they become Postulants. To take the habit made them novices. From this it is likely that the three blacks he wrote of in taking the Little Veil became postulants, or at least not more than novices. The Sisters now living do not remember having heard what became of these three young Negro girls.

Another work of the Sisters belonging to Mother Isabella's administration as Superior of the Society was that of an Asylum for the Deaf and Dumb, opened at Loretto November, 1839. This project was Bishop Flaget's. Having several hundred dollars which he could apply to charitable purposes, he induced the Sisters of Loretto to make the experiment of instructing the deaf and dumb; and, accordingly, in 1840, three deaf mutes were admitted. Bishop Chabrat, however, desired the appropriation to be turned over to the Seminary, and Bishop Flaget, complying with his wishes, withdrew the support from the Deaf and Dumb Institute, and the Sisters being unable to continue it, another great and worthy work collapsed. Bishop Flaget's niece, Eulalia, who was then a member of the Loretto Society, was at the head of the deaf and dumb school, having at the Bishop's desire fitted herself for the work by studying at the well-known establishment "La Chartreuse près d'Auray," in Britany. She was assisted in her work by Sister Philomene Bernier, and from an advertisement in the "Metropolitan Catholic Almanac and Laity's Directory" for 1841, and which advertisement appears in the same publication as late as 1843, it is stated that the institution is for the mental and moral improvement of female children who are deaf and dumb, and that all the branches taught in similar institutions in France and the United States are taught in the Loretto Institution.

Several other houses were opened during Mother Isabella's second term, the only one of which now remaining in operation is that of St. Vincent's Academy, Cape Girardeau, Missouri. Besides serving the Society so well in her official capacity, Mother Isabella was a successful teacher. She was endowed with a fine talent for painting, and some of her portraits in oil still exist, among them portraits of Bishop Flaget, a painting of "St. Joseph and the Infant Christ," one of the "Apparition of the Blessed Virgin to St. Alphonsus Rodriguez," and one of "The Orphan Boy."

Contemporary with Sister Isabella Clarke was Sister Mary Louisa Phillips, the sixteenth member of the Society. Nothing is known of her parentage, and little of her early years except that she was born in 1803. A record of various events, in her own hand, states that she "came to the monastery September 10, 1815." She was then but twelve years of age. She further records that on August 22, 1816, Bishop Flaget received the vows of Sisters Isabella Clarke, Juliana Wathen and Teresa Grundy, and gave the habit to Mary Drury (Sister Catherine) and herself.

Sister Louisa was ardently devoted to Father Nerinckx and to the Society, and, in turn, was by them greatly esteemed as an edifying religious. Those now living who knew her, experience joy at the mention of her name; her great heart found room for all, and all who came in contact with her felt the influence of her kindness and true charity. At one period Sister Louisa held the office of Sister-Eldest, and served for some time as Treasurer of the Society. For many years she was teacher of music at Cape Girardeau. To her careful interest the Society is indebted for the preservation of much of its history. Handed down through her guardianship is one of the quill pens made and used by Father Nerinckx, still treasured by Loretto. In this connection may here be quoted an item from one of Father Nerinckx' instructions to the teachers of Loretto, March 9, 1823. After recommending them to cultivate particular devotion to St. Thomas Aquinas, that they might obtain through his intercession grace to teach with success and instill virtue into the hearts of their pupils, as did that Saint, Father Nerinckx continues: "Every one of you should learn to make your own pens, and whenever you write you should have good pens and good ink; it is very hard to do good work with bad tools; get feathers and learn to make your own pens, making two every day until you can make a good one."

Sister Louisa's neat hand gives evidence that she profited by the zealous founder's instructions on this point, as her holy life was witness that she laid up in her heart all his holy counsels. In the early seventies she was brought from Cape Girardeau for the quiet rest at Loretto which her long labors had merited; her holy death soon followed, occurring on January 8, 1874. She kept with her to the end a relic of the holy founder; her sufferings in her last short illness were intense, and the heavenly light and smile that overspread her countenance a few moments before her passing caused good Father Wuyts to exclaim: "She sees Father Nerinckx."

Sister Rosalia Clarke, like her elder sister, gave herself to God at an early age. Born in 1802, she received the habit November 1, 1816. She found her field of labor chiefly in the classroom. She was a close student, and kept abreast of her times in educational matters, an example which has been assiduously followed by her successors in Loretto's many schools. She did not live to the great age of her two sisters, dying at Calvary, Kentucky, September 6, 1870.

A year later, December 25, 1817, the third daughter of these sacrificing Catholic parents knocked at Loretto's door, and, being received, was given the name of Sister Elenora. Her age was then fourteen, and for sixty-five years following she spent herself for God and her beloved Society. She possessed something of her elder sister's talent for painting, and was skilled in needle-craft, but from these more fascinating tasks she was called for the missionary life at

99

Florissant, Missouri, where, in 1847, with five Sisters, she opened an academy. The years that followed were full of trial, but good Mother Elenora won hosts of friends and admirers, who loved to recall the heroic struggles of the Sisters in their first experience in the swampy lands of their environments. After fourteen years there, Mother Elenora was called home for a much needed rest, then was sent to open a house at Edina, Missouri. In 1875 Mother Isabella expired in the arms of her sisters, and Mother Elenora, with the heart wound, received also a stroke of paralysis in the left side. For eight years God left her a cripple, but she was a most cheerful sufferer, doing what her hands found to do with the same assiduity and devotion that had marked her monumental work at Florissant. She passed to a better world December 11, 1882, the same day on which had died the first Superior of Loretto, Mother Ann Rhodes, seventy years before. These three sisters were great-nieces of the Right Reverend Edward Fenwick, O.P., first Bishop of Cincinnati. The Reverend Edward Clarke was their brother, a zealous priest and much esteemed by Archbishop Spalding. He died in 1858, his sisters surviving him many years.

During Mother Isabella's last term of office the Constitutions had been revised by the Reverend Father Fouché, S.J. These called for a single Novitiate at the Mother House. One of the four who first wore the white veil in the newly organized Novitiate was Mother Sophronia Hagan, daughter of Ezekiel and Ellen O'Brien-Hagan, and who was born in Nelson County, Kentucky, in 1823. This child was received into the Society November 1, 1839, Bishop Flaget presiding at the investiture. Her companions in the Novitiate were Sisters Mary Joseph Aubuchon, Macaria Rhodes, and Mary Xavier Conway. The second group comprised Sisters Eulalia Flaget, Philomene Bernier and another, probably Sister Teresa Bellier. Sister Sophronia spent most of her religious life in the classroom, chiefly

100

at Bethlehem, Kentucky, where she was stationed from 1846 to 1863, when she was elected General Treasurer. From 1870 to 1882 she governed the community at Cairo, Illinois. Three times she was chosen by the Society to fill the office of Assistant to the Mother Superior. She died at Loretto, Kentucky, March 30, 1904, having been a member of the Society sixty-five years.

During his sojourn in Europe in 1839 in the interests of his diocese Bishop Flaget spoke to sympathetic souls of the need there for consecrated workers. Two young French women, responding to his appeal, returned with him as candidates for the Loretto Sisterhood. One of these was Mother Philomene Bernier, who received the habit with Mother Sophronia Hagan on November 1, 1839. She began her career as a teacher in the Loretto schools, for which avocation she was by disposition and education well qualified. Her first mission out of Kentucky was to the Florissant foundation in 1847, of which in later years she was made local superior. Her last appointment was at St. Ann Academy, Osage Mission, now St. Paul, Kansas, at which place, on March 10, 1887, she surrendered her generous soul to God.

Sister Isabella Traller was another of those first subjects of the reorganized Novitiate, as well as the early gifts of the Missouri mission to the Society. Born in Baden, Germany, she came, with her parents, Joseph and Catherine Traller, to the United States in 1832. They settled in Perry County, Missouri, and were rejoiced to find a convent school awaiting them at their new home. Eight years later they saw their daughter enrolled among the Sisters. Sister Isabella received the veil December 8, 1840, at the age of seventeen years. A year later she was called to Loretto, Kentucky, to be trained at the Mother House, as the rule demanded. Her first mission was at Bethlehem, Kentucky; her second at Florissant, Missouri, going with the foundation in 1847. Music was her chief accomplishment; she possessed a voice of birdlike sweetness, and it was to her Mr. Bryan Mullanphy gave fifty dollars for singing an Irish song in a charming way. After fourteen years at Florissant, Sister Isabella passed to other schools, always as a teacher of music and German, until from the old home in Kentucky she went to join the celestial choirs and speak the language of Heaven. Her departure occurred on February 11, 1902.

Most of the earliest members of the Loretto Society were from families of English descent, who had emigrated from Maryland and Virginia. Celtic names, however, were not wanting, as we find Miss Elizabeth O'Brien among those clothed in the novice's garb, November 27, 1819. She pronounced her vows the following year and proved an efficient and devoted religious until her death at Bethlehem, Kentucky, June 30, 1842. Bishop Flaget esteemed her highly, when during her superiorship, 1832, he wrote of the favorable impression she had made: "Mother Sabina, it appears, has won all hearts; she has filled them with holy joy. The neighbors of Bethlehem are enchanted with her manners."

To make oneself so acceptable to others in a position of authority, when poverty and complicated trials are the daily portion of the superior, indicate no ordinary degree of virtue, therefore we justly ascribe to Mother Sabina a strength of character blended with gentle bearing, which go far to make a perfect ruler. Mother Sabina was the fifth Mother Superior of the Society, governing from 1826 to 1832.

Her successor in office was Mother Josephine Kelly, who ruled from 1832 to 1838. Her parents, Thomas and Martha Hartley-Kelly, were residents of Baltimore, and when Father Nerinckx, on his way home from his second trip to Europe, stopped over in that city, and told the Catholic people of the vast harvest of God on the frontier and none to garner it, she, with her sister Eulalia, offered herself for the work. Six other young women joined them, and of their long journey to Kentucky we have read elsewhere in this volume. The young aspirants commenced their religious life upon the flatboat, hence they were not appalled at the poverty they met in the wilderness of the Middle West. Sisters Josephine and Eulalia began their active life as Lorettines very soon after their reception. After teaching at the Loretto Mother House, Sister Josephine was transferred to Bethania as superior, where she remained until elected Mother Superior in 1832. After her term of office had expired, she went as local superior to Gethsemani, where she died, February 5, 1847, her remains afterward being brought back to the Mother House. Her memory is sacredly enshrined in the Society of which she was so useful a member.

Sister Eulalia Kelly was a prime mover in several foundations in southeastern Missouri and Arkansas, none of which subsisted for many years, owing to the poverty of the country in those early days and the inconvenience of travel. However, there was always work to be done; the good seed was sown, which produced fruit in God's own time. Sister Eulalia returned to Kentucky, and passed some years in teaching, principally at Calvary. When incapacitated by age, and her work had to be relinquished, the venerable religious went back to the home of her spiritual childhood and prayerfully prepared for a future which held no terrors for her. Death crowned her long life January 13, 1892.

Margaret, a third sister, went as a pupil to Missouri, where her older sister was stationed, entered the Novitiate there July 31, 1830, and was given the name of Josephine. She became a successful teacher at various Loretto schools in Missouri and Kentucky, and died at Loretto Mother House, April 1, 1870. Another Miss Kelly desired to follow in the footsteps of her sisters, but finding she had no vocation, she settled in the world as an exemplary matron.

Julia, the fourth member of this religious family, was born in Baltimore, March 29, 1817, and when old enough made the long journey from Maryland to Kentucky in order to be educated at Loretto. She passed from the school-room to the Novitiate, August 24, 1832, and was clothed with the habit as Sister Theodosia. Her talents were varied and of a high order. Besides the ordinary branches of the curriculum, she was proficient in French, Spanish, music and art. She was one of the band who accompanied Mother Elenora when the foundation was made at Florissant, thence she passed to St. Genevieve, later to Calvary, Kentucky, where she taught for twenty-five years. Sister Theodosia was amiable and agreeable as a co-laborer. Her last years she spent in an edifying manner at the Mother House, and there, on January 6, 1904, she entered into her eternal rest.

These earliest valiant women of the Society were not without their martyrs of charity: one, who, singularly enough, was a Belgian like their holy founder, was Sister Benedicta Poorter, born at Melle in the province of East Flanders, in the Kingdom of the Low Countries. We give her story as related in the "Life of Bishop Flaget": "In the spring of 1833 the cholera broke out in a very malignant form at Bardstown and in the neighboring counties. The first persons attacked by the disease were in the family of Mr. John Roberts, a Protestant gentleman residing about eight miles from Bardstown. Three servant men and a daughter of Mr. Roberts soon fell victims to the fatal malady. The whole neighborhood was seized with consternation, and no one would go near the house.

"At the very first intelligence of the distress in which this unfortunate family was involved, two Sisters of Loretto hastened to the succor of the afflicted, and they were soon after joined by two Sisters of Charity from Nazareth, accompanied by the Reverend Dr. Reynolds, the present distinguished Bishop of Charleston. These ministering angels of charity, totally regardless of self, devoted themselves day and night to the nursing of the sick and dying.

SISTER GENEROSE MATTINGLY.

One of them, Sister Benedicta (Poorter) of Loretto, died a few days later of the disease here contracted."

Mother Generose Mattingly, the eighth Superior of the Society, experienced a series of remarkable events in her life which will cause her always to remain a figure of interest to the history of its individual members. She belonged to one of the pioneer families from Maryland, and which, it may be said, has loyally continued its generous offering of sons and daughters to the Church. In the heyday of girlish charms, Ellen Mattingly attended school at Loretto, and a year later joined the ranks of the Sisterhood. Her probationary period was nearing completion when the startling news reached Loretto that her founder was about to leave Kentucky forever; and as the postulant desired to receive the habit from his hands, she had little time to make preparations for that ceremony. The habit that was given her was an old faded one, very much patched, and the color was neither black nor brown. As it was a loose wrapper, it required to be bound down at the waist, and the only available cincture was a tow string. Capes were not worn at that time, and a piece of white muslin, folded triangularly, was placed around her neck. Her hair was cut, and as the cap to which the veil was to be pinned was so small it did not close at the back, one end of the triangular kerchief had to be drawn up and pinned to the cap in order to conceal the opening. In this attire, and barefooted, the young candidate was conducted to the Church of St. Charles. It was Sunday, June 13, 1824, and as it was known that Father Nerinckx would that day bid farewell to his people, and that the beautiful Miss Mattingly would receive the habit from his hands, the last to be clothed by him in Kentucky, none of the congregation was missing. When the prospective novice and her companion reached the sacristy, by which they hoped to gain entrance to the sanctuary, where a place for the aspirant was waiting, they found the door bolted and barred; so the Mistress of Novices had to take her to the public entrance. There they found the entrance and passage blocked by the congregation, and an usher had to go ahead to make a way for them. It was no triumphal procession for the poor little novice, and the stool placed for her within the sanctuary, where she became the object of every eye, was, humanly considered, a pillory. At the Gospel she received the veil, a cotton fabric, woven of coarse thread, almost as heavy as gunnysack. In their excitement they pinned the veil not only to the cap but to the scalp, and the poor novice was so bewildered, and dazed and humiliated, sitting there before all the people, that she did not dare to remove the pin. Father Nerrinckx was leaving his people; never again should he minister to them, and long and earnestly he pleaded with them to remain faithful to the lessons he had given. But if it were a crucial hour to the old priest, it was not less so to the poor little novice, to whom the sermon and services seemed a time of long drawn torture. The end finally came, and the novice was led from the sanctuary to the convent near by. There no one paid any attention to her, for the community was weeping and wailing over the loss it was about to sustain in the departure of its beloved founder. After Father Nerinckx had breakfasted he came to the convent on horseback, where the Sisters were assembled in the yard to receive his last words and his blessing.

Before leaving, Father Nerinckx gave the new novice her obedience, which was to go to Gethsemani the following morning. She rode on horseback and wore a sunbonnet over her veil. Her companion was a colored man named Bill. Reaching Gethsemani, she found there more excitement over the approaching visit of Bishop Flaget, and she was detailed to the task of making ready the room he was to occupy. In the midst of her hasty preparations the priest in charge came in, and seeing the young novice was barefooted, asked where were her shoes. She replied

106

that she had none, since the pair she had worn on her journey was borrowed, and, with the horse she had ridden, had been sent back to Loretto with the servant. The priest declared it would be shocking for her to appear in bare feet before the Bishop, and brought her his boots. They were, of course, much too large, and so heavy she could scarcely lift her feet, and when the Sisters saw her struggling to traverse the space between the priest's house and the convent human nature got the better of rules of conduct, and though they were in strictest silence, they could not restrain their laughter. After two such deadly blows to her vanity we may feel certain it never troubled Sister Generose again.

The last to be clothed by Father Nerinckx in Kentucky, she was the first of two superiors to rule the Society by episcopal appointment, instead of election, the second being her immediate successor, Mother Berlindes Downs. She was also the first Lorretine, and it is said the first nun in the United States, to celebrate the diamond jubilee, seventy-five years since her entrance into the religious life. This auspicious occasion occurred in June, 1899, and was rendered doubly memorable by the presence of the then Apostolic Delegate to the United States, the Most Reverend Sebastian Martinelli, several other Church dignitaries and reverend clergy. The Most Reverend John Lancaster Spalding, a relative of the jubilarian, had to postpone his visit till a later date. To complete the glory of the event, Pope Leo XIII benignantly sent his congratulations and his blessing. Besides being the oldest member of the Society, Mother Generose was also the oldest member of the Alumnae Association. So glorious a year was sufficient to crown this virtuous life. The angel of death was waiting, and the venerable religious gladly followed his guidance to the land of eternal Jubilee, November 4, 1899, being in her ninety-third year.

The most unique figure in Loretto's history is that of Mother Berlindes Downs, whose humility was her distinguishing characteristic. As a little orphan, Lucy was placed in the Sisters' care while the saintly founder still lived and watched over the infant Society. This child, who had nothing specially attractive about her but her innocence, was treated as a favorite lamb by the austere priest. True, his attention consisted chiefly in reproving and correcting her faults, still it was evident his far-reaching eye beheld something of her future career. She was a real child. Once fearing the Sisters had written of some of her pranks to Father Nerinckx during his absence, she extracted the telltale paper from his pocket, tore it to pieces, and thus escaped one scolding. Lucy and another little orphan, Isabella Holden, had but one pair of shoes between them, which they wore turn about to gather chips or go outside in cold weather. Once, on the occasion of a Sister's funeral, it was Isabella's time to wear the shoes, and she secured a place in the procession. Lucy cried to go also. Kindhearted Mother Agnes Hart told the Sister-wardrobian to give Lucy a second pair of stockings, as the snow was not deep, and while in the cemetery the good Mother extended her own foot for the child in the stockings to stand upon.

In time the orphan grew in body and good behavior, so when, at the age of fourteen, she applied for admission into the Society, she was accepted, receiving the habit May 15, 1828. By no means destitute of talent, she cared little for study, and considered domestic occupations more properly her sphere than the schoolroom; yet in her mature years she proved herself an able business woman, taught and helped perhaps more by Heaven than by professors of human science. Her special devotion was to St. Joseph; she called him her banker, and ever appealed to him in time of need.

Mother Berlindes was of insignificant stature; in her face were no elements of beauty even in youth, but those who came in contact with her felt some sort of attraction for which they could give no account. Bishop David, that constant friend of Father Nerinckx and Loretto, whom she was privileged to attend in his illness, manifested his esteem for and confidence in her sterling character and piety.

She was long Mistress of Novices when vocations to religion were numerous and striking. It was under her administration that a colony of Sisters was sent to Santa Fé in 1852; on learning of their distress in their journey her mother-heart was sorely afflicted, and, to use her own words, she ate and drank her tears until she learned of their safe arrival at their destination. After the dire calamity of Loretto's fire, in 1858, Mother Berlindes was again elected Superior of the Society whose Mother House and church were in ashes and treasury depleted. What could any woman do under such circumstances? Now was an occasion for St. Joseph to show his power.

Plans for the new building were drawn up, the brick was burned in 1860 on the premises; some rock quarried for the same purpose; in the fall the foundation was dug. Convent and church were finished in 1863, with no debt. To this day it is a marvel how that little woman accomplished what she did, with no means at hand. Her assertion was ever the same—"St. Joseph always had the money ready as it was needed." When Mother Berlindes applied to the bishop to consecrate the church, he said, "Do you not knew a church cannot be consecrated while there is any debt on it?" With open-eyed astonishment he received this reply, "There is no debt."

To her last illness, which lasted but a few days, this devout client of St. Joseph performed as many little household tasks as her strength permitted. When she was no longer able to rise, the Sisters realized the end was near. Mother Berlindes died of pneumonia at Lebanon, Kentucky, five days before the feast of her beloved protector, St. Joseph, March 14, 1885. She was brought for burial to the Mother House, and laid within the church her exertions had reared with the assistance of her dear Saint.

LORETTO.

The little orphan, Isabella Holden, who generously shared shoes with Lucy Downs in their childhood days, soon followed Sister Berlindes to the Novitiate, receiving the habit of Loretto and the name Sister Regina, July 2, 1828, at the age of seventeen. Like Mother Berlindes, Sister Regina filled for a time the office of Mistress of Novices, and she was a very efficient music teacher. She was noted for her charity and amiability, as those declare who knew her, comely in appearance, queenly as her name, and blessed far above the ordinary with the gift of song. When helpless from infirmity, she was wheeled into the choir from the infirmary, where her birdlike voice, not trammeled by pain, sang the praises of God. After years of patient suffering, her fervent soul soared Heavenward within the octave of the Assumption of Heaven's Queen, August 17, 1871. Her eldest sister, Elizabeth Holden, entered the Society as Sister Susan, at the age of fifteen, August 15, 1822. She lived a faithful, worthy religious until her death, July 2, 1891.

Another of those early religious whose names will ever be held in veneration in the Society is that of Sister Mary Petronilla Van Prater. Sister, or Mother, Mary, as she was regularly called, entered one of the Missouri houses in 1842, probably Bethlehem or St. Genevieve's. She had no novitiate, but worked with the Sisters, going with them to all the exercises of the community. She went with the colony to found the house at Osage Mission, and in 1862, Mother Bridget having to go to Loretto on business, and afterwards being sent to Cape Girardeau, Mother Mary was made Superior of the Mission, holding that office for three years. She was a hard worker and most earnestly interested in the Society.

Mother Mary came of a fine French family, her father having a large plantation in Cuba. His home was in Havana. One night, at the time of the massacre of the whites by the blacks, negroes broke into his house and murdered

110

him. The other members of the family fled in their night clothes to the seashore, where they spent the night in a limekiln, taking ship the next morning for America, and settling in Perryville, Missouri, where Sister Mary had a wealthy sister and many relatives. In Havana they had possessed all that this world could give them, and Mother Mary often spoke of the time she fled in her night dress to the ship. After many years Mother Mary's brother went back to Havana to see about the property, part of which he recovered, and she used a portion of her share to erect the beautiful chapel at St. Ann's of Osage Mission. Mother Mary always had charge of the chapel, and even as superior she retained this office, which was her delight.

CHAPTER IX.

FOUNDATIONS IN MISSOURI AND ARKANSAS.

WHEN the progressive pioneer spirit was developing the sparsely inhabited West during the second quarter of the nineteenth century many a new enterprise was short-lived. Towns, built with fair prospects, withered and disappeared, or lingered to take on new life after several decades. It was a period of beginnings and progress, when mistakes and failures often ministered to success. Not all of Loretto's foundations were endowed with permanency, yet they contributed to development and progress. They planted where others came to water and reap the harvest.

St. Genevieve, Missouri, was one of the places where they laid the foundation and others built thereon. It was a spot consecrated in their eyes, since here Father Nerinckx had breathed his last. Owing to untoward circumstances, it was not until 1838 that the Lorettines were able to make a foundation here, which they dedicated to Our Lady of Mount Carmel. Mother Odille Delassus, a daughter of the Spanish Commandant of New Bourbon, Don Pierre Carlos Delassus, with seven Sisters, opened in this year the school at St. Genevieve. From the first a blessing seemed to rest upon the undertaking, and its condition was flourishing. Ten years later it sent forth the foundation of the Osage Mission, and had St. Genevieve no other gem in her crown this were enough, since the care of the Indians had been one of the darling projects of Father Nerinckx. In 1858 Loretto sold the property to the Sisters of St. Joseph of Carondelet, Missouri, who still conduct an academy there.

From St. Genevieve, in 1838, Sister Agnes Hart, with two other Sisters, went to Pine Bluff, Arkansas, where St. Mary's convent was opened, October 11, 1838. A year

112

later, August 20, 1839, she passed from the scenes of her earthly labors to find eternal rest. Sister Agnes Hart rightly ranks among the great women with which the Society was from its inception blessed. She was the first pupil of Loretto to enter the Society, and none ever gave herself to it more loyally. Among the early founders of branch houses in her native State she was, from the beginning, associated with the mission at Bethlehem, Perry County, Missouri, and, as we have seen, planted the banner of her beloved Society elsewhere in the West. She was, furthermore, the last Sister buried according to the ancient custom, without a coffin. Kind hands lined her grave with roses, for the people felt they were burying a saint. Years later, when the inroads of the river required the disinterment of many, the body of Sister Agnes was found entire and petrified, an occurrence which added to the reverence in which this zealous religious was held by the community. Not only did they give honorable position in the new cemetery to the remains of Sister Agnes, but through their pastor, the Right Reverend Monsignor Lucey, an inscribed monument was erected to indicate her last resting-place.

Among the kind benefactors of those early days at Pine Bluff should be mentioned Mr. Crede Taylor and Mr. Francis Vangine, who donated part of the land to the Sisters on which then stood two frame buildings, and some log cabins. The school was continued until 1842, when the Sisters moved to St. Ambrose, Post Arkansas, where the community remained until 1845, when it was recalled to the Mother House at Loretto, Kentucky. Another short-lived establishment of the Sisters in Arkansas was that of St. Joseph, at Little Rock. Founded in 1841 by Sister Alodia Vessels, with three companions, it also was closed in 1845, the Sisters following the St. Ambrose community to Kentucky.

Two of the foundations of this time remaining to the present day are St. Vincent's Academy, Cape Girardeau,

LORETTO.

Missouri, and St. Benedict's Academy, Louisville, Kentucky. The former, established in 1838, is second only in the tradition-loving heart to that of the Mother House itself. Founded, as we have already stated, by the transfer of the convent of Bethlehem, in Perry County, St. Vincent's Academy is practically the continuance of the first mission of the Lorettine Society out of its native State.

The Lazarist Fathers, who so befriended the Lorettines at the Barrens, desired to have them as co-laborers at Cape Girardeau, and through the efforts of the Reverend John Timon the Sisters opened school there in a rented building which was erected in 1819 by Commander Laramie, who had been the Spanish representative of the station when that part of the country belonged to Spain. The building was occupied by the Sisters until the purchase of their new home in the early part of 1839. Trusting in Providence, as their holy founder had counselled, the Sisters entered upon their new mission, with their familiar poverty still close at hand. They were sometimes obliged to permit their pupils to remain in bed until seven o'clock in the morning because they had no breakfast to give them. They were obliged to send to Illinois for provisions, and when these arrived the better part was reserved for the children; when food was scarce the Sisters, thinking of themselves last, were often threatened with starvation, and many a time made their dinner of roasted potatoes and salt.

Poverty and privations as harsh they had elsewhere experienced, but in Cape Girardeau the Sisters of Loretto were called upon to meet a new foe in the bitter prejudice that was entertained against them by the villagers in the beginning, and, later, the political persecution which fell to their lot. In 1865 the State of Missouri passed a law forbidding any person to teach or preach who had not taken the oath under the new Constitution, which prohibited tendering any assistance whatever to the South. When the mandate reached the Cape, Judge Jackson ordered a Protestant constable to arrest the priests and nuns for not taking the prescribed oath; but the officer resigned rather than engage in a work that did violence to his instincts as a gentleman and, perchance, outraged his patriotic feelings. We must charitably presume that the Mr. Whitmore who did undertake the work permitted his politics—for we cannot term patriotism that which incites to war upon the innocent—to override every other principle of Christian manhood. He made continued effort to find out the names of the Sisters that warrants for their arrest might be issued. Failing in legitimate means, he waylaid little children who attended the school; but they had either been warned by their parents, or their Angels prompted their answers, for his questioning brought him no information from that source. Finally, however, he succeeded in obtaining the names of three of the community, Sisters Margaret, Olympia and Augusta Angela, and they were arrested. Six of the first gentlemen of the Cape went on their bond, under a fine of one thousand dollars each if she failed to attend court the first Monday in September. Mother Bridget Spalding, who then filled the distracting office of superior, wrote the Most Reverend Archbishop Kenrick of St. Louis, asking if the Sisters should take the oath or go to prison. His answer was that they could not take the oath without perjury, and he advised them to select a good lawyer, promising to send his attorney, Mr. Garesché, to them as soon as a case then being tried should close.

A more exasperating case, it is safe to say, never came before a court in Missouri, and for three consecutive years, winter and summer, the Sisters had to take that unpleasant trip to Jackson. Finally, Governor Fletcher and his staff paid a visit to the convent. When the Sisters told him how they were being treated, he advised them to allow Judge Jackson to try them the ensuing court term, promising then to take a hand and settle the matter. Learning

115

of this, the judge would not allow the clerk to publish the opening of the court; but through the vigilance of Reverend Father McGuerry the date was learned. With a cunning worthy of him, Judge Jackson had set the opening of the session on the exhibition day of the academy, whereupon the Sisters advanced their Commencement exercises a week. Again foiled, Jackson became so enraged that he threw the case out of court, while the Sisters' lawyer refused any remuneration for his three years' services.

Here at St. Vincent's, mother of the Missouri houses, the good work goes on, and the pleasant relations begun with the worthy Lazarist Fathers almost a century ago continue unbroken to the present day. In these Fathers, Loretto has ever found the true friend.

For long years this foundation has been a quiet, monastic home, affording the hundredfold of peace promised even in this world to those who give up all for Christ's sake, and from the scholastic halls have many pupils gone forth to make the world better and happier by reason of the careful training they had received at dear old St. Vincent's.

Several superiors who directed the Sisterhood at the Cape were women of remarkable abilities, and served the Institute well in various posts. Among these may be noted Mother Benedicta Fenwick, first superior of the place, who was God's agent for various important undertakings in the day of beginnings; Mother Constantia Murphy, who became a member of the Central Council as treasurer; Mother Catherine Connor, a sketch of whose life is given elsewhere in this volume; Mother Placide Keating, popularly known to every resident of Cape Girardeau during twenty-six years of administration there; at one time assistant of the Mother Superior, and at present local superior of Cedar Grove Academy, Louisville, Kentucky. It was under her reign that St. Vincent's appropriately celebrated a Golden Jubilee, and later a seventieth anniversary of joy.

The St. Benedict Academy, locally known as Cedar Grove, in Louisville, Kentucky, was founded in 1842. The foundation was primarily due to Father Badin, for while Bishop Chabrat bought the property with the Sisters' money, it was only after receiving the assurance of the proto-priest, as given in the letter which follows, that they entered upon the work. The letter goes to show how dear to the heart of the saintly Badin were the daughters of his well-loved Father Nerinckx. The letter was addressed to the Mother Superior of the Society, Mother Isabella Clarke:

"Portland, Ky., 19th April, 1842.
"My good daughter,

"I arrived at this place two weeks ago with Bishops Chabrat and La Hailandière, and have been ever since a recluse here. I have heard the bishop's talks, I have seen things, I have talked myself, not with the bishop (it was enough to hear him), but with some of the principal citizens of the place, and I have made my own reflections. Finally I write to you in God's presence, resting assured that you will also read and ponder in God's presence the reflections which to my mind appear to have some weight. I will begin by stating facts:

"1st   Bishop Chabrat promised to the citizens of Portland a school of the Lorettine Sisters.

"2dly   He has bought a place to that intention, and has applied $1000 of your money to the purchasing of it.

"3dly   He has already spent $1000 more in repairs.

"4thly   He is going to build an additional brick house, 30 feet by 16 feet, with an upper story and gallery—and a cellar.

"5thly   He is assured of the co-operation of Mother Josephine, and most probably of the Sisters at St. Thomas, besides the favorites he may have in other houses, so that a schism will be formed, and the authority of the Superiors disregarded, and the Constitution, and his own several obligations too. You know the man.

"The evil, or, rather, many evils, can be obviated, if you can honorably co-operate in a plan which he is determined to execute without you.

"Your objection is an apprehension that the Sisters would not be sufficiently protected in Portland. To ascertain this, I applied to a Catholic friend, who is the principal citizen of the place. This communication caused the Trustees of the Town to meet, and they sent me their Clerk to assure me that you need not have such fear, that you will be protected and welcome, and that it is the general wish to see here an establishment of your Society.

"Father Larkin is now in Louisville, in search of a house wherein to open an Academy. The Jesuits will attend the Church of Portland, and I have given my written obligation to deed to them the church lot; of course your Sisters here will be directed by the same spirit with those of the Mother house.

"God's will be done in all things and forever. Pray for "Your affectionate Father in God,

"S. T. Badin, V.G.

"1st P. S. Tell the Sisters that I wish to live in the communion of *Saints*, and none else. . . . 2dly, that I wish to live in communion with them—3dly, That I leave to them to draw the logical conclusion, which cannot be other than Christian and Catholic.

"2d P. S. Tell your valetudinarians that the Gospel calls *blessed* those who mourn and suffer—with patience and resignation, and with Christ on the Cross, and His blessed Mother at the foot of it. . . . I beg to remind your pupils that the Infant Jesus was obedient to Mary and Joseph—I must not and will not forget your blacks. They

118

are dear to God as you and I. Let them remember that our divine Saviour made his bread by using the ax and other tools.

"My affectionate compliments to the good Father Fouché.

"Thanks to God Almighty, I am in good health. I intend to remain in Portland until the congregation be better provided. They have been poorly attended since the removal of Monsignor Perché. They were cruelly disappointed at Easter, although Bishop Chabrat might have attended. They have not yet begun to make their Easter duties, and do not want to meddle in the same.

"I flatter myself that my presence in Portland will do good to Loretto.

"Have you not been venturesome in disposing of $1200? —as well as Mother Josephine in dismissing three loads of books?"

Thus encouraged by Father Badin, the Mother Superior began at once to provide for the new establishment, and the school was opened September 3, under the direction of Sister Angela Green, with the blessing and encouragement of Bishop Flaget. That autumn five Sisters of the Good Shepherd, the first in the United States, arrived in Louisville. They had come at the request of Bishop Flaget, and it was the privilege of the Sisters at St. Benedict's to give them a temporary house until their convent could be made ready for them. St. Benedict's still flourishes, wreathed with the laurels that seventy years of good works have entwined.

Incidentally, it may be noted that Father Badin's mention in this letter of "the Sisters at St. Thomas" points to the fact that Sisters of Loretto were there in charge of domestic affairs of that institution, as they were later at the colleges, St. Joseph's, Bardstown and St. Mary's, from which they were recalled in 1851. Whether they were recalled from St. Thomas' at the same time or previously is not stated. The records do not show accurately for what length of time the Sisters of Loretto had charge of domestic affairs in the colleges, but a letter of Bishop Flaget, written in 1829 to Father Chabrat, Ecclesiastical Superior of Loretto, says: "Your good Sisters give me more satisfaction . . . at St. Thomas," showing they were there at that early date.

CHAPTER X.

FLORISSANT AND OSAGE MISSION.

NO matter how men may strive to thwart the plans of God, He can and does turn all to good purpose. Interference may have prevented Loretto from spreading forth her young branches, but that very repression caused her to sink her roots more deeply, and as in nature the tree that stands most securely in the earth lifts loftiest head to heaven, so it is with the life or the institutions of men. Every thrusting back of effort Loretto received during these twenty-two years following Father Nerinckx' death was transmuted into so much stored up energy for after work; and if in the period we are now happily to pass through we witness results which, in view of the conditions of the times, appear almost miraculous, we may find a reason quite natural in the repression the Society had so long endured.

The year of 1847 is one marked in the annals of the Lorettine story. Its spring saw Mother Elenora Clarke and her five dauntless companions setting forth for Florissant, with its heart-breaking experience; and when golden September came another intrepid band entered upon the Osage Mission, as difficult as it was perilous.

Florissant, that quaint Missouri village, within call of the mighty Father of Waters, can never be other than an endearing name to the Catholics of the Mississippi Valley. In the multiplying colleges of the Fathers of the Society of Jesus it drops on the careless ear of youth as the home where their instructors were trained; congregations know of it as the novitiate where their future priests are being fitted for their calling; later, when to it turn the longing eyes of their chosen sons, parents learn to weave it with the story of their sacrifice; while in college or in church, in crowded street or on lonely plain, wherever toils a son of St. Ignatius of the Missouri Province, Florissant is the name entwined by him with those of mother, home and heaven. Thither run his thoughts most lovingly, and were it not that the Jesuit must be as divested of self in death as in life, there he would pray that his body might rest when the labors of the day were done. For Florissant a second and ever-increasing number hold memories almost as tender, since beside the Jesuit Novitiate of St. Stanislaus the Loretto Academy was established, June 22, 1847, to become the alma mater of thousands of the fairest daughters of the West.

The Sisters of Loretto were not the first female religious community established at Florissant. As early as 1819 the saintly Mother Duchesne, with four other Religious of the Sacred Heart from France, took up their abode in the building adjoining the parish church, opened a school, and later, in 1820, a novitiate, which continued until 1840, when it was removed to McSherrystown, Pa. The school having utterly failed, the house was suppressed in 1844. The pastor at Florissant was the Reverend Judicus Van Assche, S.J., and being moved to compassion by the neglected children of the community, it was but natural, in seeking for a community to replace the Religious of the Sacred Heart, he should turn his eyes to the Sisters of Loretto, founded by his countryman and to whom, under God, he owed it that he was following the desires of his holy heart in working on the western frontier. Father Van Assche was one of the many Flemish priests whom Father Nerinckx was the means of giving to the Society of Jesus in the New World, and the earnest pleadings of the old missionary for the Indian, never forgotten by his self-exiled countrymen, increased their ardor to respond to the call of Bishop Dubourg, in 1823, for a colony of priests for these dusky denizens of the forest. Father Van Assche

LORETTO ACADEMY, FLORISSANT, MO.

realized the hardships awaiting the Sisters at Florissant, but he probably conjectured that a Society founded by the austere and saintly Father Nerinckx, with whom he had come to America in 1821, and who had turned their cabin in the sailing vessel into a novitiate as strict as he and his six companions found awaiting them at White Marsh, had been early trained to endurance. So he applied to the Reverend David A. Deparcq, who on the resignation of Bishop Chabrat as coadjutor of Bardstown, had been named Ecclesiastical Superior of the Society by Bishop Flaget. The request was granted, and Mother Elenora Clarke, with five companions, was selected for the mission. With hearts sustained by the knowledge they were doing the Master's will, the little band bade adieu to the land of their birth or fond adoption, to their loved Mother House, and their religious companions, and began their long and wearisome journey to Florissant, where it was expected of them to lay another foundation of Loretto's beneficent work for religion and education, lay it abidingly and well.

The Mother House, poor itself, could give them little beyond what they carried with them, and the Sisters found nothing awaiting them but the glad welcome of Father Van Assche and his companions, almost as lacking in worldly possessions as the poor Sisters themselves. The convent to which they were escorted belonged to the Religious of the Sacred Heart, for which the Lorettines were to pay an annual rental of two hundred dollars, and there they opened their school. Fifty years later Loretto Academy at Florissant held a three days' celebration in honor of its golden jubilee. St. Louis, now grown to an archiepiscopal see, was represented by her distinguished ruler, the Most Reverend John J. Kain; the Dioceses of Nashville and Kansas City sent their bishops, the Right Reverend Thomas S. Byrne and the Right Reverend John J. Glennon, the present Archbishop of St. Louis, respectively; and many priests and people came from the various sections of Missouri and her neighboring States. In an oration paying matchless tribute to Loretto and her far-reaching work for God and man, the late Reverend James J. Conway, S.J., recounted the trials endured by the Loretto Academy at Florissant; and we are glad to adorn this history of the Society by weaving into it a portion of the eloquent Jesuit's recital.

"Their day school brought no revenue. Their boarders at the little academy hardly numbered fifteen the whole year round. Their school apparatus was homemade. Their furniture, excepting the trifles they carried with them from Kentucky, was improvised, and in some particulars decidedly original and ingenious. Thus, their carpets—for the parlor had a carpet, if not for the elegance of the thing at least to hide the chinks in the floor—were woven from the cast-off garments of a generation of Jesuit novices, a much appreciated charity to them from St. Stanislaus' novitiate. And I am told that these carpets 'were lovely,' the envy, in fact, of Florissant society of fifty years ago. The furniture was poor indeed, yet it was a comfort to the scanty fare upon which these devoted women subsisted. This was so meagre, in fact, and so difficult at times to procure that downright hunger stared the little community in the face more than once during the severe winter of 1847 and 1848. For, to add to their dearth of funds and want of revenue, the season was too far advanced to permit of their raising anything as a provision and a supply against the hard winter which followed. Those comfortless days of the foundation on Cold Water Creek recalled, and that too vividly, the hardships, the early trials, and bitter suffering of Little Loretto on Hardin's Creek. There are here to-day two life-long friends of Loretto [the Reverend Fathers Walter H. Hill, S.J., and Francis X. Stuntebeck, S.J.], who have more than once during these days rehearsed for me their vivid memories of the desperate straits in which the academy existed during the bitter winter of

1847. There was nothing imaginary in their ills. There was nothing fanciful in their dereliction. Many and many a day that fall, tells one of these reverend friends—they were both at that time making their novitiate at St. Stanislaus—I was sent down from the novitiate to the Sisters with a basket of garden vegetables, the only thing which they would have to eat for the following day, apart from the coarse cornbread which they themselves made from the corn they shelled with bleeding hands during the recreation hours, and ground or pounded into a meal in the free time between classes.

"They possessed no help—they could not pay for it—and were forced, therefore, to chop their own wood, to haul their own outdoor burdens, to tidy their own premises, to dig, to rake, to hammer, to saw. Their heat that winter, and for many a winter after, was the cold comfort of simmering greenwood. Their light during their long, busy evenings and their cold, prayerful mornings from early fall to the springtime far away, was the dull flicker of a few ghastly tallow dips bracketed about the house and grounds like pale beacons on the distant shore on a clouded night at sea. Alas! Alas! Those were trying days for Mother Clarke! She was no coward; nor did she in anything lack that energy, that determination, that boundless hope that make the women of Loretto victors or martyrs in a work of God. But, on the other hand, she was no autocrat. She was no tyrant and her community slaves. She was a mother; her followers her dearly beloved daughters. God's work at Florissant looked, as things were then, simply hopeless, or so fraught with barrenness and perilous drawbacks that it had no vital future. On the other hand, she could not live. Her house was a hollow mockery of the very rudiments of life and the rudest elements of comfort. She could not feed her children, she could not clothe the wasting strength and shivering forms of her fast-failing daughters. For she had no property; she had no money;

she had no revenue, and no friend had, so far, offered a helping hand. Her rent, two hundred dollars—an awful sum where there is no money and no hope of money—was fast falling due. The pupils she had she could not support; how then hope for, or even receive, a single pupil more! Her community sadly needed comforts; she could not even procure necessaries. The Sisters were exhausted and she could not refresh or relieve them. The convent and premises were in wretched repair, and she was simply unable to touch the one or the other. Need we wonder, then, that at length gloomy counsels prevailed? The present was desperate; the outlook was dismally foreboding. There was nothing to lose by going; but there was less to gain by staying. To beg and starve, and yet to work for another winter as they had worked, and with no substantial prospects in any direction, was ordained of no rule, and could be legitimate by no law of duty, prudence, or well-regulated charity. To die, I dare say, they little feared, but to barter so much precious existence for no return but a dreary surfeit of hopeless sacrifice, no just sense of the will of heaven, no appreciation of the certain harvest of evangelical fruit in other fields, would tolerate or much longer permit. It was a solemn moment for the Loretto of Florissant. Those days were, indeed, the crisis which was to determine whether this academy was to be, to grow, and eventually to mature into the many blessings and the glory of this fiftieth year; or whether this spot was to be marked upon the map of the Lorettine apostolate with a cross and a sodded grave raised above the remains of so many hopeless fruits pursued beneath the strain of so many crucifying toils and sacrifices.

"But—so was it ordained of Heaven—these days were, once more in the history of Loretto, only the darkest hour before the dawn. For when distress endured for God's sake has reached its climax, it is, by that subtle alchemy known to Providence alone, dissolved into the sweet surprise of sympathy and relief. Both these welcome virtues now, like messenger spirits from the great king, came a-rapping at the gate of Loretto. The first friend to come to the assistance was Father Van Assche. A long time he had seen it all, as day by day, in sorrow and silent hope-lessness, he had watched the courage of the little band battling against every odd, until all things had well-nigh given way beneath and around them. Father Van Assche was never a man of affairs; yet in this crisis he negotiated a sale which changed night into day for the Lorettines. He purchased the premises and five acres of land for one thousand dollars. But where he or the Sisters of Loretto secured in that unpropitious hour so fabulous a sum is far more than we can now know or tell. The Ladies of the Sacred Heart remitted the rent of two hundred dollars, and in the spring Judge Mullanphy made them a donation of fifty dollars in cash. Their distress had at length reached an interested public, and their friends became many, faithful and generous. Yet next to the initial effort of Father Van Assche in securing the pioneers of the academy, next, again, to the devoted persistence and labors of Mother Clarke herself and her courageous followers, the assured existence, the early possibilities and the gradual promises of this now flourishing school were due to the fostering patronage of the two most charitable ladies in the history of the Archdiocese of St. Louis: Mrs. Jane Chambers of Florissant and Mrs. Tighe of St. Louis. These truly Christian women became, in the truest sense, not merely the friends and patrons, but the almoners of the struggling institution. It was by their timely advice and open-handed solicitude that the Lorettines saved the day at Florissant."

The after years brought success to the Academy. The ever-growing reputation of the Sisters as teachers drew pupils from the broad lands of Missouri, Illinois and Kansas. Mother Clarke was succeeded in the office of superior by Mother Elizabeth Hayden, who continued so to advance the school that when she left, in 1870, to assume the control of the entire Society, the Florissant Academy had few, if any, rivals in the western country. Mother Ann Joseph Mattingly next ruled Loretto Academy.

"The changes which Mother Hayden had introduced," to quote further from Father Conway's finished oration, "the progress which she had instituted, Mother Mattingly continued. The standing which Mother Hayden had achieved for Florissant, and the thoroughness which she put into its studies, Mother Mattingly strenuously maintained. Trained in the same school of daring and determination, inspired with the same apostolic spirit, moulded in the same form of ascetic thought, these two organizers differed little in consequence in their judgment of the present and their estimate of the future. As Mother Hayden, so, too, Mother Mattingly, was not slow to realize that the just prejudice and the advancing tastes of the times, that the demand of growing competition and, finally, that zeal for the position which the Institution had attained in the public eye, called for and authorized a total change of front at Florissant.

"But, alas! the prosecution of even the most necessary plans is slow when their execution depends upon elements over which we can exert no satisfactory control. Loretto of Florissant was, it is true, independent, but by no means rich. Added to this, the times were hard, building, especially in the country, was not cheap, and the running expenses of a large school were not to be at all trifled with. Hence it was that for ten years Mother Mattingly hesitated, prayed and pondered. Finally, suspense ceased to be precaution, delay was making only discontent and creating further wants. She began, therefore, to build in 1880, and in 1882 the work of thirty-five years of hope and patient toil was crowned" by the completion of the present handsome building.

The work begun by Mother Clarke, continued by Mother

Hayden and Mother Mattingly, fell during the succeeding years into the hands of worthy successors in Mothers Dafrosa Smyth, Evangelista Bindewald, Praxedes Carty, Roberta Jarboe, and Flaget Hill. Each added her share to its progress, and, loyally aided by her associates, helped advance the work inaugurated by Mother Clarke and her five Sisters sixty-five years ago at Loretto of Florissant.

It detracts nothing from the glory due Mother Clarke and her heroic band of Florissant to claim for the Sisters setting out for the Osage Mission a larger share of our admiration. Whatever the hardships of the Sisters of Florissant, they were endured among their own race, the civilization of the white man was all around them; and though their neighbors might not be able to relieve it, they nevertheless sympathized with and appreciated the poverty they endured. But entirely otherwise was it with the valiant number conducted by Mother Concordia Henning to the wilds of Kansas, where the Osage Indians had their reservation.

These Indians were being evangelized by the zealous Jesuits of the Missouri Province, who had led them to understand the value of Christian education for their children. Their sons were being cared for by the Jesuits, and when the Reverend J. Schoenmakers, S.J., sought to obtain a Sisterhood to bestow the same blessing upon the Indian girls, he knocked in vain at the doors of the several convents of St. Louis. They were frightened by the enterprise; and, with the horrors of warfare with the Red Man still a quick memory in every western community, their fear is not surprising. In his extremity, Father Schoenmakers bethought him of the daughters of Father Nerinckx, whose apostolic heart ever yearned for the conversion of the Indian. Loretto answered the appeal of the good Jesuit as her saintly founder would have decreed, and four Sisters were ordered from St. Genevieve, Missouri, to prepare for this arduous undertaking. The chosen quartette embraced Mother Concordia Henning, Sisters Bridget Hayden, Mary Petronilla Van Prater and Vincentia Gale.

Proceeding to St. Louis, where they made some necessary purchases of clothing for their future wards, the Sisters, accompanied by Father Schoenmakers and Mr. Jarboe, embarked on the steamer J. J. Hardon about the 20th of September, 1847, and after many delays on the sandbars of the Missouri reached Westport, now Kansas City, at that period the western end of civilization. Here, however, the Sisters met hospitable entertainment from the hands of Mrs. Chouteau, who also provided many requirements for the long journey of one hundred and fifty miles still lying between them and their destination. A two-horse wagon was hired by Father Schoenmakers, and on the 2d of October the little company parted from their race and their civilization for their future life among the savages. Camping out was a novel experience for the feminine portion of the band, but with the adaptability of their sex, the Sisters soon became accustomed to it, learned to cook without being blinded by the smoke, and to sleep in the wagon without great discomfort. At Cool Water Grove they met the first of their future neighbors, the peaceable Miamis. No alarm was experienced, however, as the chief was proud to inform the party that his children had been educated by the Sisters in Tennessee. On the third day's journey they met a white man, the first of their race encountered since leaving Kansas City, and that night they encamped near the lands of the Osages.

"This was truly a night of horrors for the poor Sisters," writes Bishop Maes in "The Life of Father Nerinckx"; "the appalling stillness of the boundless prairie was broken only by the wild howls of the prairie wolves, and the darkness of the night only served to increase their terror. Left to themselves in a wild country, far from all human aid, they frequently invoked that Divine Providence which

FLORISSANT AND OSAGE MISSION.

Father Nerinckx had taught them to rely upon, and their fears soon subsided; they felt that they were under the protection of Him for whom they had sacrificed every earthly gratification."

On the fourth day they reached Mr. Papin's trading-post, where they received their first introduction to the people they had come to serve, and thus they impressed the poor Sisters, according to a letter written by one to her friends at home: "At first sight these Indians seem more like spirits of the lower regions than human beings; the grandees among them are more frightful in appearance than the lower class. The latter are filthy and almost without covering; the former are painted red, black, green, and yellow; their heads are adorned with eagle claws, shells, heads of birds, and feathers of various kinds." From the trading-post the little caravan pushed on to the mission home, where they were greeted by Father Bax, S.J., and a dozen of little Indian boys. The Sisters found a home of hewn logs, with the rudest furnishing, and little of that.

The mission to which the Sisters were called had been for several years in the hands of the Presbyterians, but they, realizing they could make no progress among the Osages, had abandoned it; whereupon the Government, at the request of the Indians themselves, who remembered olden teachers who had come among them, had placed it in the hands of the Jesuit Fathers. Yet for all this evinced willingness on the part of these Indians, they were not so amenable to Catholic teaching, and often the Sisters, reviewing the result of their efforts, may have felt disposed to question the wisdom that had sent them thither. Father Bax, S.J., bore testimony that "their sufferings, their trials, and their privations were great. They were obliged to sleep in the open air. That did not hinder two other Sisters from coming to join them a little after in their heroic enterprise." He adds also: "They are succeeding; they have already produced a considerable change, and are doing great

131

good. The talent displayed in the direction of the school, and the rapid progress of the children are admired by all the strangers who visit this community."

The Sisters were not only teachers for their poor wards, but mothers and nurses as well. Few children were reared by their parents, and those that survived came to the Sisters afflicted with sores or other bodily ailments which had earlier carried their brothers and sisters to the grave. These received the tenderest ministration from the Sisters, who washed and dressed the ulcers, and brought all their medicinal knowledge to the invigoration of the enfeebled little bodies. Many young souls it was their blessed privilege to see go forth fresh from the waters of Christian baptism; and we doubt not in that Heaven where these good Sisters awaited them, the first to give them greeting were these ransomed ones. Mother Concordia understood the sublimity of her mission, and her name was a benediction in the Osage Mission. This good religious had the distinction of having seen the opening and waning of the Nineteenth Century. She was born in 1800, received the habit in its twenty-sixth year, and died on August 5, 1899, wanting but a few months of being one hundred years of age. She had asked to have her purgatory on earth, and during her last years she was as one not of this world. Worthy was her life, the greater part of which was sacrificed for the Indians, and unfading is the crown no doubt that she has received from Him who said, "As long as you did it to one of these, my least brethren, you did it unto Me."

Mother Bridget Hayden succeeded Mother Concordia as Superior of the Mission, and many and varied were her experiences. On one occasion, while trying to conquer a stubborn Indian girl, the father of the child suddenly and unexpectedly appeared. The girl was well pleased at the opportune arrival of her father, but when she saw him taking his tomahawk to use it on her teacher, she threw herself between them, confessing her fault, and begging her father not to kill the Sister. The Indian at once replaced his weapon, and assured Sister Bridget that he would never harm her for trying to make a good girl of his daughter. From white warriors Mother Bridget had equally fortunate escapes when the war between the States made battlegrounds of divers parts of the country. On one occasion a company of soldiers came with the intention of robbing the mission. They had not inspected many departments of the convent when one of the men said to his companions, "Come away, there is nothing here but poverty!" Thus holy poverty, an obligation on all religious and apparent in their most prosperous homes, was the salvation of this mission, which was doing so much for the glory of God and the good of souls.

The special protection of God was evident in all these times of trouble, as neither the Fathers nor the Sisters were in any way injured. The soldiers often harassed the mission, and their parting gift on one occasion was the contagion of smallpox in both schools. Father Schoenmakers bade the Sisters to go to their work of nursing without fear, for God would protect them. His words were literally verified, and not one Sister was striken with the pestilence.

Pleasant indeed were the relations that existed between the Fathers of the Society of Jesus and the Sisters. Between their respective residences stood the church, the house of the Bread of Life, and also, just back of this, the house of the "staff of life." The Sisters did the baking for both houses, and when Mother Bridge received remuneration from the Government for its Indian wards, she turned the amount over to Reverend Father Schoenmakers. Four times a year the Jesuit Fathers went in a caravan to St. Louis for provisions and dry goods, and Mother Bridget had but to give in her list of needs to good Father Schoenmakers, who provided all that was necessary, paying all bills. When Mother Bridget received word from him that a band of Indians was expected, she understood that it meant the Sisters must remain up all night baking cookies; these, with tobacco, had always to be presented to the savages as peace-offerings, on receiving which they would go away quietly well pleased.

Following the treaty of 1866, the Osage Indians were obliged to abandon their beautiful home, with its happy mission, and move further West; and their lands were given over to the whites. As the religious care of the Indians, contrary to their wishes, was entrusted by the Government to the Quakers, the Sisters were debarred from accompanying their charges. Their mission was then transformed into a school for the children of the white settlers, and the handsome St. Ann's Academy was built, and until 1895 was one of the best known educational institutions of Kansas. In that year, September 3, it was totally destroyed by fire, an almost complete loss to the Society, as it was but lightly insured. It has never been rebuilt; although the Society still owns the land, and the devoted people pray for the return of the Sisters they first knew, and who are so intimately associated with the history of the place.

If Divine Providence decreed not to bring to maturity the Brotherhood which the paternal heart of Father Nerinckx had planned for his daughters of Loretto, that Providence, at the same time, has ever provided the Sisters with true and loyal friends. We have seen how the Lazarist Fathers befriended them in their first mission out of Kentucky, in Perry County, and continue that friendship at Cape Girardeau, Missouri; how the good Fathers of the Society of Jesus proved faithful to the sorely tried founders of the Academy at Florissant, and those of this Osage Mission to the brave community here. In 1852 Divine Providence brought to the American shore the worthy sons of St. Paul of the Cross, the Passionists, who established themselves at Osage Mission in the year 1894, the Jesuits having retired from the place in 1892. To these good Passionists the Sisters will ever be deeply grateful for the kind and generous assistance they rendered on the occasion of the burning of their convent home. These kind Fathers afforded them temporary shelter in one of their buildings, and left nothing undone to comfort and console the devoted Sisters, who were grieved beyond measure at thought of departing from their cherished mission home and its surroundings. Nor has their kind interest since ceased; the spirit and devotion of the Lorettines being kindred to their own, the good Passionists seem to look upon Loretto as their sister Society, and have befriended it in ways that call for lasting gratitude.

The Passionists on coming to the mission changed its name to St. Paul. The place is growing into a town of considerable importance, with a population far better educated and more religiously devout than is usual in country districts. An illustration of their faith, as well as of their fond remembrance of the Lorettines is given when summer brings the beautiful feast of Corpus Christi. In former times the Sisters were wont to prepare for the day by erecting an altar on their grounds, from which the Benediction was given. Though years have intervened since the departure of the Sisters and the convent lies in ruins, the custom still maintains among the loyal people. Still is the altar built in the deserted garden, still the long procession in honor of the Sacramental King winds through the neglected grounds, still from the flower strewn throne the great blessing falls upon the reverent throng, who doubtless see, in spirit, the cherished veiled forms of their well-remembered Lorettines kneeling, as of old, around the sacred fane. May the holy custom they have held unbroken soon again be carried on by those who inaugurated it, and the banner of Loretto again rise over the spot consecrated by the sacrificial lives of her first daughters!

CHAPTER XI.

THE MOTHER HOUSE.

THE next heroic step taken by Loretto was for the evangelization of the Southwest. Centuries before religion and education had been planted there by the Franciscan Fathers, the primitive inhabitants owning the blessing of a school before the English settlers of New England had established one for their own children. But what the gentle followers of the little Poor Man of Assisi accomplished by the arts of civilization Spanish greed and cruelty overthrew, and when eventually American possession placed the territory under the episcopal jurisdiction of the United States, bishop and priests had practically to enter upon a mission field. On the petition of the Fathers of the Seventh Council of Baltimore, a Vicariate Apostolic was established in New Mexico by the decree of Pope Pius IX, July 19, 1850, and on the 23d of the same month the Reverend John B. Lamy, of the Diocese of Cincinnati, was appointed its Vicar Apostolic, with the title of Bishop of Agathon. Bishop Lamy received consecration in the Cincinnati cathedral, November 24, 1850, from the hands of the Right Reverend Martin John Spalding, of Louisville, assisted by the Right Reverend Amadeo Rappe of Cleveland and Archbishop-elect John B. Purcell of Cincinnati, who preached the sermon on the occasion. The journey then between Cincinnati and New Mexico is almost inconceivable for us of this day, with our fast-sailing steamboats and express trains, and our air-route on the eve of realization. Two ways to reach his See were open to the new bishop: that of "the traders' trail," which, starting from St. Louis to Independence by river, led from that point to Santa Fé, about 900 miles, by wagon, through

136

unsettled prairies infested by Comanche Indians; or by New Orleans to Galveston, thence overland to Santa Fé. The latter way was chosen by the bishop, who reached Santa Fé in the summer of 1851. He was accompanied to his new home by the Reverend Joseph P. Machebeuf, and immediately bishop and priest undertook the stupendous task awaiting them.

Bishop Lamy early realized, as had Father Badin and Father Nerinckx in Kentucky, that without schools their effort for religion must be shorne of its largest results, and in 1852, going East to attend the Provincial Council of Baltimore, he cast about for a community of Sisters to return with him and undertake the education of his people. Justice demanded that the prospective volunteers should know the actual condition of things awaiting them in the distant Vicariate, and the bishop found none willing or prepared to take up the onerous burden of education in New Mexico, until his searching at last brought him to Loretto.

The dire distress of her cherished Florissant, the worse misery of the Osage Mission, to say nothing of the struggling condition and uncertainty of other foundations, were sorely afflicting Mother Berlindes Downs and her Council; but she recognized that again the call of the Lord had come to Loretto, and she dared not close her ears against it. To the assembled community the plea of Bishop Lamy was repeated, the arduous nature of the work awaiting those future teachers explained; but the Lorettines were not appalled and the response for volunteers was characteristic of the spirit of their holy founder. From among the number offering themselves six were chosen: Mother Matilda Mills, Sisters Catherine Mahony, Magdalen Hayden, Rosanna Dant, Monica Bailey and Roberta Brown. Filled with natural sorrow on the separation from home, kindred and friends, and not without alarms because of the perilous journey before them, but strengthened and sustained by

137

their Saviour in whose cause they were enlisted, the little company set forth, not knowing that the angel of death hovered over them.

They were to make the journey by "the traders' trail," and left Loretto on June 27, 1852, for St. Louis, where they were to meet Bishop Lamy, who was to accompany them. While waiting the arrival of the bishop, who was coming up from New Orleans, where business had called him, the Sisters availed themselves of the opportunity to visit the Florissant Academy. On July 10 the bishop, with a family and some other persons belonging to his suite, was joined by the Sisters, and left St. Louis for Independence, Missouri, by the steamer Kansas. In those times the country suffered from periodical visitations of cholera and other plagues, and little or no precaution being observed, travelers not only took risks with their lives from accidents by unsafe means of conveyance, assaults by Indians and wild beasts, but from contagion as well. Several cases of cholera had been among the passengers of the Kansas, and six days out from St. Louis the superior of the heroic little band, Mother Matilda Mills, was attacked by the dread disease, and twelve hours later, at two o'clock, Friday, the 16th, she yielded her soul to her Maker. Out of this expansion of 1852 the great success of the Society in the West has sprung, and as Loretto passed into existence through the death of her saintly first superior, so to attain the wonderful life that has been vouchsafed her a like grievous sacrifice was demanded.

Following Mother Matilda's death, Sister Monica Bailey was stricken with the disease, and when, two hours later, the steamer landed at Mr. Todd's warehouse, six miles from Independence, Missouri, from all appearance she was hastening to join her superior in death. The plague-infested colony ccould obtain no hospitality from the inhabitants, and they were obliged to take up their abode in the warehouse. On the following morning, July 17, Mother

THE MOTHER HOUSE.

Matilda was borne to her last resting-place in the grave-yard at Independence, the bishop and some other persons accompanying the remains. Mother Matilda Mills was at the time of her sad death about thirty-three years of age, twelve of which had been spent in the religious life. She possessed the virtues which should adorn a religious, and was beloved by all. She had been assistant superior at Loretto and a member of the Central Council two years when, appointed to lead her Society into a new and vast field of enterprise, the Angel of death overtook her on the way.

Fearful of their lives, the bishop took Sisters Catherine, Rosanna and Roberta to the town, leaving Sister Magdalen to care for the apparently dying Sister Monica. On the night of the following Monday, July 19, Sister Magdalen was also stricken, and the poor bishop found himself with two dying nuns on his hands. He removed them from the warehouse to a camp some two miles from Independence, where they received every possible attention from the two ladies who formed part of the bishop's caravan. Through this care, aided, likely, by the change of habitation, the two Sisters recovered, although Sister Monica could not proceed farther. Sorrowfully, she was obliged to watch the departure of her companions to the work her soul yearned for. Before leaving, Bishop Lamy placed the Sister in the hands of a good woman, a Mrs. Murphy, "who," wrote Sister Monica to the Mother Superior at Loretto, "received and did for me with all the tenderness and care that a mother could, though very poor, with no dependence but a son who supports her and himself on a very small salary. He came home every day, except one, to see if there was anything wanting for me. He is a waiter in a public house. One day he came running home right after dinner, in the broiling sun, to bring me a tumbler of ice cream; and almost always brought me something." From the hospitable home of the kindly Irish woman Sister Monica went to Liberty, where this letter quoted from is written, under date of September 20. There she became the guest of Mr. Graham L. Hughes, who, with his wife, was a convert to Catholicism. By these good people the Sister was supplied with all things needful for her comfort and convalescence, and when she was able to travel they sent her to the Sisters at Florissant. After residing some time at that house, Sister Monica begged to be allowed to complete her sacrifice for the souls of the West. She went to Santa Fé, where she died holily on Christmas Day, 1865.

The caravan made its start from Independence August 1, but on their first night out a storm broke upon them with unabating fury, and it now appeared to the frightened Sisters as if they had escaped the plague but to fall victims to the elements. Huddled in their frail wagons, they waited, in prayer and supplication, for the end which seemed impending; but the wrath of the tempest fell short of destruction, and the next day all were able to pursue the journey. On the following Sunday, August 8, Mass was celebrated near an Indian hut on the road by the bishop, and Council Grove was reached on the eve of the Assumption, when the Sisters confessed, and the following morning renewed their vows just before Holy Communion, according to the Rule. The last Sunday in August, the 29th, found them at Pawnee Fork, where Mass was celebrated, and they spent the day of rest. On September 7 the party arrived at Fort Atkinson, near which the Sisters had the terrifying experience of finding themselves surrounded by three or four hundred Indians. They seemed indisposed to attack the little band of whites, the bishop being able to baptize the child of a captive Mexican woman; but placing no trust in their attitude, the bishop made his next march at night, and the Sisters remained in their carriages during the day. Sunday, September 12, found them at Cimarron, having crossed the Arkansas, and two days later they

ACADEMY OF OUR LADY OF LIGHT, SANTA FÉ.

were rejoiced by the appearance of the Very Reverend
Vicar General Machebeuf, who, with a party of men and
horses, met the oncomers at Red River. On the 17th they
reached Fort Bartley, where, for the first time in nearly
two months, they slept under a roof, and Saturday, the
18th, found them at Las Vegas, their first Mexican town.
Here the Bishop remained, sending the Sisters on with
Father Machebeuf, and on Sunday, September 26, at 4
p. m., the caravan entered the ancient town of Santa Fé. It
became a triumphal procession for the band of tired, home-
sick Sisters. Beyond the city the people, with several Mexican priests, were waiting to give them greeting, and as
they advanced the throngs reached such proportions it became difficult for the passage of the carriages. Triumphal
arches had been erected, and as they entered the city the
church bells began a joyous ringing. At the door of the
cathedral a priest met the Sisters, and, after presenting
them with holy water, led them to the foot of the altar,
where places had been prepared for them. The Te Deum,
accompanied by violins and guitars, was sung, and the episcopal blessing was given by Bishop Lamy, who had entered the town the Thursday previous. The sisters were
then conducted by the bishop, the vicar general and the
clergy to the bishop's residence, a portion of which was
vacated for their use.

The Sisters first applied themselves to a study of the
Spanish language. In November they received their first
boarders, two children who had lost their mother, the good
bishop advising that it were well to begin their work with
an act of charity. It proved bread cast upon the running
waters, for when the father withdrew the children, whom
the Sisters had the happiness of seeing baptized, he paid for
their tuition. The school, under the title of Our Lady of
Light, was regularly opened in January, 1853, with ten
boarders and three day scholars; and by the following August the number had increased to twenty boarders and

twenty-two day pupils. The community was under the charge of the ever memorable Mother Magdalen Hayden, who led Loretto to her marvelous accomplishments in the Southwest. The first house soon became too small for the ever-widening work of education, and in 1857 they purchased the only two-story building in Santa Fé, which was known as "The American House," because it had a pointed roof of shingles, all the other roofs being flat and of mud. This had earlier been bought for Bishop Lamy, who had given up his own home to the Sisters; but he, finding it commodious and well suited for conventual purposes, sold it at a reasonable figure to the Society.

Archbishop Lamy, from his first visit to Loretto Mother House in 1852, when he came to ask for Sisters to take charge of the schools of his Vicariate, to his death, February 13, 1888, ever proved himself a kind and generous father, a faithful friend and protector to the valiant Sisters who had answered the appeal of his pressing need. The memory of this venerable archbishop will ever be held sacred by the Sisters of Loretto at the Foot of the Cross.

From the start success attended the efforts of the Sisters in Santa Fé, While not without their hardships and privations, they so easily adapted themselves to the new country, the spirit of their Society was so happily in accord with the free, undaunted spirit of the West, that they straightway entered upon their possessions, and until to-day to think of the educational progress of the West, secular or religious, is to think of the Lorettines and their schools and academies. In 1878 the Sisters erected a beautiful stone chapel, which has become one of the architectural ornaments of the quaint ancient city. An academy, equipped with all modern conveniences, was built in 1881, and in 1892 the group of buildings was completed by the new convent, on the site of the old "American House" and former adobe buildings.

The spring of Santa Fé's activity was constantly supplied by Loretto; and from the day the first little band set forth in 1852 with Bishop Lamy, others had followed, enduring their hardships. Long after the Middle West had been transformed by the building of railroads, the way to the great Southwest was still by the Traders' Trail; and when the Indian represented to the mind of the people of the former place a period long past, he roamed at will over the western plains, committing depredations and crimes, filling the heart of the rancher with the same fear his presence had inspired in the hearts of the earlier pioneer of the Midland. The memory of one little band that she sent to join their Sisters in far New Mexico is forever sacred in the annals of Loretto, and for one nameless, unknown grave her great mother-heart forever yearns.

In 1867 three Sisters started for Santa Fé, traveling from St. Louis with Bishop Lamy, Father D. M. Gasparri, S.J., two other Jesuit Fathers and two Sisters of Charity. On Friday, June 14th, the caravan left Leavenworth, Kansas, reaching St. Mary's, at that time a reservation of the Pottawattomie Indians, on the 21st. From that point on the party was more or less beset by savages who, however, showed no indication of fighting until the evening of the 17th of July, when fifty of them suddenly appeared and began their attack on the caravan. Six days later cholera broke out, the victom being a young man from Ohio. While he was dying the party was again set upon by the Indians, now numbering three hundred, frightful to behold in their war-paint and feathers. The whites hastily tied the wagons together for defense, the men stationing themselves in the best positions their unprotectd condition offered. Throughout the entire night the situation continued darkness adding to its terror. The five Sisters remained in a tent, tortured by fears more agonizing than their defenders could dream of, and fervently they prayed for death before falling into the hands of the maddened savages. But the angel of the Lord guarded that little band that fearsome night, and the Indians did not destroy the helpless men and women who were at their mercy. For one, however, the shock was too great, and the next day Sister Mary Alphonsa Thompson, a native of Kentucky, fell sick unto death. She received the last Sacraments, and, notwithstanding her dying condition, the journey had to be continued. since it was not known at what moment the Indians, more strongly reinforced, would return. On July 24th, at 10 o'clock, the beautiful soul of Sister Alphonsa was released from the bondage of bodily pain and earthly fears. When the halt was made that evening, they dug for her a grave in the desert plains, fashioned for her tender frame a rude coffin, and while the lone wind sobbed its dirge they gave her frail body back to the great mother's not untender keeping. In sorrow they did it, for almost with her last breath she had begged them not to bury her there, but to take her on to New Mexico; for the fear of the Indians that killed her haunted her in her dying moments, and she dreaded the mortal tenement she was leaving should fall into their desecrating hands. Under existing conditions, to comply with the poor last request Alphonsa Thompson made upon her fellow men was, they felt, impossible; but they marked her grave with a cross, trusting, perchance, that at some future time a less perplexed company would give the Sister the burial she craved. But the wild storms beating upon that open and unprotected country soon laid the marking cross as low as the lonely grave, and over both the sand of the wilderness drifted, and only the watchful Eye of God sees where little Sister Alphonsa is peacefully sleeping.

Referring to her death, Bishop Lamy wrote: "The youngest Sister of Loretto died, on the 24th of July, from fright, as I considered it, caused by the attack of the savages. She was eighteen years of age, well educated, and a model of virtue." Miss Eleanor Donnelly, the distinguished Catholic poet, made her death the subject of a

poem, well loved by every Lorettine and familiar to every
pupil of their schools:

They made her a grave where the tall grasses wave,
    'Neath the blue of the Western sky,
And they laid her to sleep where the wild waves sweep,
    Through the bending reeds that sigh.
With a swelling heart they were forced to part
    A link from that sacred chain,
And though lovely and bright, it was laid at night,
    'Neath the sods on the Western plain.

With many a prayer, they laid her there,
    To sleep in that cold, cold bed,
While on her bier fell as holy a tear
    As ever embalmed the dead.
Now the stag may bound o'er that sacred ground,
    And the eagle from his eyry scream,
But no Vesper bell comes to break the spell
    That wraps the sleeper's dream.

Ah! far, far away, perchance, that day
    A mother's heart was sore,
With an aching void for the Lamb's sweet bride
    Laid to sleep on Arkansas' shore.
O mother dear! soothe to rest each tear,
    Thou to glory a star hast given;
And the spirit chain, though rent in twain,
    Shall be clasped again in heaven.

In the morn of youth her young heart's truth
    Sought not the earth or its dust;
But her spirit's wings left earthly things
    To fold in the bosom of trust.
O bride of the Lamb, thou hast gone home!
    In the Virgin's train art thou;
And the songs that rise o'er the dome of the skies
    But echo thy virgin vow.

145

LORETTO.

Let fancy bright, on wings of light,
    Now seek that lonely grave,
Where flowers bloom and wild birds sing,
    By the dark Arkansas' wave;
Let devotion kneel, for there 'twill feel
    A throb unfelt before,
For incense rare doth fill the air,
    Though the worshipper 's no more.

There, mortal, kneel one hour to feel
    That soothing calm within,
When devotion bows o'er holy vows
    And prayer has shackled sin.
Oh! for the bliss of an hour like this,
    When the soul's deep powers thrill
With the magic tone from mercy's throne,
    And passion's waves are still.

Lonely grave by the Western wave;
    Oh, pure heart sleeping there,
The winds alone above thee moan
    Their sad, wild requiem prayer.
E'en the savage here feels a mystic fear
    As he stands by that lonely mound,
As the whispering breeze sighs through the trees,
    "Thou standest on holy ground."

Then sweetly rest, with the cross on thy breast;
    Oh! sweet be thy slumbers here!
May o'er thy head bright wings be spread
    By angels watching there!
May no ruder wind sweep o'er thy sleep
    Than the breath of summer roses,
While virtue's tear embalms the bier
    Where our martyred dead reposes.

The first Superior of Santa Fé, Mother Magdalen Hayden, was succeeded in office by Mother Francisca Lamy, a niece of Archbishop Lamy. Her successors were Mother Catharine Connor, Mother Lucia Perea, Mother Barbara Everin and Mother Rosine Green. Of the first band that accompanied Bishop Lamy in 1852, Sister Rosanna Dant, of Kentucky, still lives in Santa Fé, and at this time (1911) is engaged in active service.

Those who have succeeded the venerable and fatherly Lamy in the Archdiocese of Santa Fé, in the order named, Most Reverend J. B. Salpointe, Most Reverend P. L. Chapelle and Most Reverend Father Bourgade, have been true and devoted friends to the Sisters of Loretto, who will ever treasure their names in the book of golden memories. The present incumbent, Most Reverend John Baptist Pitaval, continues the kind interest of his worthy predecessors.

CHAPTER XII.

FOUNDATIONS IN NEW MEXICO.

AUGMENTED by accessions from the Mother House and through the local Novitiate, which was established in 1855, the house at Santa Fé was able to found other branches. The first of these was at Taos, New Mexico, where the Academy of Our Lady of Guadalupe was opened in 1863. The Reverend Gabriel Ussel proved a generous benefactor by aiding the Sisters in the erection of the convent. Sister Euphrosyne Thompson, with two Sister companions, left Santa Fé in 1863, making the dangerous trip to Taos over seventy-five miles of mountain roads in carriage. Railroads were not in contemplation then, nor have they yet gone all the way to the Taos valley. The impulsive Mexicans gave the good Sisters warm welcome, and their school opened with a fair attendance of little girls. Sister Euphrosyne remained in charge until 1875, and won the hearts of the people of Taos. In 1894 the Public School was offered to the Sisters, which they have successfully conducted to the present time.

On the invitation of the Reverend Father Salpointe, afterward Archbishop of Santa Fé, the establishment of the Annunciation Academy at Mora, New Mexico, followed, opening March 25, 1864. Sister Mary Borgia Ward was first superior. The poverty of the Sisters during the first months was almost beyond endurance; bread and beans formed an oft-repeated meal; they had to parch wheat for coffee. Sugar they had not, nor furniture beyond the simplest; their beds were thin mattresses upon the floor, and piled up in a corner during the day, according to the custom established by their holy founders at Little Loretto. One room was used for kitchen, refectory and laundry, and that was far from being weather-proof. Their good friend, Father Salpointe, was no better situated, and the Sisters tell an amusing incident of their common affliction. During a rainy season the water ran freely through roof and walls of their adobe building, leaving them without a dry spot whereon to sit or stand. In their distress they thought to seek the advice of Father Salpointe. Hastening to his house, near by, great was their astonishment to find him perched on the window-sill with an umbrella over him, reading his breviary! They concluded his predicament was equally as bad as their own.

In 1888 the entire building was destroyed by fire. The Sisters found a friend in Mrs. Walton, who allowed them some rooms in her hotel for school purposes, and only one day was lost by the pupils. A subscription was taken up, and many generous benefactors aided the Sisters. In 1905 the boarding school was discontinued, and one year later the select school was given up that the Sisters might devote themselves entirely to the Public School, which now includes the children of all the departments, and at present is in a flourishing condition, the public being well satisfied with the arrangement.

In connection with the foundations of Taos and Mora, we give the following from "Soldiers of the Cross," by Most Reverend J. B. Salpointe, D.D.:

"In 1864, April 4th, the Reverend J. B. Salpointe, parish priest of Mora, had the pleasure of receiving three Sisters of Loretto coming from Santa Fé, at his request, to take charge of a school for girls in the vicinity of his residence on the church plaza. These were Sisters Mary Borgia, Cecilia and Ynes. Soon after there was opened in the same town a school for boys under the direction of the Christian Brothers. A few months before, the Reverend Gabriel Ussel, parish priest of Taos, had founded two similar institutions in his parish. The Brothers and the Sisters who took charge of these schools were the first who left Santa Fé to extend the blessings of their work to the parishes of the diocese. At Mora, as at Taos, the Brothers remained only a few years, owing to the poor attendance of pupils, and thereby the lack of means for their support. The Sisters have persevered residing in both places, notwithstanding the difficulties they have met with on several occasions; the severest trial the Sisters had to stand at Mora was the burning of their house at the end of 1888. It was also in 1864 that the Sisters of Loretto were called to Denver by Father Machebeuf to found St. Mary's Academy.

"As we have seen before (Chap. III), the Sisters of Loretto suffered from the cholera, which, when they first started for New Mexico, deprived them of one of their number and obliged another to stop on her way and go back from Independence to the Convent at Florissant for her convalescence. This was a severe trial, but not the last they had to undergo in extending their beneficial work to the missions of Santa Fé before there were facilities for transportation as we have them at the present time. We speak here of October 31, 1864.

"At this date we were coming to Santa Fé with some Sisters as an addition to those already established at Mora. We passed Sapello late in the afternoon, and with all appearances of bad weather for the night, but the Sisters had a good covered wagon, and we intended to reach Mora for the feast of All Saints, even by traveling by night. The distance was twenty-seven miles. We started against the good advice of the priest of Sapello, the Reverend Francis Jouvenceau, who offered us the hospitality of his house. For about an hour the weather was good, when on a sudden it commenced to rain hard, and soon after to snow in great abundance. Before long the night became dark and the road hardly visible, when the horses stopped in a ravine, and could not move ahead on account either of the deep snow or of the slippery ground they had under their feet. This had to be the end of the journey. After tying up our animals to the surrounding trees, we and our boy commenced to feel the surrounding ground with our feet in order to find some sticks of dry wood to build a fire. We succeeded, not without difficulty, but the Sisters wrapped with blankets in their conveyance, refused to avail themselves of our fire. Our supper consisted of some biscuits and apples, which the Sisters furnished us from their basket.

"At this juncture we were summoned imperatively to clear the way by Father Machebeuf, who was also going to Santa Fé for a colony of Sisters for Denver. Great was the surprise for both to meet in such a predicament, and more so for the Father when he saw that he could not attempt to pursue his way before daylight, without exposing himself to the danger of missing the road and going over some precipice. At last he understood that he could not fight against the elements and determined to accept the hospitality we could offer him. He had room for us in his wagon, and the boys, with the blankets we could spare, made it as comfortable as they could near the fire. We had just commenced to slumber when we were startled by a tremendous crash, which was repeated several times by the echo of the mountains. What was it? It was nothing but the snow, whose weight had despoiled a large pine tree of all its branches from top to bottom. Then commenced our fear for the Sisters, whose wagon was between two or three of the same trees. Fortunately, or, rather, providentially, the night went on without any repetition of the dreadful noise.

"The next morning early we started, not for Mora, our destination, but for Sapello, in order to keep the feast of All Saints. The snow had stopped falling, but we had it so deep on the ground that at every three or four steps the horses refused to pull as the snow became piled up in front of the axles, and at every time we had to use a stick to remove the obstruction before we could make another start. It was, as can be understood, a rather slow and painful way of traveling; still, towards the evening we reached the house of Dr. Fernando Nolan, about four miles from the starting point. This gentleman, a friend of ours, gave the best room he had to the Sisters. and treated us not as ordinary guests, but as we needed after a long fast. We spent the night there, and the next day in the afternoon, with the help of Mr. Nolan and some of his neighbors on horseback, we made for Sapello, and the day after for Mora by another road, out of the woods and less obstructed by the snow."

Far-seeing minds soon decided that Denver was to become one of the great cities of the Western empire, destined to rival the earlier founded ones of the East. The great pioneer priest and future first Bishop of Denver, Monsignor Machebeuf, already in charge of religious matters in the growing town, began to consider plans for the Christian education of the children. Happy recollections of the Sisters of Santa Fé caused him to apply to them for assistants in his proposed work. After encouraging replies, a two-story frame house, belonging to George W. Clayton, standing on a lot facing California Street and extending from E to F Streets, was purchased in 1864 for four thousand dollars, the Sisters taking possession that year.

Thus came into existence the St. Mary's Academy of Denver, almost simultaneously with the beginning of civilization in the mountain region of the West; famous among the justly celebrated religious institutions of its own Society and of others which followed Loretto to the "Rockies," as they had followed her throughout the Mississippi Valley, across the arid sands to Texas, New Mexico and California. The pioneers of Christian education and merciful service to humanity, the Sisters of Loretto, knowing that centralization of effort produces better results, confine themselves to the education of youth; and until time shall obliterate all marks of the race upon this fair continent, as time has done with civilization as proudly builded, benerations shall pass where Loretto fearlessly led the way.

Sister Mary Joanna Walsh and two Sister companions were the founders of the Denver institution. Soon they were joined by others, all of whom were from the house in Santa Fé. The school, after a humble beginning, soon prospered; but, as no conventual establishment escapes the cross, the Sisters' Academy, in the fifth year of their establishment in Denver, was partially destroyed by fire, while Bishop Machebeuf was saying Mass on Sunday, April 18, 1869. The Sisters might have been discouraged had not the good bishop appealed to the public in their behalf, and with the willing help of many sympathizing friends, who contributed freely, they were enabled not only to repair the damage, but also to enlarge the building. This unlooked for casualty and consequent business caused the bishop to forego the pleasure of accompanying his old friend, Father Salpointe, of Mora, New Mexico, to France and of being present there at his consecration as Vicar Apostolic of Arizona. But nothing was too precious for Bishop Machebeuf to sacrifice for his Sisters. What a Flaget had been to the Sisters in Kentucky; a Rosati to those of the early foundation in Missouri; a Lamy to the Lorettines in New Mexico, that Bishop Machebeuf was to the Sisters of Loretto in Colorado. St. Mary's was "dear to the heart of Father Machebeuf," writes the Reverend W. J. Howlett in his "Life of the Right Reverend Joseph P. Machebeuf, D.D.," "and he never counted anything a sacrifice that he could do for St. Mary's Academy, and it can be as truly said that the Sisters of Loretto never abused his benevolence, nor forgot any favor which he ever did for them." And not only was Father Machebeuf their devoted friend, but his financial ability, as the following incident evinces, enabled him in many ways to assist them. We quote again from Father Howlett's work:

LORETTO.

"The valleys near Salt Lake were teeming with fruit, and before Father Raverdy left them he sent a large box of peaches as a treat to Father Machebeuf in Denver. Father Machebeuf was surprised at receiving them, but more surprised at receiving with them a bill for sixty dollars, express charges. There was no fruit growing then in Colorado except such as grew wild, and, while apples were freighted in by wagon, the peach was too perishable for a journey of thirty days. To reimburse himself for the cost of transportation, Father Machebeuf hit upon the idea of offering a number of the peaches for sale at the seemingly extraordinary price of one dollar each. But peaches were an extraordinary fruit just then, and he had no difficulty in disposing of a sufficient number at that price to pay the cost of carriage, and he had enough left for an abundant treat for himself and the Sisters and pupils of St. Mary's Academy."

As an ever-hallowed reminder of those days of pleasant relationship is the sweet-voiced bell of St. Mary's Academy, whose soothing tones for nearly fifty years have floated out over the Queen City of the Plains, and fallen like a benediction on the ears of Denver's inhabitants. It was secured for the school by Father Machebeuf in 1865.

Success continued to reward the Sisters' exertions, and a widespread reputation brought them pupils from distant quarters. In 1872 began the erection of the splendid St. Mary's Academy which for nearly a half-century did excellent work on Fifteenth and California Streets, until the encroachment of business houses obliged the Sisters to seek a more desirable location. This secured, plans were promptly carried out, and the autumn of 1911 beheld the elegant new fireproof academy on Fourteenth and Pennsylvania Streets completed. As regards patronage, it was but a transfer of pupils from the old to the new building, with many additions to swell the ranks of the time-honored institution.

FOUNDATIONS IN NEW MEXICO.

The next foundation was made in 1866, when the Reverend Augustin Truchard, parish priest of Albuquerque, called the Sisters of Loretto to open a school in that town. He had built a large house for the purpose, and the school prospered until 1869, when it was closed, owing to a change of the ecclesiastical administration in the parish. Las Vegas, 1869; Las Cruces, 1870, both in New Mexico, followed. A favored region of New Mexico, even at that time, was Las Vegas, and the Lorettine Academy of the Immaculate Conception entered at once on a successful existence, and has carried its good name to our own day. The meaning of the name, *vegas,* meadows, will convey the idea of the fertile tract embraced within the strong arms of the surrounding mountains. Sister Mary Kostka Gauthreaux was the first superior, and, with her associates, laid amply the foundation of the convent and school.

Like so many other establishments of the Society, Las Vegas once experienced the trial of fire, and the stricken Sisters saw their home and school laid in ashes. The loss interrupted, but did not stop, the work, and in another quarter of the town a better building soon arose, where boarders and day scholars annually assemble to drink at the fountain of knowledge, and, their studies completed, go forth to brighten simple, happy homes among a God-fearing people.

An oasis in the desert appears the bloooming spot to which the first settlers gave the name of Las Cruces, where the traveler will find a stately building of the Spanish mission style of architecture, known as the Loretto Academy. To-day Las Cruces is easily reached by rail, and the well-appointed coaches make the journey agreeable. But no pleasure trip was it when, at the solicitation of the Right Reverend J. B. Salpointe, of happy memory, then Bishop of Arizona and Southern New Mexico, the Sisters of Loretto, in 1870, journeyed thither from Santa Fé. Between the two points lies an immense strip of barren land, level as a floor, with high mountains skirting it at a distance on either side. About one hundred arid miles it measures from Paraje to Doña Ana, with no water to refresh either man or beast, no tree to spread its shadow upon the way, no grass to soothe the eye or rest the aching feet. *Jornada del muerto,* "The journey of death," that trail has been called, since the caravans marked their passage over it with the bones of man or horse. Known and feared less by the more enduring Indian, he frequented it, and often added to the horrors of the way by attacking the unprotected and cruelly plagued freighters and immigrants.

Sister Rosanna Dant and her four companions put their trust in God and rode to Socorro without mishap. Reverend Father Bernal came for them in a carriage, and, guarded by twelve men, they resumed their journey. Arriving at Las Cruces, the Sisters were taken to the house of Mrs. William Tully, whose elegant home was theirs until their own humble roof was prepared to shelter them. The first pupils were enrolled in Mrs. Tully's parlors. Humble as was the new convent, the Sisters were glad to occupy a home of their own, and soon welcomed help in the persons of three other mmbers of the Institute.

The Sisters' chapel of the first days was about twelve feet square, with a neat rag carpet on the floor. The altar was made of trestles and a few boards covered with white muslin, and the tabernacle was a small pine box lined with green silk. Outwardly the effect was fair and neat, especially as some of the Spanish maidens had donated their silk dresses for an antependium. A statue of our Lady enhanced the little shrine and our dear Lord did not scorn His poor abode. Mother Elizabeth Hayden, superior, on visiting this community was greatly pleased and edified; she mentioned the poverty and cheerfulness of the Sisters on her visitations to other houses and extolled obedience, which makes religious happy under any circumstances.

In 1875 a novitiate was established at Las Cruces, this

having been decided by the Mother House as best, in order to accommodate the people living so far away, who found distance and the danger of travel to Loretto obstacles in their way. It continued until 1880, when the novices were removed to Santa Fé.

In 1880 Mother Praxedes Carty was appointed superior at Las Cruces, where a heavy debt had been incurred for a new building. She set to work in earnest to clear away all obligations and make other improvements. The chapel was beautified, a new altar being donated by Reverend A. Echallier. Reverence for the last resting-place of the dear departed next drew her care and attention to the little graveyard; and this task done, she improved the grounds around the convent. The unfinished convent left to her by her predecessor was completed, and all the comforts her poverty allowed were introduced. In 1881 the railroad reached Las Cruces, and the school entered upon an era of even greater popularity.

The transfer of Mother Praxedes to Florissant, 1893, was deplored as a great loss by the people; but her successor, the amiable Mother Rosine Green, continued the work ably until called later to Colorado Springs. During the superiorship of Mother Albertina Riordan additions had to be built to accommodate the increasing pupils, especially its boarders; and to-day no institution in the whole of New Mexico and adjacent States surpasses the Loretto academy which has risen in the once silent Mesilla valley and made the desert to blossom as the rose.

From Las Cruces in 1879 went out, in answer to the appeal of Reverend Father Bourgade, the parish priest, a community of four Sisters, with Sister Mary Kostka Gauthreaux of Santa Fé as superior, to found St. Joseph school at San Elzeario, Texas. At that time no railroad reached that section, and when one was built San Elzeario was slighted, coming no nearer than three miles. A wider field of usefulness calling them to El Paso, the community, with Sister Mary Magdalen Dietz as superior, was transferred there in 1892, although retaining their property in San Elzeario. At El Paso the foundation entered immediately upon a flourishing career. The Sisters are in charge of St. Joseph's Academy and the three parochial schools. Many of the Mexican children attending these schools are from Juarez, Mexico, and other points across the Rio Grande. Holding in loving memory the zeal of their holy founder for the Indians, the Sisters of Loretto lost no opportunity for carrying out his ardent desire for the Christianizing of these wards of the nation.

In 1875 Mother Magdalen Hayden was requested by Don José Leander Perea, a wealthy resident of the fertile valley and town of Bernalillo, New Mexico, to open a school for girls of that neighborhood. He built for this purpose a house on a small tract of land adjoining the parish church, which he deeded to the Sisters on their arrival. Sister Adelaide Farren was appointed superior of the establishment, and the schoool was successfully conducted on the original basis until 1885, when, through the zeal of the Very Reverend J. A. Stephan, Director of the Bureau of Catholic Indian Missions, the present Industrial School was established, a contract being made between the Commission of Indian Affairs and the Bureau of Catholic Indian Missions which agreed to pay for a stipulated number of girls of the Pueblo Tribes. Monsignor Stephan was instrumental in obtaining from Miss Drexel, now Reverend Mother Katherine, Superior of the Sisters of the Blessed Sacrament, a donation of two thousand dollars, which aided the Sisters in the erection of their first building.

The conditions of the contract were strictly fulfilled by the Sisters, and from the report of Mr. Charles Burton, of the United States Indian Service, in 1898 the following extract is quoted:

"I noted with great pleasure the peculiar excellence of that schoool. The teachers are careful and painstaking, and the children are remarkably bright, clean and attractive. The intellectual advancement of the children is beyond that of any of the schools under my care. The buildings are ample, clean and well cared for; the grounds are very attractive. The superintendent, Sister Margaret Mary, is a woman of fine attainments and excellent character and possesses great executive ability. I therefore take pleasure in recommending that the contract be increased from thirty-four to seventy-five children."

But, alas! notwithstanding the eminent satisfaction pronounced by the agents of the Government and others, the contract was cut down from year to year, and finally withdrawn in June, 1901.

Through the zeal and untiring energy of good Sister Margaret Mary Keenan and her corps of self-sacrificing Sisters, together with help that is received from the Bureau of Catholic Indian Missions, the school is continued with the same interest as when remuneration was received from the Government. Through Sister Margaret Mary's efforts a fine twenty-five acre tract of land adjoining the Industrial Institution was secured, which supplies the large family with an abundance of grapes of many varieties, luscious fruits, and vegetables in quantity and quality. Spacious buildings have been erected and everything provided for a first-class Industrial School, where the children learn to use their hands as well as their heads. Twelve Sisters preside over the different departments—such as kitchen, laundry, sewing room and classrooms. Several premiums were awarded the school by the World's Columbian Exposition for their specimens of work in the different branches. These little Indians are ignorant of the requirements of civilized life when they come to the Sisters, understanding no language but their own Indian tongue. Their docility, however, soon leads them to conform to the more modern ways, and in a few short years it is surprising to see them leave the School possessing a good knowledge of the elementary branches, and some are adepts in music and singing.

Besides the Industrial School, the Sisters prepare a number of worthy girls to teach in the Mexican towns. No fewer than eighteen of those were teaching in the public schools in 1910. The Public School for Girls in Bernalillo has been taught by the Sisters of Loretto since 1887. On Sundays the Sisters appointed drive to the nearest pueblo to teach the Indians catechism, prayers and singing of hymns. As soon as the *cacique* announces the arrival of the Sisters, old and young flock to the little adobe chapel. The poor Indians seem to appreciate the zeal of the Sisters, and they entrust their little girls to their motherly care with the greatest confidence in *la Madre Margarita,* as they call good Sister Margaret Mary.

Surely must the spirit of their dear founder be not far from those daughters of his Society when they set forth from their school of Indian children to carry to the parents the knowledge of the true God.

At the solicitation of the inhabitants of Socorro, a flourishing town in New Mexico, the Reverend Father Benito Bernard applied to Mother Magdalen at Santa Fé, in 1879, for a colony of Sisters, which was sent, with Sister Euphrosyne Thompson as superior. The house was built by the Father and ready on their arrival. The Sisters conducted a well-patronized boarding and day academy, and for many years taught in the Public School. The foundation still continues to prosper. A good music class shows the taste of the people for the fine arts, and singing is popular as part of the day's program. Special care is taken by the Sisters to prepare their pupils for First Holy Communion.

Santa Fé saw another school of the Lorettines established in 1886, when, at the solicitation of the Most Reverend Archbishop Salpointe, they accepted the Saint Catherine school for Indian boys, Sister Loyola Hernandez being put in charge. In 1889 the Benedictine Fathers conducted it for one year, when it passed into the care of Mother Katherine Drexel's Sisters.

In 1886 five Sisters, with Sister Mary Joanna Walsh as superior, were sent to the distant mission of Salinas, California. They had high hopes of a flourishing foundation in the school of the Sacred Hearts of Jesus and Mary, but conditions did not prove to be what they had been represented, and the Sisters, much to their regret, were withdrawn in 1888.

CHAPTER XIII.

The Mother House.

THE venerable Mother House rejoiced in this waxing strength and ever-increasing usefulness of her children abroad. While she gave to them freely, she suffered no diminution of her life-sustaining powers, and as an individual educational institution still led the most ambitious of her daughters. Among the cultured of the South and East were numbered many of Loretto's pupils, while the West, passing by her branch houses, sent to the mother foundation many of its fairest daughters. In those more leisurely and gentle days Loretto was considered favorably situated, and over the smooth roadways that had replaced the buffalo traces and woodland paths of pioneer days rolled the carriages of wealth, bringing visitors or pupils to the academy; while not infrequently the occupants were young maidens returning to their alma mater to beseech her to receive them as her spiritual daughters, or fair strangers who had heard from afar the worth and wisdom of the Lorettines, and, called to the higher life, sought admission among their number.

History and tradition were weaving their deathless spell around this height; Art had brought hither some of her priceless treasures from the Old World, and immortal Science sat there enthroned. Culture dwelt there as one among her own people, and over all hovered Religion. Hence, with the passage of years, Loretto became one of the interesting places of Kentucky, and within the stately academic walls that had risen above the first log cabin many whose names shall be remembered, "While Fame her record keeps," were made welcome, and carried back with them to the fret and turmoil of their eventful lives the lasting recollection of Loretto's hospitality, her peace and magnetic charm. Many noble exiles about this time were wanderers in the States, among whom was Louis Philippe, before the fortuitous developments of time had placed him on the throne of France. A thorough Frenchman, he naturally sought out a French bishop; therefore he became the incognito guest of Bishop Flaget, and with that devoted friend was often a visitor at Loretto. Some years later, Louis Napoleon visited it in the same manner. Among our own renowned who deemed it an honor to partake of Loretto's far-famed hospitality was Henry Clay, who, on one memorable occasion, presided at the commencement exercises. In his eloquent address he complimented the students, lauded the faculty for its advanced and comprehensive manner of instilling knowledge, and concluding, fervently exclaimed:

"Knowledge availeth not without virtue. Clothe yourselves, then, young ladies, in the garments of purity, and thus prepare to enter into the glory of the Lord."

At the present time it is hard to conceive the difficulties resulting from lack of books, school furniture and other accessories now considered indispensable, met with by teachers in the schoolroom during the first decade and more of Loretto's existence. Notes preserved of instructions given by Father Nerinckx to the Sisters in the school at Loretto show that he realized their difficulties, and that his purpose was to form and train teachers qualified to meet any difficulties which varying conditions and exigencies of time and place might bring. The tenor of his instructions further shows that the fundamental principles of religion formed the foundation upon which he would have them base all their work, and the purest Christian motives to be the support upon which they should rely for inevitable success. To quote some of the memoranda that have been preserved:

"He encouraged us to love our work and the office in

which we were placed, as being the will of God, for we did
not place ourselves in it, but were placed in it by our superiors, who had authority over us, and whose command we
ought to respect as coming from God. He recommended
the virtues of humility, patience, meekness, mildness, and
cheerfulness; that these virtues once implanted in our own
hearts would teach us how to instruct the children under
our care, to love them all alike, and to act to them all in a
loving manner; reminding us that what we did or left undone for their advancement would be judged by Christ as
done or not done to Himself.

"He said that this Society was a nursery or garden, and
the appointed teachers were the cultivators of this beautiful
garden, and he begged them in a most humble manner to
be attentive in discharging their duty and, as it were, to
place the hearts of their pupils in the hands of the Blessed
Virgin Mary, that she might be their mother in life, and
in death conduct them to Heaven."

Among the minute directions relative to transient conditions there are some that would be salutary in every effort
to develop Christian character; as, for instance, this provision for the meritorious use of time:

"The scholars, not to lose time and labor, ought to be
often put in mind of doing all their actions for God's honor,
glory and love. It may be done thus, at the common
Standard of the Society:

"V.   O Suffering Jesus!
R.   O Sorrowful Mary!
V.   I give you glory, thanks and praise;
R.   O bless my work and guide my ways!"

These instructions, so assiduously inculcated by their
venerated founder, not only enabled the Sisters to succeed
amid the adversities of pioneer days, but prepared them to
meet and solve the problems the future would unveil.

Father Nerinckx' progressive spirit animated the Sis-

LORETTO ACADEMY, KENTUCKY.
Seniors of 1912. Our Lady's Court. Guests' House.

ters, and, foreseeing that more than the primary branches
would be called for in their schools, they prepared for the
exigency. Reverend William Byrne, President of St.
Mary's College, himself a gifted and efficient teacher,
taught the Sisters some of the higher branches. In 1826
the school was opened on a new basis. Reverend Ignatius
A. Reynolds, of St. Joseph's College, Bardstown, Charleston's future bishop, had been sent to Baltimore to master
physics, chemistry, etc., and on his return he taught a class
of Sisters from Loretto, who repaired to St. Thomas' Seminary, near Bardstown, for his convenience. In the meanwhile other professors had prepared the Sisters in rhetoric,
composition and literature. Pianos were procured and
teachers engaged; a Swedish pianist, later a French lady,
Miss Herminie Gruit, a pupil of Henri Herz, gave lessons
on the piano, harp and guitar. Professor Collière, a distinguished opera singer, gave the Sisters vocal lessons.
Father Fouché taught them French, bookkeeping and
higher mathematics. A portrait painter from the East
taught them painting. In 1829 the Institution was incor-
porated under the laws of Kentucky. Its elegant buildings,
completed in 1834, afforded comfortable accommodations
for a large number of pupils. The school was directed by
a Board of Trustees, of which the Right Reverend Bishop
Flaget was Moderator; and at the close of the year the
pupils were examined by some of the principal professors
of St. Mary's College. The following, according to the
prospectus, were the branches taught: Reading, Writing,
Arithmetic, English Grammar, Geography, with the use of
maps and globes, History, ancient and modern, with Chro-
nology and Mythology, Rhetoric and Composition, Botany,
Optics and the elements of Mechanics; Hydrostatics and
Astronomy; Chemistry and Natural Philosophy, French,
Needlework, plain and fancy, Marking, Lace and Bead-
work, Drawing, Painting on satin and velvet, Music, Vocal
and on the Piano, Harp and Guitar, Dancing. Lessons

and exercises were given in polite literature. French was taught by French ladies. Music and painting early became a distinguishing feature in Loretto's curriculum, and teachers from other schools came to perfect themselves in these arts. Among these were Sisters of the Holy Cross from Notre Dame, Indiana, who, according to the records of both Societies, studied music and painting at Loretto.

The Community being numerous, fullest and most prompt attention was given to every department, while the teachers had been carefully selected with a view not only to talent and learning, but also to disposition and aptitude to fashion and habituate the young mind to what was useful, elegant and proper. Thus did Loretto lay the foundation of her methods of instruction, which in the present day brings her such high repute.

Constant industry and improved methods were reclaiming the farm from its native wilderness; good stock was introduced into its pastures, while the cultivation of its fields provided plenteous fare for the household. The country at large was experiencing that bounty of Fortune which in the veiled future red-handed War was sharpening his weapons to destroy, and Loretto, secure in the belief that her severest trials were past, rejoiced in the happiness of the times.

Thus the dawning of 1858 found the Mother House, within four years of its golden mile-post on the far-reaching road of Time: before two months of the New Year elapsed a heap of ashes and charred embers pointed out where church and convent had stood. On the night of the nineteenth of February, in warmth and security, Sisters, Novices and pupils lay down for their quiet sleep; at two o'clock in the morning they were rudely awakened by the terrible cry of "Fire!" The fire had originated in the kitchen, and when discovered the entire house was in a blaze. Hurrying into the church, the Reverend Father Wuyts, then the chaplain, moved the Blessed Sacrament to a room in the brick house which Father Badin had built in 1816. Before his return, though short was the distance, the devouring flames had enveloped the church, and he had scarcely time to notify the Sisters, who were striving to save some of the valued and valuable furnishings, of their imminent danger.

The shocking knowledge of their doom did not leave the Sisters helpless, as is often the case; and long years of training stood them in good stead that hour. Those whose duty it was brought the children and Novices instantly out of peril, while the others rushed to save in the departments of their individual calling. To this swift action we owe it that no loss of life is to be recorded, and that all Loretto's treasures were not sacrificed to the flames. Superhumanly aided, they tore their priceless paintings from the walls, dragged out the chests containing the equally priceless vestments and altar vessels which Father Nerinckx, Bishop Flaget and other thoughtful friends had procured for them while abroad, and snatched documents and papers, more priceless still, from the very teeth of the fire. Then, when the flames had reached the victor's place, they withdrew from their heroic efforts, and while around them whistled the wintry winds, watched, with streaming eyes, the annihilation of the work the slow years had builded up. The valuables they had saved were insignificant with those which had been lost, while of clothing they now possessed nothing beyond the hastily donned garments on their backs. Their library, a costly and valuable one, was lost, and when the roof of the church went down, it carried into the seething fire the chimes which Father Nerinckx had brought from Europe and which had no counterpart in America; but past all their losses was that of their private papers, historical documents, and those belonging to and relating to Father Nerinckx which, by some fortuitous circumstance, had escaped Father Chabrat's bonfire. From this last loss Loretto can never recover, while it is one in which the history of the Church in Kentucky must likewise share.

LORETTO.

It is such a trial as this that proves the spirit, and Loretto, though overwhelmed, was not subdued. While still the embers smouldered among the ashes of their home, and they shivered under the heavy snow that began to fall in the afternoon, the Sisters' thoughts began to turn to the new structures they would erect, for the idea of abandonment did not enter their minds. It is also such times of distress that prove our friends, and Loretto found she was not lacking in these. Among the first to hasten to the relief of the suffering Sisters were their friendly neighbors, the good Sisters of Nazareth. Shortly before the burning a letter had come to Loretto from the truly apostolic Mother Catherine Spalding, one of the founders of the Society of Nazareth, appealing for assistance for the orphans of which her community had charge, and closing with the touching assurance of cordial and sisterly affection, "that," she wrote, "should ever exist among the communities of our holy religion;—for, after all, we should make but one common family to carry on the different works of our common and divine Master,"—a sentiment which, from the beginning, Loretto has cherished. When opportunity arrived, Nazareth showed that the sentiment of Mother Catherine had its root in the heart of the Society, and a large box of supplies was speedily dispatched to Loretto. Every article that could be thought of needful for wear and use in a household was included, their consideration even extending to a paper of needles; and so truly is this, her chief instrument, appreciated by womankind its inclusion in the box from Nazareth never fails to receive the distinction of special mention, and it is an historical fact that some of those needles are still treasured by the older Sister at Loretto, who, doubtless, will pass them on as prized relics to their successors. With equal gratitude were the kind benefactions of other friends remembered. The list would be long, filling pages, but the following deserve special mention: Bishop Spalding, the Right Reverend Abbot of Gethsemani, the Jesuit Fathers in St. Louis and elsewhere, the Trappists in Dubuque County, Iowa, the Sisters of the Good Shepherd, the Sisters of St. Dominic at St. Catherine's, the Dominican Fathers and St. Rose's congregation, the Sisters of Charity in St. Louis, Bishop Lamy. Kind friends from far and near hastened to give relief; the branch-houses were swift to send help; individual contributions were received, and immediate needs, at least, were provided for. But the Sisters were obliged to dismiss school in order to give shelter to the religious family, thus cutting off their only source of revenue and at a time when it was needed most. Then, indeed, did they recall the maxim of their holy founder, "Never forsake Providence and He will never forsake you."

At this crisis Mother Berlindes Downs was elected for the third term to the office of Mother Superior, and proved a woman chosen by God to lead the Society out of its Egyptian night. We have seen elsewhere the sublime reliance of Mother Berlindes upon Divine Providence and her never-failing patron, St. Joseph; but her faith was of that order held by a certain general, who tersely bade his men to trust in God and keep the powder dry; a faith that always accomplishes things, since miracles include efforts on the part of man to meet God's assistance. Mother Berlindes prayed hard, and worked harder, and the impossible, to human seeming, resulted.

Out of its ruins Loretto rose. More stately, more imposing and more substantial were the convent and academy, larger and more beautiful the church, which, on its completion, brave Mother Berlindes could offer to the bishop for consecration, standing as it did entirely free from debt. The interrupted work was recommenced, and, with its former patronage restored when ready for acceptance, Loretto resumed her unusurped place among the leading educational institutions of the country.

The work of foundations that Santa Fé was carrying

on so successfully in the Southwest was being pursued in like manner by the Mother House and other houses in Kentucky and Missouri. St. Benedict's Academy of Louisville had in 1857 taken charge of the day school connected with the church directly opposite the academy, where the Sisters continued teaching with good results, especially as to the religious education of the children. Kentucky's next foundation was that of St. Joseph, in Daviess County, in 1863, and was made by Sister Agnes Carrigan as superior and four companions. It enjoyed a period of success, but when the school was most flourishing and affairs assuming the permanency that time alone can bestow, fire destroyed the convent, December 30, 1870, and the Sisters were obliged to return to Loretto. Some years later they were succeeded by an Ursuline community, which is still doing excellent work there, under the patronage of St. Joseph.

Lebanon was next enrolled under Loretto's banner when, in 1864, Sister Felicitas Webb, sister of the Honorable B. J. Webb of Louisville, to whom posterity owes an unending debt for his labors in gathering the fragmentary history of the Church in Kentucky into permanent form, in his "Century of Catholicity in Kentucky," and other writings, conducted a colony of Sisters to the capital of Marion County, where they opened St. Augustine's Academy under favorable auspices. That locality being largely Catholic, the school has always enjoyed a good patronage. Besides the academy, which is for girls, the Sisters also conduct a Lebanon school for boys and a school for colored children.

At Flint Island, Kentucky, in 1867, a school, under the patronage of St. Teresa, was opened by Mother M. Joseph Aubuchon and four companions. At the end of two years the Sisters left for a more desirable locality, but some good was accomplished during their stay. At Flint Island there was a church station as early as 1810, and the Catholics were administered to by Father Badin and Father Nerinckx. In the diary kept by the latter it is stated he received a gift of three hundred acres of land for Church purposes on his visit to it in company with the newly ordained Father Robert A. Abell.

New Haven followed in 1868, when four Sisters, at the request of the pastor, the Reverend Francis DeMuelder, took charge of St. Catherine's parochial school, with Sister M. Eucheria Byrne as superior. A cordial welcome from the good people of New Haven awaited them. Until better arrangements could be made, the unselfish pastor occupied the sacristy, giving the Sisters the use of his house. This inconvenience was cheerfully borne both by them and the pastor. The school has continued to the present, productive of much good.

In 1869 the Lorettines made their first advance into the eastern part of the State, and the Covington Diocese, in opening their school of St. Charles at Paris. Thither, in the pursuit of his missionary work, had often gone their saintly founder, making the long journey on the back of his good horse, Printer. A record of one of these trips has been preserved; when a messenger called him to the home of a Mr. Keith, in Bourbon County, eighty miles away. As the messenger stated he had left the man in a dying condition, zealous Father Nerinckx immediately set forth, and after riding for a day and a night reached the home of his distant parishioner to find he had already passed to his reward. Father Nerinckx consoled the stricken family, prayed with them for the soul of the departed, nor left until he had followed the remains to their last resting-place. In the garden spot of Kentucky, with a growing, influential and well-to-do Catholic congregation, it would seem that here a religious community, especially one native of the soil, would abide and flourish. In addition, a site, spacious, picturesque and healthful, was secured. From the quiet street it fronted to the convent door swept an ample lawn, set with pine and other forest trees, with a tiny dell like a dimple on a smiling face; to the north, to the George-town Pike, lay the orchard, fit recreation ground for meditative nun or frolicking girl; at the rear, the convent gardens, the cow pasture, leading down to the creek. In this ideal spot the Loretto Sisters lingered until 1875; while the stay of some of their successors was even briefer. In due order there followed Benedictine Nuns from St. Walburg Academy in Covington, who were succeeded by the Sisters of Notre Dame from Cleveland. These, too, abandoned it, and then came the Visitation Nuns from Maysville, who, after efforts as brave as their predecessors, too, had to yield to circumstances which they could not control, and cast their fortunes in the far West, establishing themselves at Tacoma, Washington. The fair conventual property then passed into Protestant hands, and a secular school was opened, and later, Negroes owned it for educational purposes. The property was divided into town lots, and now "Convent Heights" is one of the residential portions of the thriving, wealthy town. The Lorettine community was in charge of Mother Constantia Murphy.

Elizabethtown welcomed the Sisters of Loretto in 1870, when Sister Superior Simplicia Moffitt, with four companions, opened St. Mary's school. About four acres of land surround the school, which still exists for the education of the Catholic youth of that neighborhood.

At Louisville, in 1871, the Sisters opened two parochial schools, the first in St. Joseph's German parish, with Sister Mary Cleophas Julius, superior, and three companions, but which continued only three years, as another German school made this one unnecessary. The second, the Immaculate Conception school, was a more permanent establishment for the German Catholics, and was opened by Sister Everildes Rooney, superior, and two other Sisters. Sister Mary Edward Meagher later joined the community and remained its superior for thirty years.

The early seventies saw another parochial school opened

172

NOVITIATE.

Chaplain's Residence.　Church of Our Lady of Dolors.

in Louisville, 1873. The Reverend Father Disney, during his pastorate, solicited Sisters for the parish of the Sacred Heart. A community of three, with Sister Mary Philippa Cantwell as superior, was sent to the work, which it and its successors did well until the suspension of the school, in 1877.

At Earlington a mining company donated land for a school and church, and to this Sister M. Berchmans Doran, accompanied by three other Sisters, went in August of 1875 to open the school of St. Bernard. At first the company built a frame house for the Sisters, which was later replaced by a more substantial one, and occupied until 1889 by the Sisters, when they were recalled to the Mother House. In 1875 the Sisters took charge of St. Bridget's school, Louisville, where they found ample opportunity to exercise patience and zeal. Many of the adult members of the congregation had to be instructed in their religious duties, and the children stood sorely in need of training; but the face of things was soon changed, and the mission brought salutary results.

After the school of St. Francis Xavier, opened at Raywick in 1878, and which was held by the Sisters for a short term of years, Kentucky knew no other foundation until 1886, when the school of St. Charles was organized. As the site of the first school opened by Mother Mary Rhodes, the Sisters naturally felt the spot should be occupied by some of their Society. Wherefore, on a cold December day, five Sisters drove to St. Charles and entered a new house of rough boards which had been erected for them, and which seasoned sufficiently to let in snow and rain, there being no plaster. With the best will to carry out their appointed work, the Sisters of the present day cannot stand what had been endured by the original foundation; when they returned to the Mother House for their vacation the project was considered unwise, and, the superior dying, the Sisters were not sent back to the unsuitable domicile. Moreover, with the country so thickly set with Catholic schools, educational and religious conditions are vastly different from those of 1812; else Loretto's daughters would have stood by their post, at whatever hazard or sacrifice. In 1890 another short-lived school was opened at Chicago, Ky., under the patronage of St. Francis, continuing five years.

CHAPTER XIV.

FOUNDATIONS IN VARIOUS STATES.

MISSOURI, the second home of the Lorettines, and bound by many tender ties to the Society, was likewise blessed with a number of foundations during this span of years; and while some, as in the mother State, have passed from existence, still during their period of life they exerted a beneficial influence upon the community at large, and by instilling virtue and religion, with education, in the hearts of the children, advanced the interests of humanity and laid the obligation of gratitude to Loretto upon the future.

In 1862 the Sisters opened the St. Mary's day school in the old College parish, St. Louis, which was continued until 1864, when the Sisters were transferred to Cairo, Illinois. Sister Mary Ferdinand Sweeney was in charge of the first community.

When her term of superiorship at Florissant had expired, in 1865, Mother Elenora Clarke was named superior of a new foundation at Edina. The first benefactor of the Sisters in their new abode was Mr. Peter Early, who provided them with a house and lot. The sterling worth of the Catholics in that cold section of Missouri insured an attendance of sturdy pupils, whose minds and hearts opened readily to the instructions of their teachers. A moral stimulus may be traced, also, to the one-time pastor, Reverend D. H. Phelan, present redoubtable editor of the *Western Watchman,* who awakened his people to an appreciation of the thorough and Christian education afforded by the Sisters' school, which in the near half-century of its existence has lost none of its early prestige. To-day, as in former times, its pupils are eagerly sought as teachers for points around Edina, while in other spheres they are equally successful. The improved school building, due chiefly to the efforts of the former pastor, Reverend C. E. Byrne, is looked upon with honest pride by the inhabitants, and a quiet, comfortable home is found within its walls for the present community. Incidentally, it may be added that the Edina foundation was the occasion that gave to Catholic journalism the *Western Watchman*. During the early years of the Sisters' life in Edina religious bigotry lived and was not ashamed to display its vindictive face. Father Phelan took up his trenchant pen with telling effect, and his gallant championship of the Lorettines of Edina was the beginning of the campaign in the cause of truth, that he has so valiantly waged now for nearly half a century in the *Western Watchman*.

The parochial school of St. Michael was opened in St. Louis, 1869, by Sisters from the Florissant Academy, in charge of Sister Mary Simeon James, which continues to the present, with every indication of a long career of usefulness. St. Louis also received the next Missouri foundation when the Sisters were placed in charge of the school of the Sacred Heart, in 1871, three Sisters, in charge of Sister Mary Roberta Jarboe, going daily from St. Michael until 1891, when they took up their residence in a house adjoining the church.

The St. Louis Loretto Academy was erected in 1874 at Twenty-sixth and Pine Streets, the property, about five lots, having been given by the late Mrs. Ann Hunt for school purposes, with a condition that should the Sisters dispose of the property the sum of $12,000 be paid to the St. Vincent de Paul Society. The first faculty consisted of ten members, with Sister M. Simeon James as superior. Immediate success crowned their efforts, and lasted for years, even after traffic had rendered the location unsuitable for a school. In 1903 the Sisters disposed of the Pine Street property, paid the $12,000 to the St. Vincent

LORETTO ACADEMY, ST. LOUIS, MO.

de Paul Society, and secured a desirable site on Thirty-fourth and Lafayette Avenue, where they have erected the present handsome academy. Their beautiful new chapel was dedicated by the Most Reverend J. J. Glennon, assisted by a number of the clergy, secular and regular, on February 1, 1910. In the sermon on the occasion, His Grace extolled the work of education, which, he said, "requires greater self-sacrifice and higher consecration of purpose than devotion to a life of charity in the alleviation of bodily suffering; after all, charity in this significance, caring for souls, teaching the poor in spiritual things to know God, was a special work of our Lord. Companionship with Mary at the foot of the Cross implies contact with the spirit of sacrifice that enables the Sisters of Loretto to find strength and courage to go out from this institution to the various parochial schools of our city to teach God's little ones to know Him and to love His teachings."

The Sisters of Loretto have been teaching the parochial school of the Old Cathedral parish since 1875, and pleasant relations have ever existed between them and its long-time pastor, the Reverend Eugene Coyle, whom the Sisters justly look upon as a father. To him they are indebted for many of the sacred vessels belonging to their present chapel on Lafayette Avenue. In 1876 Reverend P. L. McEvoy engaged the Sisters to conduct St. Kevin's School, now the Immaculate Conception, which they continue to the present, and which, under the able management of the Reverend Edward J. Shea, has become one of the finest parish schools in St. Louis.

The St. Mary's Academy at Moberly was established in August, 1877, and continues its beneficial influence in that section of Missouri. A school for boys is also under the care of the Sisters, and the pupils from both bear creditable testimony to the careful training given by their teachers.

Perched on an elevated plateau of the Ozark Mountains,

the beautiful city of Springfield prides itself on its healthful climate, romantic surroundings and educational advantages. One among many schools, Loretto Academy presents its name to the public, and is well known as a select boarding and day school. It was humble in its beginning. Its founders, five, with Sister Mary Oda Smith as superior, arrived in Springfield August 28, 1878, and were kindly welcomed by the Reverend Father Kussman and some of the ladies of the parish, who entertained the Sisters with hospitality, and then conducted them to their new home, a small cottage of five rooms, adjoining a two-story brick building. The house was clean, but without furniture of any kind, and in consequence the Sisters had to sleep on the floor the first night. The next day they were introduced by good Mrs. Horine to Catholic storekeepers, the kind lady giving security for the Sisters, who were without money, having but ten cents to their credit when they had paid the freight charges on their piano. Trials were early the Sisters' portion in this foundation. Two of their number were taken sick, and they had to close the parish school until other teachers were sent; but their superior, a most edifying religious, zealous and fervent, sustained their courage, often assuring her Sisters that if but one soul were saved their labor should be most bountifully rewarded.

The generous patronage of the Catholics and some non-Catholic parents soon gave the Sisters reason and resources to enlarge the building, until the present aspect of the house and grounds speaks well for the industry and progress of those who conduct the institution. Under Mother Clarasine Walsh notable improvements were made, while Mother M. Flaget Hill added to the interior decorations and playground arrangements, so that the school is admirable in many respects and the convent complete as a home for the religious. The Sisters are sixteen in number and, besides the academy, teach two parochial schools.

FOUNDATIONS IN VARIOUS STATES.

Marshall became the next home of Loretto, when, in 1884, Sister Dolores Jackson opened the St. Savior's Academy. It was successful for several years, but owing to its proximity to other academies conducted by the Lorettines it was relinquished in 1907 to the Sisters of Notre Dame de Sion, an exiled French community, which desired to locate in the United States. St. Louis in 1886 and Kansas City in 1889 were the next Missouri foundations. In the former is the satisfactory parochial school of the Visitation, where proper arrangements have been made for graded classes and a comfortable home provided for the teachers. Having no other than the ordinary difficulties to contend with, the teachers can give undivided attention to the work of the school.

The Kansas City foundation known as St. Patrick's school was begun by Sister Mary Simeon James, who, with her assistant teachers, soon made the school popular. In 1893 the Sisters were withdrawn to open the school of St. Charles Borromeo, in St. Charles, Missouri, where in 1894 the new convent and school were erected, and since then various improvements have been made. The well-known missionary Jesuits, Reverend Fathers Rosswinkel and Lambert, were pastors at St. Charles when the Sisters were invited to control the schools. In 1894 Reverend Father O'Dwyer, pastor of the Sacred Heart parish, Kansas City, Missouri, sold the present Sacred Heart school building to the Loretto Society. Sister Mary de Sales Hynes was sent, with a little band of Sisters, to take charge of the flourishing school, which had been conducted by the Sisters of Providence of Indiana. The school still holds an average attendance of nearly three hundred and fifty children, with eight Sisters in charge.

Illinois saw the first establishment of the Lorettines within her boundaries at Cairo, 1864, while the country was in the throes of the war between the States. Troublous was the period of foundation, and such in lesser or greater

179

degree was its existence. The community of St. Mary's
Academy of St. Louis was transferred to Cairo in the year
above named, and the new institution was placed under
the patronage of St. Joseph. The Sisters had come on the
invitation of the Right Reverend Bishop Junker, and the
inducement offered was a plat of swamp land covered with
logs when not submerged by the high water. This tract
was donated by the Cairo Land Company, a corporation
composed of non-Catholic gentlemen, their object being,
no doubt, to aid them to build up a city. The gift, as is so
frequently the case with benevolent donations, had a condition attached in the proviso that if the Sisters ever sold
the property for other than educational purposes the sum
of two hundred dollars a lot should be paid to the Land
Company or its heirs. The late Reverend L. A. Lambert,
editor of the New York *Freeman's Journal*, was pastor at
St. Patrick's Church, then the only one in the town. He
aided the Sisters by collecting from everybody, Catholic
and Protestant, and soldiers, of whom there were many at
that time in and about Cairo.

The first building attempted was only partly erected
when it was blown down and much of the lumber was carried off by the soldiers for tents and other purposes. In
order to erect their building the Sisters were obliged to
borrow from $12,000 to $15,000 at a high rate of interest.
Meanwhile, one of their best creditors was forced to make
an assignment, and in order to avoid publicity the Sisters
had to procure payment of their debt immediately. In their
distress they turned to St. Joseph. Their novena closed
on March 26 (1879), and that morning, before they arose,
a flash of lightning during an electric storm struck the
cupola of their convent, totally destroying the building by
fire before it was paid for. But it is an ill wind that blows
nobody good. Fortunately, the building was insured, and
the insurance money liquidated the debt which was the
cause of so much anxiety to the poor Sisters. They were

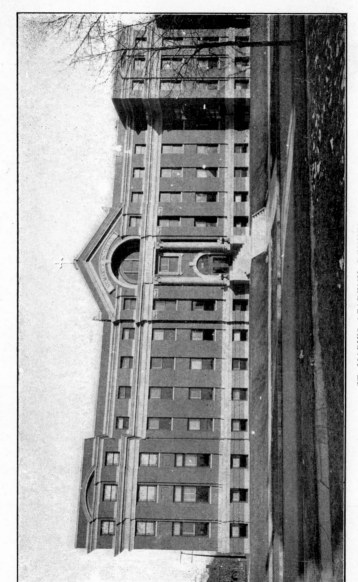

ST. MARY'S ACADEMY, DENVER.

now homeless and penniless, and were about to be withdrawn by their superiors, when the people of Cairo petitioned that they be allowed to remain. With the aid of contributions from the branch-houses of the Loretto Society, part of the inheritance of one of the Sisters, and slight contributions from the people of Cairo, the new school building was begun. It cost between $12,000 and $14,000. In 1896 the Sisters permitted the parochial school to be conducted in their building, the parish paying a rental of one hundred dollars a year for the use of three rooms. Besides the donated land, the Sisters had purchased eight lots in Cairo. Negotiations were entered into with the parish in 1903 to dispose of the property to them. Countless difficulties arose entailing almost endless communication by letter, repeated visits to Cairo, etc., in all of which a lasting debt of gratitude is due to Mr. J. D. Healey, of Henry Hiemenz Realty Company, St. Louis, who donated his valuable services.

The school at Cairo was opened by Sister Ferdinand Sweeney, after whom Mother Elizabeth Hayden did good service in advancing it along successful lines. During its existence it accomplished good, and between it and the two parochial schools taught by the Sisters, and their patrons and pastors, good understanding existed; but the natural difficulties obtruded too frequently to make the place desirable.

Cairo is, furthermore, associated with a sad page in Loretto's glorious history. "On the noblest tree of the forest," has said a writer, the Reverend Hugh McGeveny, "even in the blush and flush of spring, there are some withered leaves. They do not affect the vitality of the trunk that bore them, but their deadness mars the beauty of its life. . . . Some of us children of the Church are like these dead leaves." These dead leaves now showed on Loretto's tree, but were soon swept by the hand of Divine Providence from its vigorous branches, and lie smouldering in the past.   Sister M. Ferdinand Sweeney, who led the foundation to Cairo, had been received into the Society in the autumn of 1852.   She possessed attractions of the highest order.   She made a good beginning; virtue, piety, even wisdom, guided her way; the term of probation passed, and with the idea that a young saint lived in their midst, the community rejoiced to see her appointed Mistress of Novices.   The study of writings beyond her spiritual capacity, with a consciousness, now enlarged to inflation, of her inherent powers, overbalanced a character originally finely poised, and Sister Ferdinand began to dream of a reform in the Society, saw herself acclaimed the St. Teresa of the Lorettines.

Between 1861 and 1862 two Sisters, followers of her misdirection, withdrew to the home of one of them, where Sister Ferdinand was to join them when they had secured an opening for their "new reformed Society of Loretto." Meeting with no encouragement in their rash design, the deserters returned to Florissant and tried to make reparation.   It will be sufficient to add that one of these Sisters became mentally unbalanced; the other left the Society. In 1862 Sister Ferdinand was placed in charge of the newly opened day school of St. Mary's in St. Louis, and when the application came for a foundation at Cairo she was commissioned to visit the place and investigate its prospects. Upon her recommendation it was accepted, and she was sent with a faculty to found the St. Joseph Academy.   An opening for the realization of her search after "higher perfection," as she termed her dissatisfaction with her Society, seemed here to present itself, and a brisk correspondence with the unhappy ones she had caused to become unsettled ensued.   But among her many attainments that of prudence was lacking; and a too swift assumption of authority, with too much intercourse with the outside world, caused Sister Ferdinand to be recalled to the Mother House, where Mother Berlindes Downs was then Mother Superior.   She

was assigned to St. Mary's College, where a few Sisters
had charge of the wardrobe and infirmary, until her superiors obtained light how to deal with so delicate a case.

After some months in Kentucky, Sister Ferdinand, pro-
fessing to be penitent, was again forgiven, and the Council
in May, 1864, at her own request, named her one of the
community to open St. Mary's Academy in Denver. She,
with Sister Mary Jerome, started for St. Louis, provided
with money for the western trip. In St. Louis she tarried
to visit secular friends, who declared it a pity to send so
fine a woman to the rough mission in Denver, and advised
her not to go. Sister Ferdinand yielded, and communi-
cated with her misguided Sisters at Florissant. Then the
would-be reformer, the poor, self-deluded seeker after
"higher perfection," performed an act that destroys every
remnant of belief in her honesty of purpose and holiness of
intention: she sent a telegram to Mother Elizabeth, the
Superior of Cairo, summoning her immediately to St.
Louis. Supposing she was called by proper authority,
Mother Elizabeth started; learning otherwise on arriving
at St. Louis, she returned in haste to Cairo, to find Sister
Ferdinand, who, with one of her chosen ones, had reached
Cairo during her absence, the self-appointed superior of the
Academy and Community of St. Joseph. Strong in her
knowledge of duty, Mother Elizabeth remained at her post
awaiting orders from the Central Council, which attitude
and her uncounted upon sudden return rather upset the
plans of the reformers. Father Lambert, his eyes now
opened to the true state of affairs, frankly showed his dis-
approval of Sister Ferdinand's conduct. Realizing that
there was no chance for the success of her venture in Cairo,
Sister Ferdinand turned toward Chicago, Illinois, where
the Right Reverend James Duggan permitted her to open a
school. She even received new members, and in the eyes
of the world the community for a brief interval was successful. But unless the Lord build the house, they labor

in vain who build it. The work of Sister Ferdinand was
not of God, and after a few years the institution disbanded,
the scattered members for the most part desiring to return
to Loretto. The question of receiving them, in case any
applied for admission, had early been referred to ecclesiastical authority in the person of the Right Reverend M. J.
Spalding, Bishop of Louisville. His decision, that those
who left with final vows could not be received, those in
their probation, being young and easily deluded, might be
considered, was now followed. Sister Ferdinand had taken
with her to Chicago three Sisters of Loretto, one from
the St. Louis house, one from Florissant, and one from
Cairo. The last named, at the intercession of her relative, Archbishop Elder, reentered Loretto and became a
worthy Sister.

And what of her who led others astray? Left alone,
she passed in her despair into the darkness of infidelity,
and, attacked by cancer, was nearing a doleful end. But
the great mother-heart of Loretto, though she had pierced
it so cruelly, never cast her off from her affection and her
prayers. Learning of the unhappy condition of her who
had once been one with them, the Sisters of Loretto besought the Reverend F. Sautois, S.J., who had given Sister
Ferdinand the habit, to seek her in the non-sectarian hospital and make a last effort to save her soul. Prayer and
zeal again prevailed, the prodigal was reconciled to her
God, and with the angels, Loretto rejoiced more over this
one soul saved than over the ninety-and-nine that needed
not repentance.

Danville and East St. Louis next received the Sisters in
Illinois. At the former place St. Patrick's school was
established in 1882, and was closed eight years later; while
the school at East St. Louis, also under the patronage of
Ireland's saint, established in 1888, still continues with encouraging prospects. This school was begun by five Sisters, with Sister Avellina Coleman as superior, who placed

it on a good footing, and left the way comparatively easy for their successors. The present year about three hundred and fifty children were enrolled.

Southern as Loretto was, in virtue of the birth of its founders and of the women who for years afterward made up the Society, and who still form an appreciable portion of it, as well as of its establishment and the permanence of its Mother House in Kentucky, it was not until 1873 a branch was established in the South east of the Mississippi; but established, it flourished like the proverbial bay tree, and among Loretto's best known, most flourishing foundations is that of St. Mary's of Loretto in Montgomery, Alabama. Enthroned upon a terrace, this academy stands as if overlooking the city in whose progress it modestly takes its share. Two buildings, one the original mansion, with its colonial pillars, the second more modern but little less stately, form a picture it is pleasant to recall. Mother Harriet Moore and her five companions found devoted friends among the warm-hearted Southerners, who aided in building up the school of that early day, and whose descendants are still patrons of the institution. Mother Symphorose Warren was successor to Mother Harriet, and died while in office. Mother Mary Flaget Hill was then appointed, and when her term expired Mother Mary Kevin Coffey, Mother Evangeline Gorman, Mother M. Borromeo Hynes, and the present incumbent, Mother Mary Xavier Cunningham, followed in the order named. St. Peter's school for boys has always been taught by the Sisters, and both academy and parochial school are in a flourishing condition.

At Birmingham the Sisters opened the Holy Angels Academy in 1880, but being too near to the academy at Montgomery, it was retained only five years, the community returning to the Mother House.

Kansas was again entered by the Lorettines in 1882, when Sister M. Augustine Beaven and a community organized St. Patrick's school at Parsons, to the great satisfaction of the residents, who regarded St. Ann's Academy at Osage as the star of that locality. When St. Ann's was burned the Sisters at Parsons felt more or less isolated, and they were withdrawn in 1896.

The lure of the West, which in the century and more past fell upon her early founder and drew him to his sublime mission on the then frontier, was felt early by Loretto. When Denver was a mining camp on the outer edge of civilization, if indeed not beyond it, Loretto, responsive to the old, old call, drove down her stakes in the clearing, and St. Mary's became an integral part of the hazardous life of the Colorado of the early sixties. The first community, as we have seen, came from Santa Fé, which city they left June 21, 1864, and the following July 9 arrived at their destination, traveling by stage coach. They were received by Mesdames A. Perry and John Marshall, who prepared for them their first meal in the home of their ambition. Rude was their home and poor, but Loretto trains her daughters to make the best of things where improvement is impossible; and the Sisters found themselves no worse off than the hardy, determined people with whom they had cast their lot. When the great wave of prosperity swept over Denver, Loretto rode on its crest.

The second foundation of the Society in Colorado was made at Pueblo in 1875, on invitation of Reverend Charles Pinto, S.J., later the Very Reverend Superior of the Jesuit Mission of Colorado and New Mexico. Mother Joanna Walsh and Sister Mary de Sales Hynes visited the place, and were hospitably entertained by Captain J. J. Lambert and his wife. In the latter part of January, 1875, Sister Mary de Sales Hynes and a companion returned to open school, at the earnest solicitation of the Right Reverend J. P. Machebeuf. The historic "Blue House," with the adjoining "White House," was secured as being the most suitable to be had at that time, and the children gradually assembled within the schoolrooms. In September the Sisters were located in the Barber house, Grand Avenue and Twelfth Street, and later the property at Tenth and Elizabeth Streets was purchased through the influence of their kind friend, Captain Lambert, who, by the present Holy Father, has been titled a Knight of St. Gregory.

From this humble beginning Loretto Academy has grown to its present proportions; it was humble when Pueblo was humble, and grew with Pueblo's growth. Thirty years ago Pueblo was a struggling frontier town; to-day it is a commercial center, rich in the blessings education and religion bestow. In the drawing down of this blessing Loretto has had her great share. So successful was the school previous to 1879 that an addition had to be built to the house, and again in 1884 the Sisters were obliged to enlarge the building, the number of boarders requiring more rooms and classes needing ampler space during recitation hours. The silver jubilee of the academy was celebrated in 1900. Four Sisters have died in Pueblo since the school was opened and lie at rest in God's Acre there.

Conejos next rejoiced in the beneficent influence of Loretto, when, in 1875, responding to the prayer of the people, the Jesuit Fathers petitioned Bishop Machebeuf for a school. The bishop bade the people to have the house prepared and the Sisters would come; so adobe buildings were put up for the pastors and the Sisters, the former arriving first and taking possession of the house nearest completion. Mr. Lafayette Head, already a benefactor of the Church, donated more land, and as soon as practicable the Sisters, four in number, arrived, Sister Vicenta Gonzales being in charge of the community. The poor Sisters found in Conejos no human consolations; they were lodged in inconvenient and unattractive quarters; and while the support from a private school of Mexican children proved sufficient for their simple needs, it was not sufficient for building. The Sisters, during the late years, have taught the Conejos Public School, which they still continue, and which is reputed as one of the most successful in that locality.

Sister Fara Maloney, a member of the first community, fell a victim to the smallpox, which raged in the town the winter of '77-'78. She died January 5th, and was buried with unusual demonstrations by the warm-hearted inhabitants of the place, who had begun to appreciate her worth. She was the last victim of the dreaded scourge of that year.

Loretto's fourth foundation was at Colorado Springs, where ground was purchased in 1885 by the Corporation of St. Mary's Academy, Denver, and plans for a school drawn up. Mother Pancratia Bonfils superintended the erection of the new academy, which was finished in 1887, the school having been conducted meanwhile in a rented building. Mother Catherine Connor was superior of the first community in the new academy. In 1902 permission was granted to the parish by the Loretto Society to erect an addition to the convent building for parochial school purposes, and where the high school grades are taught. Here, as elsewhere in this open-hearted State, the Sisters found generous benefactors, who kindly befriended them on many occasions.

Loretto Heights, about seven miles from Denver, became Loretto's next foundation in 1891. In the West the schools of the Society had begun to prosper even beyond the Sisters' expectations, particularly in Denver, where, at one period, fortunes were as quickly made as they are generally lost. St. Mary's academy, long the pride of the city as an educational center, by its overcrowded attendance convinced the Sisters that the time had come to provide a separate building for the boarders. Accordingly, ground was purchased first in North Denver, but this site proving unsuitable, a portion of it was sold and the proceeds used to secure a forty-five-acre tract about seven miles outside

LORETTO HEIGHTS ACADEMY, LORETTO, COLO.

the city limits. Here was erected Loretto Heights Academy, the building being ready for occupancy in 1891, when Mother Pancratia Bonfils was appointed superior. Not long had this gem of architectural beauty been completed when the panic of 1892 fell heavily on the country at large, and especially on the progressive City of the Plains. During the construction of the building the Sisters had borrowed from two prominent insurance companies money as it was needed, depending largely on the ready sale of their valuable city property, which expectation seemed to place the undertaking beyond all anxiety for the future. But property that had been purchased and held at fabulous prices depreciated; money was hard to borrow, and the rate of interest high. These conditions, together with the general depression of business and many financial failures, threatened disaster to the school.

The Mother House, notwithstanding the fact that she had coped with difficulties in the past, and at times experienced a real dearth of means, was wholly without debt; yet she was powerless of herself to afford adequate assistance to the academy at the Heights, while existing debts on the branch houses precluded the possibility of obtaining aid from them.

For nearly six years Loretto Heights Academy, with what aid other branch houses of the Society could bestow, warded off the fate which had befallen many business enterprises throughout the State. In 1895, when the mortgages on St. Mary's Academy and Loretto Heights had expired, anxiety was felt by all concerned, especially by the bondsmen. The Society was not willing to renew the loan with the insurance companies at the former high rate of interest and on former conditions. Some other solution of the problem, therefore, must be sought. By the advice of the Right Reverend Thomas S. Byrne of Nashville, appointed Ecclesiastical Superior of the Society in 1896, the Council of the Mother House decided to concentrate the indebtedness of the entire Society and negotiate a loan to cover the amount. Owing to the financial conditions of the times, such an undertaking called for patient perseverance; however, the loan was obtained in June, 1898, at a lower rate of interest, the insurance companies were paid and the bondsmen released, the Loretto Mother House holding herself responsible for the debt. To her credit and that of her loyal branch establishments, who came nobly to her aid, she had the happiness of seeing the mortgages lifted from all her properties in 1908 and Loretto Heights Academy, which had been the cause of so much apprehension, was saved.

As the child that has cost its mother the greatest pangs is dearest to her, so is Loretto Heights precious in the eyes of the Society, and, knowing no jealousy, to it in pride and affection turn its sister houses. And well is it worthy of Loretto's love, Loretto's pardonable pride! Of this treasure of the Society let one who has seen it with eyes alive to beauty and art, to fix the picture they behold, tell us, the late Reverend James J. Conway, S.J., from whose superb address at the golden jubilee of the Loretto of Florissant we have quoted, and now quote, as he described for his audience Loretto Heights:

"The scene beneath us, and vanishing into hazy vistas far away and beyond us, was one to fix an epoch in a lifetime. To the east—five miles away—like a mammoth relief, standing out against the sloping perspective of the eternal prairies, lay the granite nucleus, the central mass of red brick homes, the faubourgs and princely villas in the north and east, the shanties, the *baraques,* the wigwams in the south and west, the smoking smelters, the spires, the steeples, the palaces, the hovels, the avenues, gardens and parks of the Queen City of the Plains. To the south, far away as eye could reach, stretched the broad savannas of the Platte. At our feet, on the west, its monotony broken only by a panoramic aspect of picturesque Fort Logan, rolled a very world of grassland far away to the foothills and the mountains piled, base upon summit, around the cloud-piercing peaks of Pike and Fremont, and ranging southward, like a spectral horizon, to Manitou and the Garden of the Gods. Behind us in the north, almost within touch, although fifty miles away, towered aloft in everlasting grandeur—their snowcapped summits glistening in the midday sun—the uplifted masses of the Rockies.

"How grand! I thought; yet how much fuller of mystery and prayerful hope I felt as the voice of the mighty vision was heard within my soul. These Heights, I seemed to hear, are her latest and Loretto's grandest works. They stand—Heaven do grant that they may never crumble!— they stand, a monument, a symbol, and the motive of a heartfelt prayer to Him Who has perused each page in the story of her apostolic zeal; to Him Who has closed the last chapter in the biography of that soul for labor which animates her being; to Him Who will open the book of her life-sacrifice to record the future works which the Lorettine, God abiding with her spirit, will accomplish for the honor and the glory of that Divine Majesty which she loves and has served so well. Ah! a monument, indeed, they stand, those lofty Convent Heights above the Colorado Plains! A monument of what Loretto's zeal will dare and do to make the institutions of the Church the noblest in the land! A symbol, too, they stand of Loretto's holy work, whose heaven-fixed aim it has been always to raise all things upward, from the earth, nearer to heaven, closer to God—the purest of aims, the sublimest of works, the loftiest of the motives of life!"

If the stranger should be so enthralled, no wonder that the heart of Loretto should cleave to that radiant daughter, sprung from her bosom, nourished by her life, set like a star upon the brow of the morning; nor that her superiors were ready to drain their hearts' last drop of blood for its preservation. To God alone be praise that in the beautiful chapter of Our Lady of Loretto they have lately builded to Him, Loretto's children worship, and that the white statue of Our Lady still looks down from its niche above the convent's classic portal.

The successor in the See of Denver of good Bishop Machebeuf, Loretto's longtime friend and first benefactor in Colorado, was the Right Reverend Nicholas C. Matz. His constant kindness and encouragement and many favors to the Sisters have ever been gratefully appreciated.

CHAPTER XV.

SOME PROMINENT MEMBERS.

MOTHER BERLINDES DOWNS having served her second term as mother superior, her successor in the important office (1852-1858) was Mother Bridget Spalding, who, as other members of her family in Loretto, other religious societies and the priesthood, wrought great things for the honor and glory of God and service for her fellow man.

Martina, the daughter of Edward Spalding, was born near Calvary, Kentucky; and at the age of thirteen years received the habit from Father Nerinckx, March 25, 1824. Like many of her family, Sister Bridget was endowed with superior intellectual gifts, but the traits of her lovable character made a greater impression upon those with whom she lived and, later, those whom she was called to govern, than could have been made by learning as wide and deep as that of her illustrious cousin, Archbishop Martin John Spalding. That she was equally appreciated by her relatives is shown in an old letter from her father, begging permission for Sister Bridget to stay a week at Calvary Convent, near the old home, and once to visit her infirm grandfather, Benedict Spalding, "with whom Martina was a great favorite." After some years of study and teaching, Mother Bridget was elected mother superior in 1852, and advanced the interests of Loretto with the powerful influence of an energetic will and devoted heart. When two terms of office had expired she was appointed, 1858, local superior of Cedar Grove Academy, Louisville, in which position she remained until her holy death, July 4, 1871. Her remains were interred at the Mother House, where the mother superiors who have passed away are laid to sleep, near the relics of their saintly founder.

Mother Bertha Bowles, Loretto's twelfth mother, was of the finest type of Kentucky womanhood. She was of majestic height, stately presence, gentle manners, and spoke slowly in dovelike tones. Attentive to duty, she gave every one else credit for doing the same; if her long career of local superior and her double term as mother proved she had some faults, the one most prominent was being too indulgent, a defect we can readily condone.

From the day of Mother Bertha's reception of the habit, August 15, 1828, when not yet sixteen years old, until the day of her death, January 14, 1896, she was a faithful toiler in the Lord's vineyard, especially after her election, August, 1864, to the highest office of the Society. A civil war, still convulsing the country, and domestic trials within called for a fearless, but a tender-hearted superior, who was vouchsafed by Providence in the person of Mother Bertha Bowles.

A name deeply interwoven with Loretto's varied history both at home and abroad, is that of Hayden, three daughters of this estimable family being among the early members of the Society, and all of whom served it long, well and faithfully. Mr. Thomas Hayden and his wife, Bridget Hart-Hayden, came from Ireland in 1820, settling at the Barrens, Perry County, Missouri, where patient industry built up in the course of years a comfortable home for the numerous offspring with which God blessed them. Mary Ann, the youngest of the three Lorettine Haydens, known in religion as Mother Elizabeth, succeeded Mother Bertha in the office of Mother Superior. She was born November 5, 1818. Piously reared, she showed a predilection for the conventual life as soon as the world presented itself to view in its most attractive guise. Admitted as a postulant at Bethlehem Convent (Mo.), August 15, 1837, she received the habit November 5th, the Right Reverend Bishop

194

Rosati of St. Louis presiding at the ceremony. Sister Elizabeth's life was more varied, as to locality, than the lives of her older sisters; her zealous works were not, however, more widely known than their heroic missionary labors.

After profession, 1839, the young religious was sent to Cape Girardeau, Missouri, thence to Arkansas, in 1840, and to Loretto, Ky., 1845. Elected general treasurer of the Society in 1849, her executive ability soon manifested itself, and was fully shown when, in 1856, she was appointed local superior of Cedar Grove Academy, Louisville, Ky. Having put this school on a sound financial footing, she was transferred to Florissant, 1861, to replace Mother Elenora Clarke. In 1864 Mother Elizabeth took charge of the school in Cairo, Illinois, and, 1870, she was elected Superior of the Loretto Society. For six years did she carry this responsible burden, visiting the various houses of the Society, which involved wearisome travel along routes sometimes dangerous; and when the Constitutions required a successor to be elected the late mother was immediately sent as local superior to the important house, St. Mary's Academy, Denver. Here her health began to fail. She was recalled to the Mother House at Loretto, to prepare for the great change, and started on the last, long journey November 5, 1884, having reached her sixty-eighth year.

Joanna Hayden, the first of the Hayden sisters to enter the Socicety, was the eldest of eight children. She was born at Rath-Clough, Ireland, August 12, 1813, but came with her parents to America in 1820. For education, Joanna, now twelve years of age, was entrusted to the Sisters of Loretto, whose school at Bethlehem, in the same county, was beginning to be more widely known, and she entered as a boarder, with an eager desire to acquire all the knowledge suitable to her age. She studied her teachers, too, and with wonderful decision of character made up her mind to become a religious. When her father next visited her she asked him if she might take the little veil, and he, thinking this to be some ornamental addition to her dress, readily agreed and promised to pay for it. Joanna, full of joy, acquainted her teachers with her father's ready compliance, was admitted as a postulant and, in due time, clothed with the habit of a novice. Later on, her father paid her another visit. She appeared before his astonished eyes in the religious garb, for which he was totally unprepared; great was his indignation, and even after due explanations had been made, he insisted upon his daughter resuming her secular dress and going home with him, saying she was too young to take so important a step. The girl, being under age, obeyed her father's commands, but did not lose sight of her high calling. She grew into an attractive and lovable woman; suitors were not wanting, though they were unsuccessful.

Mr. Hayden's sudden death proved another obstacle to Joanna's plans; but after staying two years with the bereaved mother, this faithful child at last was permitted to enter the Novitiate at Bethlehem, Perry County, Missouri, May, 1833, being then twenty years of age. Having finished her novitiate, Sister M. Magdalen pronounced her vows in 1834, went to Loretto, Ky., to complete her studies, whence she returned in 1836, and after one year was transferred to St. Genevieve, Missouri, in 1837, and to Cape Girardeau in 1840. After a term as local superior at Bethlehem, Mo., and at the Cape, Mother Magdalen was called to the Mother House in Kentucky, 1850, and appointed Mistress of Novices. When a colony was organized for the mission in New Mexico in 1852, she was one of the chosen few. During the perilous journey the superior of the little band of Lorettines, Mother Matilda Mills, died of cholera, and Mother Magdalen succeeded to the office. Reaching Santa Fé September 16, 1852, she was duly installed as head of the community by Bishop

Lamy, on the feast of the Holy Rosary. Then followed a long career of zealous usefulness in the distant West, including some thrilling experiences in the line of mountain travel; danger from prowling Indians and swollen torrents; struggles with poverty, and the usual vicissitudes of a new foundation in a strange land. Wonderful were the results of Mother Magdalen's energy and the Sisters' indefatigable labors. Eight schools, most of which developed into academies, were established in New Mexico, Colorado and Texas, and when, in 1902, the Golden Jubilee of Our Lady of Light, Santa Fé, was celebrated, the drama for the occasion introduced not only the stirring tableaux of early travel and later incidents, but also a beautiful figurative representation of the Santa Fé house sending abroad rays of light, each ray representing a foundation.

This valiant woman gave her heart and physical powers to the work God had entrusted to her until 1881, when rheumatism and gradual paralysis brought her to a helpless condition, which was her cross for thirteen years. Despite her sufferings, her mental powers remained bright and enabled her to assist her successor in office, while a remarkable cheerfulness was a source of edification to all to the end. She died in 1894. Few deaths awakened such widespread and sincere regrets; she was lamented as only the saintly and unselfish can be.

Margaret Hayden, the third Lorettine of this family, was born August 25, 1814, in Perry County, Missouri, and shared the joys and sorrows of that Christian home with younger sisters and brothers. She, too, was sent to Bethlehem for education, thence to Cape Girardeau when the Sisters opened school at the latter place. Her older sister's entering the Convent prevented Margaret from even expressing her own views, until she saw she was not absolutely needed at home, and could follow the call of God without neglecting any duty. She accordingly began her postulantship at the Cape, July 6, 1841, and was clothed

197

with the religious habit September 19th of the same year, receiving the name Sister Bridget. After profession she was assigned to work among the Indians at Osage Mission, Kansas, 1847, appointed superior there in 1860, of Cape Girardeau convent in 1863, and thence transferred back to Osage Mission, which became St. Ann's Academy for young ladies, and prospered under Mother Bridget's administration until her death, January 23, 1890, at the age of seventy-six.

The full record of Mother Bridget's labors and those of her devoted Sisters during the early days of hard beginnings and while the Indian children were their special charges can never be put on paper. Thankless and repulsive tasks were almost their daily portion; only Heaven can obliterate the memory of those mission days, and Heaven will not fail to compensate for hardships so heroically endured. Her name was a household word to the white settlers of Saint Paul, as the mission is now called; no political hero nor public benefactor was more widely and more sincerely mourned than the humble, tenderhearted Mother Bridget Hayden.

Another venerated name in Loretto's story is that of her who succeeded Mother Elizabeth Hayden in its highest office. Maria Smythe was born March 13, 1818, in the town of Little York, Pennsylvania. Her father, Edward Smythe was a native of Ireland, but came to America when a child, to grow up into a true American, and was always firm in the Faith of his fathers. Her mother, Katherine Kain, was a native of Maryland, as pious and loyal as her husband, hence Maria's early days were passed in a hallowed atmosphere. The good father was carried away by death almost as soon as his little daughter could lisp his name, and thus mother and child were drawn closer together. They made their home in Gettysburg and Baltimore; in the latter city the child received her elementary education from the Sisters of Charity, and on the family's removing to Louisville she was sent, by the advice of Bishop Reynolds, to Loretto Academy, Marion County, to finish the course of study.

Kentucky's academic halls of that early time were not of the style and proportions of the present-day structures; still this young Maryland girl, following in the footprints of Mary and Anna Rhodes, was attracted to the Society they had helped to found, and entered as a candidate, February 14, 1837, receiving the habit just three months later, from the hands of Bishop Chabrat. Mother Josephine Kelly was mother superior at that time.

The five years of Sister Dafrosa's probation were spent at Loretto; thence she passed to Calvary Convent, near Holy Mary's church, where she remained for twenty-seven consecutive years as teacher, directress and superior, the school growing in popularity during the term of her administration. In 1870 she was elected general treasurer of the Society; after three years another election placed her in the office of first assistant, and she was given charge of the Novices, which delicate and important post she held to the satisfaction of those concerned until 1876, when the votes of the Society rewarded her virtues with a heavier cross, that of mother superior. Being no longer eligible for re-election, in 1879 Mother Dafrosa replaced Mother Ann Joseph Mattingly as local superior of the Florissant community, directing that house for six years.

Time was beginning to wrinkle the brow and bend the shoulders of this faithful religious, so it was evident she very reluctantly accepted the result of the election of 1885, which called her to assume once more the responsibility of governing the Society. Submitting to God's will so long as she felt able to do so, she discharged every duty with strict fidelity until she realized the age-worn shoulders were too heavily taxed, and then she wrote privately to the bishop, begging him to accept her resignation and direct the community to elect a successor for the unexpired term. Mother

LORETTO.

Catherine Conner was duly elected, 1893, and Mother Dafrosa retired, with the fond hope of facing no more the trials and distractions of official positions, intent only on preparing to meet her God. It pleased the Divine Majesty to prolong her life nearly eight years. She passed away April 28, 1900, aged eighty-one years and eleven months.

Hardinsburg, Ky., was the native town of Rose, daughter of Zachariah and Ann Beaven-Mattingly. Confirmed in the church of the Seven Dolors at Loretto by Bishop Flaget, 1843, the young girl appeared to imbibe a devotion to our Sorrowful Mother which, after being a pupil of Loretto, ripened into a desire to consecrate her life to God. She became a Novice April 2, 1852, receiving the name of Sister Ann Joseph, and generously offered herself for the western missions as soon as she was professed. Santa Fé was her destination; thither she traveled in 1855, to remain until 1864, when, a few months after the opening of St. Mary's Academy, Denver, she was named superior of the new establishment. Transferred to Florissant, Mo., in 1870, it fell to her lot to erect a new academy at this place which she did not enjoy even for a day, being elected mother superior in 1882, before the community of Florissant had moved into its new quarters. At the Mother House the newly elected superior learned that here, too, a building had been partly planned and she should have to turn her attention to a third erection. Though rather dismayed at the prospect, she began the tedious work, for which Providence had fitted and destined her. She completed her task in 1888, before her term of superiorship expired, passing again from the scene of her labors without enjoying their fruit, but going this time to Florissant, where every stone had become dear to her heart. Having been local superior at various houses, she retired to Florissant in declining health, and died there on Christmas Eve, 1903.

Among the novel experiences of this notable Lorettine

THE GENERAL COUNCIL OF 1904.

was an attack by Indians while on her way to Santa Fé, 1855, with her companions, Sisters Mary Borgia Ward, M. Joanna Walsh and M. Monica Bailey, the last of whom, it will be remembered, was prevented by illness from accompanying the first band in 1852. Of the attack, which occurred July 16, Mother Mattingly has left us the following account:

"The caravan with which we were traveling having halted for breafast, Father Machebeuf had his tent erected and offered up the Holy Sacrifice of the Mass, at which all the Sisters received the Holy Communion. After thanksgiving we had our breakfast, seated at the improvised table, and were talking cheerfully when a cry was heard, 'Indians; Indians!' Looking towards the east, we saw the whole bluff covered with Indians on horseback, their faces and arms painted in warlike style. They swooped down on our camp like so many eagles. We were ordered to get into our ambulances, the curtains were buttoned down, and the duck curtains (storm-sheets) were tied down over these. We were left thus in the circle in the midst of about two hundred mules and horses, and around us the wide plains, without a tree or any object of protection except our frail ambulances. The temperature was about ninety degrees. Soon the savages entered the circle and were anxious to see what was in the ambulances, but the drivers sat each in the front of a vehicle, and as the Indians would try to peep in he would use his whip on them.

"The merchants, who owned the wagons and the merchandise with which they were filled, were very generous to the savages, and gave them many presents of blankets, calico, cotton, sugar, tobacco, molasses, etc., etc. Father Machebeuf gave them many medals. The Indians had a captive Mexican, whom Father Machebeuf was anxious to redeem, but in this he did not succeed.

"After keeping us shut up in our air-tight tents from ten o'clock in the morning till four o'clock in the afternoon, about half of the Indians left, but quite a number of them hung around till five o'clock, when the caravan started for a better place to camp for the night. When a convenient spot was reached, we descended from our conveyances, where we had been imprisoned for seven hours, and we literally could not stand on our feet for some time."

The Sisters had left Louisville on the 12th of May, and it was July 24th before they arrived at Santa Fé.

Sister Joanna Walsh, a companion of Mother Mattingly on this perilous trip, was a cousin of the three Hayden sisters, and as such was welcomed to the Novitiate, August 15, 1853. She was born in Ireland and was a sister of Reverend James Walsh, S.J., whose austere piety she reproduced in her own life. Generous of herself, she embraced the opportunity of going to Santa Fé as early as 1855.

The opening at Denver in 1864 saw Sister Joanna in the breach again, facing the trials of a new foundation, where everything was comparatively crude. Sister Joanna was appointed local superior of St. Mary's Academy in 1870, and called to the Mother House in 1875 to replace the mistress of novices, who had just been elected mother superior. Obliged by ill health to relinquish this post, she was stationed successively at Salinas, California; St. Ann's, Kansas; Florissant, Mo., and in 1897 at Loretto, Ky., where she filled the office of assistant mistress of novices until her holy death, October 3, 1910. Sister Joanna's spirituality deeply impressed all those who knew her; her humility was evident to the youngest novice; her devotion calculated to inspire every one who beheld her kneeling erect in the presence of the Blessed Sacrament. Her dying eyes turned instinctively toward the door which led into the church.

As teacher, directress, local superior and general officer, Mother Cecilia Roden's name stands out prominently in Loretto's annals. Born in Ireland, she came to this country in early childhood, dwelling for a time in the East, but had her later home in St. Louis, where she applied to enter the Novitiate of Florissant, at the age of sixteen, October 31, 1856. Her companions regarded her as an angel of piety and innocence: tears of devotion often bedewed her cheek during meditation; spiritual exercises never wearied her, yet her daily life was practical as the most commonplace could wish; study and work were not neglected.

Science and literature were her forte; for music she had no taste whatever; as a class-teacher she gave satisfaction from the start, while advancing years matured her judgment and heightened her success. She had great aptitude for conducting sodalities and leading the pupils to piety. In appearance there was nothing commanding, yet she won respect and possessed a countenance of great sweetness. Those who enjoyed her intimate acquaintance recall many instances of her native wit, which proved an innocent amusement during recreation hours. Most of Mother Cecilia's life was confined to the classroom; twice she was elected general treasurer and several times appointed local superior. She died at the academy on Pine Street, St. Louis, June 23, 1894.

Among the chosen spirits who flocked to Loretto during the early fifties, and whose life left there an odor of sanctity, was Sister Raphael McArdle. Born in Ireland, she came with her family to this country, settling in Canada. She entered the Florissant Novitiate September 8, 1858. Her superiors soon discovered that despite the modesty of her speech her talents were above the ordinary. She succeeded in the scientific and literary pursuits to which she applied herself without losing the sweet simplicity of her character; indeed, throughout life she was more remarkable for concealing than for displaying the rather unusual amount of knowledge she possessed.

Sister Raphael's first mission was to St. Louis, thence

she was transferred to Cairo, Ill.; later, about 1890, to Cedar Grove Academy, Louisville, Ky.; to Denver, Colo., in 1892, where she taught successively at St. Mary's Academy, Loretto Heights Academy, and in Pueblo. As her first mission, so was her last, to St. Louis, where she ended her active life and spent a few years quietly preparing for eternity, into which she entered April 25, 1910.

Another of Loretto's treasured names is that of Sister Winifred Leahy, who, bringing the energy of her Irish character to the home of her adoption, proved an efficient laborer in the Loretto schools, deeming education next to salvation, as many of her wayward pupils can testify. Never was there a more earnest student in every branch to which she applied herself, beginning with the botanical specimens at an early hour, and watching the planets and constellations as long as she was allowed to turn her attention to earthly things. Her entrance was at Florissant, November 21, 1852, where she dwelt altogether twenty-nine years and six months. She was deeply interested in everything that concerned the Loretto Society, and certainly did well her part in trying to advance its welfare. Laboring till the end, it seemed rather a surprise to herself that illness compelled her to put down her class book, after which she lived scarcely two weeks. She died November 8, 1903, at Loretto, Ky.

Among the daughters of Missouri who hastened to enroll themselves with their devoted teachers was Marie Louise Madigan. A native of St. Louis, she attended school at the Florissant Academy, and at the early age of fifteen passed, in 1862, from the classroom to the Novitiate, receiving the name of Sister Dositheus. To her the world was a sealed book, but she needed not its false wisdom when grace enlightened her heart and mental pleasures opened a delightful vista to her talents. She continued in the convent the studies which she had been pursuing, and became proficient in nearly every branch of the academic curriculum, including modern languages. Her translations from the French were considered strikingly accurate; she was requested to do such work for important occasions, and even theologians pronounced her efforts remarkable. Employed in almost every Loretto academy of the Middle West, Sister Dositheus' reputation as a teacher reached farther than she knew, for she remained childlike throughout life, and did not appear to realize her extraordinary gifts, hence no unruly pride spoiled the sweet simplicity of her character. Typhoid fever carried off this valuable member, November 8, 1892, while she was engaged in teaching at the Loretto Academy, Pine Street, St. Louis, Mo.

The name Webb is a distinguished one in Kentucky, and Mother Felicitas Webb upheld its reputation in the ranks of the religious life. Of English extraction, the family of Jane Webb had emigrated westward and settled near Bardstown, Ky. The young girl received her education from the Sisters of Charity at Nazareth, Ky., and entered the Novitiate of Loretto August 15, 1855. She was assigned to the school in Lebanon soon after her profession, and sent to Cedar Grove, Louisville, in 1869. Twice was Mother Felicitas appointed mistress of novices, twice elected assistant to the mother superior, local superior in three houses, the last St. Ann's Academy, Kansas, in 1895, but the buildings were destroyed by fire soon after her arrival, and the shock proved so distressing to the poor superior she preferred to spend the rest of her days without such responsibility. Living thenceforth as a private religious, Mother Felicitas prepared in an edifying manner to give an account to God of the long years he had vouchsafed her. She entered into rest at Loretto, Kentucky, January 20, 1908.

Another member of the Society native of Kentucky was Sister Euphrosyne Thompson, her family living near Loretto, in Marion County. She was one of four sisters who

LORETTO.

entered the Society in early youth, passed from her novitiate to Cedar Grove, Louisville, Ky., in 1856, and made the long, tedious journey to Santa Fé, New Mexico, in 1858. In the far West lay the mission of her life. At the voice of obedience she went to Taos, 1863; later to Las Vegas, to Mora, to Socorro, where she was superior, and a second time to Las Vegas, now to preside over the community. Here she ended her long life of toil, January 26, 1908. She had faced the hardships of pioneer life, encountered one flood and saw one convent burn. It was her sister who died on the plains while journeying westward to begin her missionary career. Sister Euphrosyne contributed much to the happiness of those with whom she lived, being of a cheerful, sociable disposition and always ready to oblige others.

Later admitted to the Society than those previously mentioned, but no less revered, was Ellen Hynes, who, at the age of seventeen, received the habit at Loretto on April 12, 1867, and the name of the founder's patron saint, Borromeo. Sister Borromeo retained her girlish freshness in appearance for about forty years after she put on the religious dress, and never showed any decided symptoms of age. Florissant was the scene of her active life during the greater part of her career; there she taught various branches and gave music lessons. Though gifted with talents above the ordinary, Sister Borromeo will always be best remembered for the sweetness of her disposition and suavity of manner toward every one. The depressed in heart, looking on her heaven-lit countenance, found comfort, the good felt drawn closer to God; she was much beloved, and well deserved to be, for her great charity embraced all. Her closing years were spent as superior of the convent at Montgomery, Alabama, whence she repaired to Florissant, Mo., in failing health, and from that home of many years winged her way to eternity, November 26, 1907.

SOME PROMINENT MEMBERS.

Sister Mary Catherine Connor was born in the County Wexford, Ireland, and was brought up as rigidly as a Puritan. The world had early proven distasteful to her young heart and led her to retire into a convent as soon as circumstances permitted. Miss Connor entered the Loretto Novitiate then at Florissant March 25, 1857. Being endowed with rare musical talent, our young novice soon became proficient in the hands of skillful instructors, and very soon she herself became an adept in the art, and taught for years to Sisters and pupils the various musical instruments, harp, guitar, mandolin, piano, etc. When necessary, she lent a helping hand also to teach the various class grades, from the lowest to the highest branches of science.

In 1866 she was elected treasurer of the Society, and after her term of three years was appointed local superior at Cape Girardeau. Six years later she was called to Loretto to serve as treasurer a second term, acting also as directress of the academy; elected assistant to the mother superior from 1885-88; local superior and mistress of novices, and in 1894 Mother Superior of the Society. During the forty-five years of Sister Mary Catherine's religious life she was most devout and fervent. She loved her Institute intensely and labored most zealously for its benefit. Hers was a character of the most inflexible kind, so far as conscience and principles were concerned. An austere ascetic herself, she was ever kind and considerate towards others. She died at Florissant Convent, February 4, 1902, most revered by those who knew her most intimately.

CHAPTER XVI.

ECCLESIASTICAL SUPERIORS.

DURING these four score years and over of our history Catholicism had made steady progress in Kentucky, more especially in that portion of it contained in the Diocese of Louisville, to which city the See of Bardstown had been transferred in 1841. The few log churches of 1812 had given place to more appropriate ones of frame or brick, and these had been greatly multiplied; the priestly line had been increased by native fervor and foreign zeal, and various societies of religious men and women were well established and carrying on the charitable or educational works of their institutions.

For thirty-eight years Loretto had found in Bishop Flaget a kind and loving father. His letters to superiors and others breathed forth his paternal love for the Society which was the first to spring up in the virgin soil of his prolific See; and his many acts of benevolence, coming as they did from one so truly of God, proved his high regard for it and its accomplishments. He kept it in his heart, treasured it as the priceless gift of Father Nerinckx, dying, had bequeathed to him and to his successors forever. "Loretto, my dear Loretto," he calls it in his letters, and again, writing to Mother Sabina O'Brien, on New Year's Day, 1829: "I open all my episcopal treasures to pour them with both hands on you first, and on all your dear daughters and mine, without exception and without distinction. I truly and sincerely love them all in God and for God, and recommend myself and my diocese earnestly to their fervent prayers."

Under his successor, the Right Reverend Martin J. Spalding, Loretto may be said to have expanded as a flower blessed by the sun and dew of heaven. No greater prelate than Archbishop Spalding has blessed the American Church. As coadjutor to the venerable Flaget, his first solicitude was to promote Christian education in the diocese. To this end he gave special encouragement to religious communities, upon which he relied for teachers, and Loretto has ever gratefully acknowledged his generous benevolence. When he was called to a higher and broader field of labor, with its heavier responsibilities, in the archbishopric of Baltimore, in 1864, the gentle, ardent Lavialle was elected to succeed him in that of Louisville. While President of St. Mary's College for several years, Bishop Lavialle had been near Loretto and ever ready to render benevolent service. When fire destroyed the convent in 1858, he exerted himself to relieve the distress of the Sisters and to encourage and aid them in rebuilding; thus he became highly esteemed as counselor and friend. As bishop, his interest in the Society and desire to promote its welfare were redoubled, but he was called to his eternal reward before he could carry out his generous designs. During the two years of his administration he gave the impulse of his own zeal and devotion to the diocese, and won the hearts of his people, who readily recognized the accuracy of the poet's couplet:

"Lavialle, to all the world a friend,
Who never could one mortal heart offend."

The Sisters of Loretto established only two schools in the diocese during Bishop Lavialle's administration, but all their institutions felt the effects of his beneficent influence, which strengthened and encouraged their zeal, then heavily taxed by the missions they had so generously undertaken in the West.

The appointment by Bishop Flaget of Reverend Alexander Deparcq as Ecclesiastical Superior encouraged the Sisters in the faithful observance of their Rule and in veneration of their saintly founder. Fellow-countryman of Father Nerinckx, Father Deparcq came to Kentucky in 1818, and was ordained the following year. Assigned to missions that Father Nerinckx had so long attended, he finished the church at Lebanon which Father Nerinckx had begun, and labored most zealously for forty-four years, chiefly in the Counties of Marion, Casey, Mercer and Adair. He had caught the spirit of Nerinckx, Flaget and David, and his zeal was fruitful. The people loved him, and Bishop Flaget held him in highest esteem. His services to the Community during twenty years as Ecclesiastical Superior won for him the lasting gratitude of the Sisters. He died at Calvary convent in 1864, and his spiritual daughters laid his remains in their own cemetery at Loretto.

The successor to the amiable Lavialle, the Right Reverend William George McCloskey, first Rector of the American College in Rome, was consecrated Bishop of Louisville in the Eternal City, May 24, and arrived in the diocese in October, 1868. Finding that no one had been appointed to succeed Father Deparcq, the bishop, wishing to promote the best interests of the Society, in 1869 appointed Reverend Francis Wuyts Ecclesiastical Superior of the Sisters of Loretto. Father Wuyts was a Belgian, ordained in Europe in 1851, and engaged in parochial work in Mechlin; responding to the appeal of Bishop Spalding, he came to Kentucky in 1853. He spent a year at Calvary with Reverend A. A. Aud to acquire facility in the English language, and was appointed chaplain at Loretto in 1854, where he resided until his death, in 1891. For many years he was actively and very efficiently engaged in missionary work, having in charge the congregations attached to the churches of Holy Cross and of St. Vincent, at New Hope. He built the church of St. Francis of Assisi and organized the congregation at Chicago, Ky. He was a learned theologian and a zealous pastor, whose counsel was often sought by his fellow priests and by bishops.

LORETTO ACADEMY, KANSAS CITY, MO.

ECCLESIASTICAL SUPERIORS.

The one work dearest to his heart was to promote the welfare of the religious Congregation established by his fellow-countryman. Whatever he could do for the Sisters of Loretto was a labor of love. When appointed ecclesiastical superior, Father Wuyts was brought officially into closer relation with the affairs of the Community. Henceforth whatever concerned the welfare of the Society was of prime interest to him. To encourage the Sisters in the observance of their Rule and protect them from embarrassment in the administration of their own affairs was his chief aim. He gave them the benefit of his wisdom and mature judgment, without infringing upon their rights by usurping control. He taught them to love their work of teaching, insisted upon its excellence as the most fruitful, perhaps the most necessary, of all the works of mercy.

When Father Wuyts died it was with sad hearts and a deep sense of their loss that the Sisters followed him to the grave in their own cemetery. They erected a granite shaft, typical of the tower of strength he had been to them, and upon its base inscribed the epitaph he had written during his last illness:

"D. O. M.

"Belga fui, non sum, sum civis et incola mortis.
Flens flentis Matris turba memento mei.
Quod sum mox eritis: Dominum spem ponite vestram;
Matris ab uberibus spes mea Jesus erat."

"I was of Belgium, I am no more; I am a citizen and an inhabitant of death.
Weeping Daughters of a weeping Mother, remember me.
What I am you soon shall be. Place your hope in the Lord.
From my mother's breast my hope was Jesus."

The death of Father Wuyts marks an epoch. The Reverend C. J. O'Connell of Bardstown was appointed ecclesiastical superior. He was ardent in his devotion to Loretto and applied himself with his characteristic energy to promote the welfare of the Society. Just then, however, a financial panic prevailing in the country gave rise to many difficult questions touching the interests of the Community. Before these problems could be solved Father O'Connell was superseded by Reverend Thomas F. Gambon. As difficulties multiplied the superior and her council prudently turned for advice and direction to the Apostolic Delegation at Washington. Realizing the intricacy of the difficulties, the Most Reverend Delegate, Archbishop Satolli, appointed the Right Reverend Thomas S. Byrne, Bishop of Nashville, to direct the Community. By his prudent care, untiring efforts and wise counsel, Bishop Byrne rendered inestimable service, for which Loretto acknowledges a lasting debt of gratitude. In 1898 he gave a testimonial fully assuring the Most Reverend Archbishop Martinelli, who was Mgr. Satolli's successor as Delegate, of the satisfactory condition of the Society. Bishop Byrne was relieved of the charge to which he had been appointed, but His Excellency, Archbishop Martinelli, in his fatherly solicitude was vigilant, and extended his protection to the Loretto Society. The Reverend Henry Westermann was appointed Ecclesiastical Superior. His good will could not relieve the anxiety of the Sisters. Understanding the nature of the questions that had been involved, and that might easily arise again, Archbishop Martinelli directed the Sisters to take their Constitutions and Rules to the Holy See for further examination and approval. Accordingly, as soon as necessary preliminaries could be arranged, Mother General Mary Praxedes Carty, with her companion, Mother M. Wilfrid LaMotte, set forth for Rome, where they arrived December 5, 1903.

The examination to which the Rule and Constitution were subjected resulted practically in the elimination of the modifications that had been introduced without warrant during the past, and restored them as near to the original

ECCLESIASTICAL SUPERIORS.

Rule drawn up by the founder and approved by the Holy See, in 1816, as the changes in conditions of life wrought by the vicissitudes of time will permit. The Decree of Confirmation was placed in the hands of the Mother General May 18, 1904. The long years of waiting, the trials patiently borne, were rewarded in God's own time and way, and Loretto, on the eve of her centennial, attained her rightful place among the religious Congregations of the Church. With hearts swelling with gratitude to Divine Providence, the Mother General and her companion hastened on their homeward journey. Never did holy joy reign more completely at Loretto, if we except, perhaps, that hour when Bishop Flaget first set foot within her portals, than on the tenth of June, when glad *Te Deums* welcomed the travelers home.

To carry out the provisions of the approved Constitutions as directed it was necessary to elect the general officers of the Society as soon as practicable. The election took place at Loretto Academy, Florissant, Mo., July 26, 1904, and resulted as follows: Mother General, Sister M. Praxedes Carty; First Assistant—Mother Vicaress, Sister M. Francisca Lamy; Second Assistant, Sister M. Laurentia Simms; Third Assistant, Sister M. Rosine Green; Fourth Assistant, Sister M. Evangelista Bindewald; Secretary General, Sister M. Rosine Green, and Procuratrix General, Sister M. Domitilla Furlong.

The title Mother is given to each of these general officers, and the Constitution permits one of the assistants to be chosen secretary general. Upon the Mother General, aided by her assistants, depends the administration of the affairs of the Society. Prospects now brightened; manifold blessings, the fruits of being directly under the protection of the Holy See, were soon plainly manifest, and the Sisters, reanimated and encouraged, applied themselves to every call of duty with renewed vigor and fervor.

Three years later Mother General Praxedes, with

LORETTO.

Mother Evangelista Bindewald, knelt again at the feet of the Holy Father to implore the final seal of approval. The Decree of final confirmation was issued December 30, 1907.

Loretto's anxiety as to her Constitutions was gone. The hearts of the Sisters throbbed with joy and gratitude. Again they raised their voices in hymns of glad thanksgiving when they learned that their first Cardinal Protector was His Eminence Cardinal Satolli, who, while Apostolic Delegate at Washington, had visited several of their houses and befriended them in many ways. The Sisters gave happy expression to their sentiments, recounting how past anxieties had given place to joy and gratitude in the realization of what had been so long desired. One, with skillful pen (Sister M. Wilfrid LaMotte), expressed sentiments awakened by the fact that every one who had gone to Rome to ask favors for the Sisters of Loretto had knelt at the feet of a Pontiff named Pius: Pius VII, Pius IX and Pius X:

THREE TIMES TO PIUS.

Back, back, back. The century was young,
A dark cloud spiritual o'er this land hung.
Life seemed so hard, sweet heaven so far away,
When one was praying for a brighter day.
This generation may not see full light,
Yet they are growing who will claim their right:
If these dear children could be trained to love
And serve their God. Good Nerinckx gazed above.

The years ran on. O'er marble steps there trod
One in apparel poor, but rich in God,
Who in meek confidence had crossed the sea
To bow in suppliance at the Pontiff's knee.
"Father of Christendom," the good man said,
"Whose pastorate o'er this wide earth is spread,
In yon fair land where Freedom's banner waves
Are countless souls the evil one enslaves.

214

ECCLESIASTICAL SUPERIORS.

"To rescue souls, the children must be won,
Salvation's lessons during youth begun,
Ah! Holy Father, have we been too bold?
A mustard seed, e'en now, its buds unfold.
To crave your blessing on this cherished plan
Has been my hope; for this all risks I ran."
Upon the paper gazed the Pope in tears,
"A tiny seed. God prosper it thro' years."

Another Pius sat upon the throne,
His rank the ninth; the worldwide cross his own;
His eye far reaching and his great heart warm
To keep his distant children safe from harm.
The West improved; the Church had prospered there
In freedom's sunshine to proportions fair,
But cockle, too, had been more freely sown,
And with the Master's wheat in boldness grown.

Loretto's vineyard broadened day by day;
Although the sower's hand cold, pulseless, lay,
His spirit lived; the blessing Pius gave,
Thro' trying years proved powerful to save.
A mitred brow next brought the Rule to view,
To Pius Ninth, the blessing to renew,
Which he, a former Pius, had bestowed,
Ere yet Loretto's star with radiance glowed.

Years bore their burden toward the eternal shore,
When at the Vatican was heard once more
A timid knock. Loretto's daughters came
The Final Blessing for their House to claim.
To claim? Yea, with long trust fulfilled,
They sought what Pontiff promised, if God willed,
And felt, when Pius Tenth their cause had heard,
His lips, so wisely just, would speak the word.

And he did speak it. Not in reckless haste,
For calm deliberation is not waste

LORETTO.

Of precious time; but with things duly weighed
Long prayer and patience amply were repaid.
And he did speak it. Lord, Thy Name we bless,
Thy providence in this great work confess.
Thrice hath a Pontiff Pius heard our call;
Loretto's gratitude enshrines them all,
Loretto's annals hand the blest names down;
Two blessed, encouraged, and one gave the crown!

Bereft when Cardinal Satolli was called to his eternal
reward, Loretto was consoled when another faithful friend,
Cardinal Martinelli became her Protector. She had long
acknowledged her obligations for his generous assistance,
fatherly solicitude and many kindnesses.

Soon the salutary results of the confirmation of the Constitutions began to be manifest. The sense of security it
gave the Sisters is a great stimulus to their zeal and devotion. The strict observance of their Rule becomes more
attractive, and the aims, both spiritual and temporal, for
which the Institute was first founded, seem more sure of
realization. A steady increase in membership, which began
in 1904, is an assurance of God's blessing, which is further
revealed in the successful development of their institutions,
strengthening their resources, enabling them to meet some
of the demands made upon them for new schools, and, as
for instance, at Denver, Kansas City and St. Louis, for
new and larger buildings.

Thus, with the accumulated strength of a century of
sacrifices and faithful service, with renewed vigor and redoubled fervor, with the same spirit still buoyant and reso-
lute that animated her venerated founders, Loretto comes
to her centennial to add the gleam of the first purely American star to the brilliant galaxy of religious communities
in the Church.

CHAPEL, LORETTO ACADEMY, KANSAS CITY, MO.

CHAPTER XVII.

SCHOOLS AND BENEFACTORS.

THE call that brought Loretto into existence was the necessity for primary schools to save the faith of the children of Kentucky pioneers; the necessity for parochial schools is many times more urgent now for Catholic children throughout the country. Mary Rhodes and her companions heard the call whispered by "the still, small voice"; it rings now in clarion tones from the central watch-tower of Christendom in the appeals and commands of the Vicar of Christ to all the faithful, to protect the children from irreligious and materialistic influences, and equip them with Christian principles and training for the battle of life. The system of secular schools conducted upon the pagan idea of educating the child only for life in this world, regardless of God or eternity, claims the child in the cradle and the kindergarten. To counteract the pernicious influence of this system and secure Christian education and training for childhood and youth, the Supreme Teacher has spoken in the Decree *Quam Singulari,* emancipating childhood from the bondage of an unjust custom, and defining duties of parents and pastors which cannot be adequately discharged under present conditions without parochial schools. There can be no true education without religion, for true education is that training and development of both the moral and intellectual faculties which will enable the young to gain the end in view, namely, victory in this life's warfare and the victor's crown in eternity. It is only in the Catholic parochial schools, colleges and academies that childhood and youth can receive the religious training necessary and suitable for the formation of Christian character. As the solidity of the foundation determines the strength

217

and value of the superstructure, the primary school is of
first importance. Whether the child is privileged to continue through higher grades, even to the apex in the university, or is launched upon the troublous sea of life from
the primary school, there the foundation for his future is
laid. Few men, no matter what distinction they may attain
in their life-work, ever get much beyond the circle of
thought outlined for them in the primary school. If the
true mainspring of motive is rightly adjusted there in relation to spiritual interests and mental and moral elements,
it will serve with salutary results the future man and
woman in the strenuous everyday struggle for success. Religion is essential to this, and consequently religious teachers are indispensably necessary. This concept of the primary school, presupposed in the decrees of the Holy Father,
is fundamental to a correct idea of the full scope of the
Catholic school system, and, in face of the fact that more
than half the children never reach a school of higher grade,
gives to the parochial school the place of first importance.
Moreover, the parochial school opens the fairest field for
the performance of the spiritual works of mercy, particularly that of instructing the ignorant. Every religious
order devotes itself chiefly to some one or more of the
spiritual or corporal works of mercy, without, of course,
neglecting the others as circumstances permit and occasions
demand.

The necessity for Christian education turned a lowly
cabin into a schoolroom. From that school divine Providence brought forth Loretto, and plainly pointed out teaching, instructing the ignorant, as the special work, the particular mission to which the energies of the Sisters of
Loretto at the Foot of the Cross should be devoted. In
harmony with all His ways, God allotted to the first native
American Institute the highest mission,—teaching. True
to this divine call, Loretto has multiplied her schools.
When occasions demanded, she willingly took up other

works of mercy, the care of the orphan, nursing the sick, and the like, but when the emergency passed she promptly returned to her own particular work. The broad scope of her divinely appointed mission demanded more than human strength unaided by the grace of God could hope to accomplish, but Loretto knew that fidelity to her mission would merit that God should strengthen her to accomplish what His grace had enabled her to begin. During several decades before the present flourishing parochial system was inaugurated Catholic schools in this country were practically private enterprises. Loretto, like others, relied upon her own resources and patronage in establishing and maintaining her schools. In all her academies she taught the primary classes as well as the academic courses. In many instances she established parish schools at her own expense, some of which she still maintains. She was already in the field when Archbishop Hughes pleaded so eloquently: "Let parochial schools be established and maintained everywhere; the days have come, and the place, in which the school is more necessary than the church."

The great prelate voiced the inflexible truth. The Catholic Church stands firm and maintains that among her own children, at least, education shall not be divorced from religion; and, if driven to that resort, which she shall never be, she will part with her churches rather than part with her schools. The result of this unalterable decision is already being perceived. The Catholic element in this country is coming to be recognized for its stability, for its stand for morals, in the nation and in the individual; its recognition of God and obedience to His laws. It is the anchor of the Republic of the Fathers, caught in a storm of change, whose fury is yet to come. When it passes, two forces will stand; Christianity, as represented by the true Church of Jesus Christ, and the new Paganism of the future.

To protect the faith of her children the Church must

have schools for them under her own control. The up-building of the parochial school system in this country was a herculean task entailing sacrifices innumerable, especially on the part of teachers. Nobly and generously have Catholics in general responded to the demands made upon their means, but the sacrifices demanded of teachers were far greater. Their part of the work could be successfully accomplished only by those of consecrated lives, willing to labor for a bare subsistence here, looking to God for reward hereafter. This could be illustrated by pointing to lack of material equipment in the way of school buildings and their accessories and indispensable requisites. Money could supply these material deficiencies, and the generosity of the faithful could furnish the money; but to give religious instruction, train children in religious practices and keep the Catholic schools fully abreast of the non-Catholic schools in respect to the secular studies, demands of teachers the sacrifice of everything that could interfere with exclusive devotion to their work. Only the teaching religious Orders and Congregations could supply such teachers. Only Heaven's record can show the ceaseless activity and tireless industry of such teachers, aided by God's grace, that have been expended in the upbuilding of the parochial school system. To maintain and extend the system exacts sacrifices as great as ever. Material requisites are better supplied, but the teacher's task has not diminished, and the future invites to difficult fields, near and afar, beset with poisonous weeds of unbelief, where children are crying for consecrated teachers to guide them to the light of truth and to the way of right living. The harvest is great, but the laborers are few.

For this work Loretto budded and bloomed in the forest a century ago. In this work she has lived and labored, never faltering, through every phase alert and progressive, apace with every advance, aiming ever at the Christian ideal of education, which means preparing the child for life in the world to come as well as for life in this world, making spiritual interests supreme, yet developing all that belongs to culture, refinement, happiness and success in the realm of nature and humanity. Careful preparation is a prerequisite for any profession; it is doubly important for the Christian teacher, for whom teaching is a life-work, looking forward to no other rank or higher station in this world, the service which claims Heaven for reward.

To prepare her Sisters for this noble work, Loretto forms them to habits of solid study and close application and constancy of purpose. The foundation for this course is solidly laid in the thorough religious training given in the novitiate. She opens her novitiate to young women whose previous intellectual attainments have awakened aspirations to consecrate their lives to the sacred cause of promoting Christian education. The year and a half, and more, they spend there is of supreme value in preparing them for their sublime calling of teaching. The drill in the principles of religious life, with self-improvement as the aim ever in view, prepares them to concentrate all their energies and intellectual faculties upon attaining the Christian ideal of education in their work as teachers. From the novitiate the young Sisters pass to the normal school, where the course is directed to the acquisition of accurate knowledge and familiarity with the best methods of imparting it. Thus prepared, the Sisters enter upon their duties in the classroom. The normal school is located in connection with Loretto Academy, St. Louis.

Like other teaching Congregations, Loretto has been unable to meet the demand made upon her for teachers. In view of the necessity for maintaining and extending the parochial school system and the insufficient number of teachers to supply the ever growing demand, it is plainly an important matter, demanding especially the attention of parents and pastors, to encourage vocations to religious teaching communities. With her accustomed zeal, however, Loretto has in recent years opened some twenty parochial schools in seven different States and as many different dioceses. Some of these schools, beginning with seventy-five or one hundred pupils, have since attained an attendance of four or five hundred. To mention each would be a monotonous repetition of similar experiences; for the difficulties attending the founding and maintaining schools vary more in degree than in character, whether they result from the conditions the Sisters found in Bisbee and Flagstaff, Arizona; in David City and South Auburn, Nebraska; Huntsville, Alabama; or Toronto and Wellsville, Ohio, or in the large cities, as St. Louis, Kansas City and Denver. To the Sisters, however, such experiences never become monotonous. Whatever concerns the success of their work and the welfare of the children in the school is of sufficient interest to them, each kindly face that welcomes them to a new school is remembered, each kindly act of encouragement awakens their gratitude, and they devoutly invoke God's blessing upon those who make sacrifices to establish and maintain the school, the parents who overcome difficulties and bear hardships to keep the children in school, and especially upon priests who labor in maintaining the school with the same spirit of self-sacrifice as themselves.

When the sisters devote themselves to teaching with such dispositions as these, what wonder that they are everywhere in demand? But who can measure the sacrifices they make to counteract influences that would blight the lives of the little ones whom they have labored to guide in the way of righteousness? As the mother loves her child, so does the Christian teacher love the souls of her pupils and fear for them. Her heart is in her work because she desires to see its results in Heaven. This is the spirit Loretto inculcates and assiduously cultivates in her teachers.

With the progress of her parochial schools Loretto has

kept apace in her academies. Two causes combine to their growth, the excellence and thoroughness of the course given and the desire of pupils who have known the Sisters in the primary grades to continue with their favorite teachers. To meet this demand Loretto erected new and larger buildings on new sites for St. Mary's Academy, Denver, and Loretto Academy, St. Louis, and established the Loretto Academy, Kansas City. In these, as in her other academies, nothing is neglected to facilitate the realization of the Christian ideal of education.

In 1901 the Lorettines purchased five acres of land on Broadway and began to make preparations for a convent school in Kansas City, Missouri. The Right Reverend J. J. Glennon laid the corner-stone on April 24, 1903, and on completion of the building the community from Broadway occupied it, classes being opened on the following September 15th, with Mother M. Louis O'Connor as superior and Sister Louise Wise as directress of studies. God blessed the new venture, and Our Lady of Good Counsel, in whose parish the convent was situated, seemed to guide events according to the designs of her Divine Son, and Loretto Academy has become one of the city's leading and most promising institutions. The Sisters' chapel is much admired, being devotional and very artistic. The fourteen windows, representing mysteries in the life of Our Lord and His Blessed Mother, were made in Munich, and are works of art. They were donated by friends of the Society. The splendid *Pietà* which crowns the main altar is a gift from Miss May Curry, while many other donations to this sacred shrine have been made by well-remembered friends.

Wherever the Sisters of Loretto have established or conducted schools, whatever trials and hardships they have met with, they have always been assisted and encouraged by true friends and generous benefactors, towards whom they have ever cherished a deep sense of gratitude that prompted many fervent prayers. This sense of gratitude

223

springs instinctively from their devoted hearts, and they cherish it as a sacred duty because Father Nerinckx enjoined it as an obligation. In his own handwriting, they still preserve his precious memorandum:

"The Society, under the special protection of the Sorrowful Mother, has still a particular obligation, to pray for her benefactors as are those persons that any ways have assisted them in spirituals and temporals by prayers, advice, words, works, or goods or property of any description: of course, the head of the Church, their bishops and confessors, the persons that by subscription or other gifts and liberalities have laid claim to their pious remembrances! the Catholics of Flanders in Europe having a most eminent place amongst the benefactors of the Church in Kentucky in general, and more in particular of the Loretto Society, as well as their nice ornaments, chalices, &c., &c., come from their liberality, besides a smart support and provision for the houses, it will be nothing but justice to have their names on the records of the Society for everlasting remembrance of the religious liberality of the givers and for the constant gratitude of the receivers.

"The American benefactors and well-wishers ought not to be neglected: they were mostly living in the counties of Washington and Nelson, or rather the congregations of St. Charles, St. Ann, Holy Cross, and Holy Mary's."

True to the instructions of her founder, Loretto preserves the list he gave her, and has added to it until it has grown to a volume. It would be impossible to recount the notable favors from particular benefactors for whom she cherishes special remembrance. The Reverend Eugene O'Callaghan and his aged brother, Jerry O'Callaghan, Mr. J. M. Elder and a host of others whose gifts and services sustained them in many a trying hour; Monsignor Antonio Fourchegu and so many other priests whose self-denial and sacrifices have insured success in parochial schools where otherwise the Sisters would not have been

CHURCH OF OUR LADY OF DOLORS, LORETTO.

able to surmount the obstacles; and the bishops whose friendly interest and protection have been ever a shield and guide. For them all Loretto pays the tribute of her gratitude by invoking every day the blessing of God upon them. When for the welfare of the Society the mother general went to Rome she met kind friends and benefactors all along the way, as if sent by Providence to lead her step by step. Loretto holds each in grateful memory and loves to recall each token of kindness and friendly interest, but her heart throbs quicker at the names of the three illustrious Cardinals, Satolli, Martinelli and Falconio, successively Apostolic Delegates at Washington, for their vigilant protection and fatherly direction.

CHAPTER XVIII.

MEMORIALS OF FATHER NERINCKX.

WHEN April leads the year of 1912 up to the twenty-fifth day, a century shall have passed since Mary Rhodes, Christina Stuart and Nancy Havern, prostrate before the rude altar in the log church of St. Charles, promised God, in the presence of Father Nerinckx and his congregation, to renounce the world and devote themselves to the service of God in the religious state. From that solemn act sprang forth Loretto.

The marvelous changes in the world of men during these one hundred years are nowhere more marked than in our own country. When Loretto came into being the young Republic was engaged in an unequal struggle with Great Britain, and staggered from that conflict to find itself beset by Indian foes. Its sublime declaration of independence was then regarded as an experiment doomed to failure by the nations that to-day reckon nothing of world-wide interest without its counsel. In Kentucky the forests and the canebrakes have disappeared, with the wild beasts and savages they sheltered, and the ax and plow of civilization have converted the dark and bloody ground of the Indian into the beautiful land of the white man. Rich and populous cities have replaced the stockades, and stately homes the isolated hut of the more venturous frontiersman. Science has spanned her turbulent rivers, tunnelled her mountains, and brought forth her hidden minerals. Education assiduously cultivated has pointed the way to distinction for her sons and daughters in every rank of life.

From her historic height Loretto has witnessed the manifold changes at home and abroad, and experienced them within herself. In the great race she has maintained the

226

steady pace of the victor, and that without separating herself from that source of strength which alone can sustain unto the end. Faithful to the teachings of her holy founder, "Do not forsake Providence, and He will never forsake you," she has come up to the celebration of her century of life, crowned with honor and veneration, approved by God and man. Faithful to the memory of her founder, to whom, under God, she owes her existence, Loretto has treasured the tomb that encloses his mortal remains. From the day that strangers bore his dead body to the stricken little community of Bethlehem convent, in Perry County, Missouri, Loretto's reverence for Father Nerinckx has enlivened her devotion and strengthened her fidelity to the lessons he taught.

When the funeral obsequies were over and his body was buried in their convent graveyard at Bethlehem, the Sisters in reverence caused an appropriate tomb to be erected without delay. When nine years of entreaty finally obtained the consent of Bishop Rosati to the removal of the precious remains to Kentucky, a tomb was prepared in the cemetery at the Mother House, in which they were deposited December 16, 1833. Here novices in their first fervor, Sisters in trials or triumphs, and the aged in their patience, loved to pray; and as time's erosion wore the marble slabs, Loretto erected a new monument surmounted by the Calvary group, as a centennial tribute to her venerated founder.

Admirably appropriate was the choice of a Calvary group for the monument. His life had been spent in an effort to keep the image of Calvary before his people, he had chosen the foot of the cross for the dwelling-place of his little Society of "The Friends of Mary." He taught them to venerate St. John the Evangelist, whom the dying Jesus gave to His Blessed Mother, and to cherish devotion to the faithful few who at the Foot of the Cross gave untold comfort to the agonizing Saviour. He appointed the

227

Feasts of St. John, St. Mary Magdalen and St. Dismas as particular to the Society, that the Sisters of Loretto might ever feel more intimately associated with those who were at the Cross to the end under the special protection of "the Disciple whom Jesus loved."

The home of the Sisters of Loretto is on Calvary. Every hour of the day they must place themselves under the cross of Jesus and in compassion repeat, "O Suffering Jesus! O Sorrowful Mary!" But no stretch of the imagination is needed for this; they have not to go back through the centuries to stand by that cross, for the world of to-day is but Calvary two thousand years old. The same Victim offers Himself now as then, and uninterruptedly, from the rising until the setting of the sun, is the divine One crucified by sinners, so that the first Good Friday has never come to an end. It were a great honor to be called to serve on any part of that holy mount, but to be summoned to stand under the Cross with Mary! Oh, what a vocation! What a sanctuary! What a holy place to live! What a blessed place to die! Surely in such a place it is easy to carry out that part of the Rule which enjoins that, during silence, the Sisters shall hold converse with the Spouse of their hearts and make the "sufferings of Jesus and the sorrows of His Immaculate Mother the familiar subjects of their thoughts and affections;" surely it is no place for thought of self, where a God is immolating Himself; no place for disunion and uncharitableness, where a God is dying of love even for His executioners; no place for worldliness, for pride, where a God is drinking the dregs of humiliation; no place for love of pleasure and ease in presence of such agony of pain; no place for unforgiveness within hearing of those pleadings of the Divine Heart, "Father, forgive them, for they not what they do!" If these unworthy defects are sometimes found in Mary's children, it is because in a moment of weakness they forget whereon they stand. But love excites to action, and the Sisters of Loretto, hearing

the agonizing cry of Jesus, "I thirst," and the words of
their holy founder: "Gain souls, hunt souls, catch souls,
court souls, draw souls, carry souls, deliver souls, shelter
souls, buy souls! Souls! Souls! Nothing but souls, for
the love of Jesus, the owner of all souls!" are strengthened
to endure arduous labors in the education of youth, and,
following the example given them on that first Good Friday by their Sorrowful Mother, they plead especially for
those souls who are in their last agony. Like ministering
angels, the Sisters are in spirit at the squalid pallet of the
poor woman dying in lonely cabin, or by the luxuriant
couch of the agonizing King in his palace, by the poor
soldier who dies far away on the battlefield, as well as by
the child who is tenderly cared for in devoted home:—so
that no soul in agony, from the highest to the lowliest,
goes before the judgment seat of God without their assistance in that awful hour, and for this pleading the Sisters
choose a most propitious hour, the holy hour of "Three-in-
the evening," which wears a "crimson crown" and is
"Priest of the hours forever," the one which Jesus made
"His own last hour"—

> "O Heart of Three-in-the evening,
>   You nestled the thorn-crowned head
> He leaned on you in His sorrow,
>   And rested on you when dead."

The Calvary group upon his tomb makes doubly dear to
the Sisters the hallowed spot where the sacred remains of
their founder repose.

Excavations for the new monument revealed the vault
containing the hallowed remains. The vault was opened
and the bones reverently removed to the church, where the
Sisters rejoiced at the privilege of reciting the Community
prayers in presence of the precious relics. It was a stimulus to their devotion when they recalled to mind that it
was July 18, the anniversary of that July 18, 1805, when

Father Nerinckx arrived at this very place, the home of Father Badin. When the vault was repaired the sacred deposit was reverently replaced.

The beautiful monument, surmounted by the Calvary group, is a most appropriate expression of the sentiments of the Sisters for that hallowed spot. It stands majestic in height, inscribed at the base as follows:

In Memory of
Rev. Charles Nerinckx,
A Native of Flanders, who died August 12, 1824, in Missouri. His remains were translated to Kentucky, in 1833, by Brother Charles Gilbert, at the request of the Loretto Society, and interred at this place by Right Reverend Bishop Flaget and the Rev. G. I. Chabrat, Superior of the Society.

MR. NERINCKX

Came to Kentucky in 1805, and devoted himself zealously to that laborious mission, during which time he was nominated to the Diocese of New Orleans. But he refused that dignity, and, in 1812, he, with the approbation of the Holy See, instituted the Lorettines or Friends of Mary, and died in performing the visitation of the Order, at Ste. Genevieve, Missouri, aged sixty-three.

Loretto's Mite
of
Esteem and Veneration
For its Founder.

Do not forsake
Providence,
And He will never
forsake you   C. N.
230

MEMORIALS OF FATHER NERINCKX.

In front is a slab bearing the words:
Our Founder.
O Suffering Jesus! O Sorrowful Mary!

Graceful statues of angels on either side, with slabs in front, mark the graves, and are inscribed in memory of Mother Mary and Mother Ann, the first two superiors of the Society.

Located in the center of the cemetery, surrounded by the graves of so many faithful members of the Community, it is a scene that revives in the heart of every Sister of Loretto the tenderest sentiments of devotion to their founder, to the Rule he gave them and to the Society he established. It recalls to their minds his farewell letter and his tender exhortations summarized in the Morning Manna. The words of counsel with which he was wont to encourage and guide the first generous Sisters of Loretto, which they carefully garnered in their hearts and transmitted, still echo from his tomb with inspiring force and meaning:

"It is the will of God and the Blessed Virgin's pleasure that the Society should exist. Happy those souls that are in it, and happy those souls that may hereafter be good members of it, and again happy those souls that out of it have already passed the gates of eternal bliss!"

"If you all would be faithful to your God, be strict observers of your Rule, which He has given you. He will enable you to suffer for His sake whatever difficulties you may meet with. But if you are careless in the discharge of your duties, He will not assist you in affliction; neither can you expect Him to listen to your prayers, and the unfaithfulness and sloth of one may bring many to utter destruction. So I beg you for God's sake to be fervent in all things, consider the importance of your undertaking, the dignity of your vocation and Whom you are serving. Well, my children, God bless you!" And the Sisters of Loretto to-day are as prompt and generous to respond to

231

the counsels of their holy founder as were those who were privileged to receive them from his lips.

The Via Matris Dolorosæ erected along the avenue leading to the cemetery is peculiarly appropriate as a reminder of the favorite devotion of Father Nerinckx, which he bequeathed as characteristic of the Sisters of Loretto. The unique distinction of having the first Stations of the Seven Sorrows erected in statuary in America fittingly belongs to Loretto Mother House, and is much appreciated. It is the conception of Loretto's chaplain, the Reverend Edwin Drury. The Stations were canonically erected, with befitting ceremony, on the Feast of the Seven Dolors, September 17, 1911.

Another impressive reminder of the devotion in which his memory is cherished is the beautiful statue of Father Nerinckx, the gift of the Loretto Alumnæ Association. It was solemnly unveiled on June 15, 1910, in the presence of the Right Reverend Denis O'Donaghue, Bishop of Louisville, Very Reverend J. P. Cronin, V.G., many clergymen, and a large number of the Aumnæ and friends of Loretto. The good bishop expressed his great pleasure, and then introduced Very Reverend C. J. O'Connell, who delivered an eloquent panegyric. The poetic muse found voice in Mr. Thomas Walsh's rendition of his own very appropriate and beautiful poem.

With Father Nerinckx this volume began; with him let it close. Love for Jesus and Mary absorbed his being, and any devotion that would kindle a like affection in the hearts of his people he eagerly seized upon. He brought with him the devotion to the Sacred Heart, and preached of its saving power. He organized in 1809, in St. Charles' church, the first Society of the Holy Name in this country. With the vision of a man of God he anticipated many works whose value the present is but beginning to realize, and in the ever-widening circle of time it will become apparent to the many what was early recognized by the few, that one according to the heart of God walked this earth in the person of the humble Belgian priest.

To other hands we here resign this history of Loretto, whose next chapter will record the solemnity of her centennial celebration. What the future holds for her no man knows; as was her past, it shall be woven day by day, year by year, unto the end. This, however, we may expect: unto the end Loretto will abide in the spirit of her holy founder, unto the end his watchword will continue to be hers:

"For the love of Jesus and Mary,
For the good of my neighbor."

APPENDIX.

Ecclesiastical Superiors of Loretto.

1—Rev. Charles Nerinckx, Founder and Superior.........1812-24
2—Rev. Guy Ignatius Chabrat, Superior..................1824-34
3—Rev. Walter Coomes.....................................1834-35
4—Right Reverend G. I. Chabrat..........................1835-46
5—Rev. David A. Deparcq.................................1846-64
6—The Right Rev. Bishop of Louisville...................1864-69
7—Rev. Francis Wuyts.....................................1869-91
8—Very Rev. C. J. O'Connell.............................1891-95
9—Rev. Thomas F. Gambon.................................1895-96
10—Right Rev. Thomas S. Byrne...........................1896-98
11—Rev. Henry Westermann................................1898-01

Cardinal Protectors of Loretto.

1—His Eminence Francis Cardinal Satolli.................1908
2—His Eminence Sebastian Cardinal Martinelli...........1910

Mother Superiors of Loretto.

1—Ann Rhodes, by Election..............................1812
2—Mary Rhodes, by Election.............................1812-22
3—Juliana Wathen, by Election..........................1822-24
4—Isabella Clarke, by Election.........................1824-26
5—Sabina O'Brien, by Election..........................1826-32
6—Josephine Kelly, by Election.........................1832-38
7—Isabella Clarke, by Election.........................1838-42
8—Generose Mattingly, by Episcopal Appointment........1842-44
9—Berlindes Downs, by Episcopal Appointment...........1844-46
   Berlindes Downs, by Election.........................1846-52
10—Bridget Spalding, by Election.......................1852-58
11—Berlindes Downs, by Election........................1858-64
12—Bertha Bowles, by Election..........................1864-70
13—Elizabeth Hayden, by Election.......................1870-76
14—Dafrosa Smythe, by Election.........................1876-82
15—Ann Joseph Mattingly, by Election...................1882-88
16—Dafrosa Smythe, by Election.........................1888-93
17—Catherine Connor, by Election.......................1893-96
18—Praxedes Carty, by Episcopal Appointment............1896-98
   Praxedes Carty, by Election..........................1898-01
   Praxedes Carty, by Election..........................1901-04
   Praxedes Carty, by Election..........................1904-10
   Praxedes Carty, by Election..........................1910

234

APPENDIX.

FOUNDATIONS OF THE LORETTO SOCIETY CHRONOLOGICALLY ARRANGED.

1812—Loretto Mother House, St. Charles, Hardin's Creek, Ky.
1816—Calvary, Holy Mary's, on the Rolling Fork, Kentucky.
1818—Gethsemani, near Pottinger's Creek, Nelson County, Ky.
1819—Mount Mary's (now St. Mary's College), Kentucky.
1821—Bethania, near Fairfield, Nelson County, Ky.
1821—Jericho, Mechlin, Belgium.
1823—Mount Carmel, Breckinridge County, Ky.
1823—Bethlehem, Perry County, Mo.
1824—Mount Olivet, Casey County, Ky.
1824—The Negro Sisterhood, Loretto Mother House, Kentucky.
1825—La Fourche, Loretto Convent, Louisiana.
1829—Fairfield, Kentucky, St. Michael's Parochial School.
1830—Bethlehem Academy, Hardin County, Ky.
1831—Apple Creek, Perry County, Mo., St. Joseph's Parochial
       School.
1832—New Madrid, Mo., St. Mary's Convent.
1832—Fredericktown, Mo., St. Michael's Convent.
1833—Lebanon, Ky., Boarding and Day School.
1837—St. Genevieve, Mo., Our Lady of Mount Carmel.
1838—Pine Bluff, Arkansas, St. Mary's Convent.
1838—Cape Girardeau, Mo., St. Vincent's Academy.
1840—Loretto, Ky., Loretto Deaf and Dumb Asylum.
1841—Little Rock, Arkansas, St. Joseph's Convent.
1841—Cape Girardeau, Mo.. St. Vincent's Parochial School.
1842—Post Arkansas, St. Ambrose's Convent.
1842—Louisville, Ky., St. Benedict's Academy.
1847—Florissant, Mo., Loretto Academy.
1847—Osage Mission (St. Paul), Kansas, St. Ann's Academy.
1852—Santa Fé, New Mexico, Convent of Our Lady of Light.
1857—Louisville, Ky., Our Lady's School.
1862—St. Louis, Mo., St. Mary's Academy.
1863—Cairo, Illinois, St. Patrick's Parochial School.
1863—Daviess County, Ky., St. Joseph's Convent.
1863—Taos, New Mexico, Our Lady of Guadalupe Convent.
1864—Mora, New Mexico, Annunciation Academy.
1864—Denver, Colorado, St. Mary's Academy.
1864—Cairo, Illinois, St. Joseph's Academy.
1864—Lebanon, Ky., St. Augustine's Academy.
1865—Edina, Mo., St. Joseph's School.
1866—Albuquerque, New Mexico, Loretto Convent.

APPENDIX.

1867—Flint Island, Ky., St. Teresa's Convent.
1868—New Haven, Ky., St. Catherine's School.
1869—New Haven, Ky., School for Colored Children.
1869—Paris, Ky., St. Charles' School.
1869—St. Louis, Mo., St. Michael's School.
1869—Las Vegas, New Mexico, Immaculate Conception Academy.
1870—Las Cruces, New Mexico, Loretto Academy.
1870—Las Cruces, New Mexico, Parochial School.
1870—Elizabethtown, Ky., St. Mary's School.
1871—Louisville, Ky., St. Joseph's Parochial School.
1871—Louisville, Ky., Immaculate Conception School.
1871—St. Louis, Mo., Sacred Heart School.
1871—Denver, Colorado, Boys' School.
1872—Lebanon, Ky., School for Colored Children.
1873—Louisville, Ky., Sacred Heart School.
1873—Montgomery, Alabama, St. Mary of Loretto Academy.
1874—Cairo, Illinois, St. Joseph's Parochial School.
1874—Montgomery, Alabama, St. Peter's Parochial School.
1874—St. Louis, Mo., Loretto Academy.
1875—St. Louis, Mo., Old Cathedral Parochial School.
1875—Pueblo, Colorado, Loretto Academy.
1875—Earlington, Ky., St. Bernard School.
1875—Bernalillo, New Mexico, Indian Industrial School.
1875—Louisville, Ky., St. Bridget's School.
1876—St. Louis, Mo., Immaculate Conception (formerly St. Kevin)
        School.
1876—Las Vegas, New Mexico, Parochial School.
1877—Conejos, Colorado, Sacred Heart School.
1877—Moberly, Mo., St. Mary's Academy.
1878—Moberly, Mo., Boys' Parochial School.
1878—Raywick, Ky., St. Francis Xavier's School.
1878—Springfield, Mo., Loretto Academy.
1879—Socorro, New Mexico, Our Lady of Mt. Carmel.
1879—San Elzeario, Texas, St. Joseph's School.
1880—Springfield, Mo., Immaculate Conception School.
1880—Birmingham, Alabama, Holy Angels' Academy.
1881—Mora, New Mexico, Public School.
1882—Danville, Illinois, St. Patrick's School.
1882—Parsons, Kansas, St. Patrick's School.
1884—Marshall, Mo., St. Saviour's Academy.
1885—Colorado Springs, Colorado, Loretto Academy.
1886—St. Charles, Ky., St. Charles' Parochial School.
1886—Santa Fé, New Mexico, St. Catherine's School.
1886—St. Louis, Mo., Visitation School.
1886—Salinas, California, School of the Sacred Hearts.
1887—Florissant, Mo., St. Ferdinand's Parochial School.
1887—Springfield, Mo., Sacred Heart Parochial School.
1888—East St. Louis, Illinois, St. Patrick's School.

APPENDIX.

1888—Bernalillo, New Mexico, Public School.
1889—Kansas City, Mo., St. Patrick's School.
1890—Chicago, Ky., Santa Clara School.
1891—Loretto, Colorado, Loretto Heights Academy.
1892—El Paso, Texas, Loretto Academy.
1892—El Paso, Texas, Sacred Heart Parochial School.
1893—St. Charles, Mo., St. Charles Borromeo's School.
1894—Kansas City, Mo., Sacred Heart School.
1896—St. Louis, Mo., St. Edward's School.
1896—St. Louis, Mo., St. Rose's School.
1897—Lebanon, Ky., Boys' Parochial School.
1897—Loretto, Ky., Loretto Normal School.
1898—Webster Groves, Mo., Loretto Seminary.
1899—Normandy, Mo., St. Ann's School.
1899—Toronto, Ohio, St. Francis' School.
1899—David City, Nebraska, St. Mary's School.
1899—Flagstaff, Arizona, St. Anthony's School.
1900—Wellsville, Ohio, Immaculate Conception School.
1900—South Auburn, Nebraska, St. Joseph's School.
1901—Santa Fé, New Mexico, St. Francis' Parochial School.
1901—Kansas City, Mo., Loretto Academy.
1901—Huntsville, Alabama, Loretto Academy.
1901—Maysville, Ky., St. Patrick's School.
1902—Colorado Springs, Colorado, Parochial School.
1903—St. Louis, Mo., St. Cronan's School.
1903—El Paso, Texas, St. Mary's School.
1905—El Paso, Texas, St. Ignatius' School.
1906—St. Louis, Mo., St. Pius' School.
1906—Maplewood, Mo., Immaculate Conception School.
1906—Springfield, Mo., St. Agnes' School.
1907—Kansas City, Mo., Our Lady of Good Counsel.
1907—Bisbee, Arizona, Loretto School.
1910—East St. Louis, Illinois, St. Francis Regis' School.
1911—Denver, Colorado, St. Leo's Parochial School.

APPENDIX.

THE BEGINNING OF CALVARY (1816).

Sister Christina Stuart, second member of the Loretto Society, as superior of a colony of Sisters, opened school at Holy Mary's, June 10, 1816, in a house which had been prepared as a Widows' Home (the widows were to observe a modified form of the Loretto rule). It was at this place, on November 15, 1805, just one year after his arrival in America, that Father Nerinckx laid the corner-stone of Holy Mary's Church, the first of the dozen churches built by him in Kentucky. In 1823 Father Nerinckx built a new convent and chapel at Calvary, which cost him nearly $400; the Sisters moved into their new monastery, previously blessed, on the eve of Corpus Christi, May 28th.

Some time in the year 1820, three or four Sisters of Calvary were cutting wood, when a roebuck (chevreuil), pressed to extremity by dogs which were on the point of seizing it, fell almost dead at the Sisters' feet. They looked upon this as a merciful and tender dispensation of Providence, as on that very day they knew not whence they should obtain food for their next meal.

Calvary Convent, the eldest daughter of Loretto, followed the latter's custom in regard to the tuition fees to be received from the pupils. The following were the requisites:

"Provisions to be brought in by pupils: 100 wt. good Bacon; 10 lbs. Sugar; 10 lbs. Coffee; 5 bushels Potatoes; 5 bushels Meal; 100 wt. Flour; 5 lbs. Tallow; 20 lbs. Lard.

APPENDIX.

ITEMS FROM CALVARY'S FINANCIAL RECORDS (1823).

1823	$	s.	d.
Jan. 2—Received of Mr. Bernard Abell for spinning, 139 wt. of pork, at 4$ per hundred................ and 9 gallons of soap at 6 pence per pint.	5	3	4¼
Received of Mr. Aaron Spalding, for his daughter and grandaughter's schooling, in shoe-maker's work	3	0	9
Received of Mr. Basil Hayden, for his daughter's schooling, 200 wt. of flour at 9s per 100........	3	0	0
and 2 dutch-ovens & lids, 21s each...........	7	0	0
Received of Mrs. Ann Raley, for spinning, 48 pounds of bacon, at 4½ pence per lb..........	3	0	0
and one bushel of salt..........................	1	4	0
Received of Mr. Joseph Spalding, for his daughter's schooling, some leather..................	2	0	0
Received of Mr. James Elder, for spinning, 17 lbs. Tallow, at 9 pence per pound.............	2	0	0
Paid for 12 tin cups.............................	2	0	0
Paid for 1 axe...................................	3	0	0
Paid for 2 hoes..................................	2	4	6
Paid for the making of 6 pairs of shoes for the family at Gethsemani, at 3s per pair..........	3	0	0

APPENDIX.

GOD'S ENVOY.

Read by Thomas Walsh, Esq., at the Unveiling of Nerinckx
Memorial, June 15, 1910.

O Saintly Priest of blessed memory,
Bright envoy of God's kingdom, thou art throned
In glory, strength and power. Thou art crowned
With holiness and beauty, like the stars
Of midnight in the heavens. Thou art robed
In garments whiter than the snow that drifts
Across the hills at sunset. Thou art blest,
And seated with the Ancients that bow down
Before the Everlasting. Thy renown
Increases with the years, and fills the land
With legends of thy sanctity, and deeds,
And works of mercy.

           Thou wert sent,
A shepherd in wastelands to reclaim
The wandering fold from pitfall, flood and fell,
To flowery meadows and refreshing shade,
Beside the waters of eternal life,
In vales of Paradise. Thou wert sent,
A flaming torch of splendor through the mists,
And darkness of the wilderness, to bear
God's message to His people. Thousands heard
Thy voice within the wilderness, and saw
The light that led them to the gates of Heaven.

           Calm and bright,
And joyous as the light of setting suns,
Thy glory shines upon us from the past,
Reflected in the splendor of thy toil,
Performed in His name. Thy labors done,
And work well finished thou wert summoned home
To rest within the beauty of God's house,
Wherein His glory dwelleth. From thy home
Of everlasting joy beyond the stars,
And sweet, eternal rest, we call on thee;
Remember us this day in Paradise,
And bless thy children in this holy place.

                    THOMAS WALSH.

APPENDIX.

Lines written on the occasion of the Diamond Memorial of the Loretto Society, and dedicated respectfully to the Sisters and pupils of St. Mary's Academy, Denver, Colorado.

By Reverend M. Carmody, Central City, Colorado.

I.

A fair new land lay 'neath the western sun;
A land of beauty rare and promise grand;
Nor fabled Ormus, nor the wealth of Ind,
Could match this treasure, which, with lavish hand,
Nature had dowered her: great Jehovah's wand
Had waved, resistless, o'er her sleeping bed;
And, at the Arch-Enchanter's stern command,
Columbia raised her fair, majestic hand
And gazed on lake and mount and plain in peerless beauty spread.

No fairer scene had 'raptured human eye
Since the great Artist limned creation's halls;
No richer pearl had Nature's palace decked
Since Nature's Author reared her golden walls;
For one bright gem Columbia vainly calls;
And naught 'vails Nature's wealth, though spendthrift-given,
And naught but ill a nation's course befalls
When, like a bark unanchored, tempest driven,
She lacks the shining beacon-light that points the way to Heaven;

Perfect religious life; a chosen few
To point the destined goal and lead the way;
To glorify humanity, and shed
On feeble womanhood God's choicest ray.
Old Europe reigned o'er these with potent sway,
And to the young Columbia proudly turned,
With radiant youth and glittering jewels gay,
And while her conscious face with blushes burned,
Her newer rival fiercely thus with haughty glance she spurned:

"Proud Sybarite, you boast of lands and gold,
Where are your altars with burnt offerings sweet?
Your countless subjects from my courts you've won,
Like mushroom rank sprung from the rich oak's feet;
For you to babble boastings now, indeed, 'twere meet!
Know you the saintly crown that erst I wore,
When you were yet a silent, sad retreat,
And naught disturbed the weight of gloom you bore
Save Jove's all-deaf'ning thunder crash and ocean's maddening
    roar?

APPENDIX.

"Gaze on my thousand cloistered holy fanes,
Where Godlike sacrifice for men doth dwell;
Behold my myriad throngs of saints in flesh,
Who Christ's great love to suffering mortals tell;
No band of holy women hast thou borne,
Who may in future works thy praises swell,
When thou shalt be of false luxuriance shorn,
The Niobe of nations, God abandoned and forlorn;

"For this, Columbia, shalt thou fade and die.
I see thy greatness crumble into dust;
I see thy palaces and temples proud
Thy regal monuments and halls accurst,
Thy splendid courts all stained with crime and lust,
Thy goddess science and thy genius grand,
All, all, swept from thy grasp by one fell gust,
A lightning stroke, a desolating brand,
A fierce simoon, Nemesis dire, runs riot o'er thy land."

II.

In Heaven's court is loud and long acclaim
In praise of Mary's spotless virgin name.
The silvery bells are ringing,
The perfumed censers swinging,
The choir of angels singing
    A Gloria to their Queen;
While troops with white wings glancing
And form and grace entrancing,
With rescued souls, advancing
From every clime are seen;

From Europe's highly favored lands,
From Asia's vales, from Afric's sands,
In glorious file they came,
Each bearing on a fillet bound
Close to the head, in circlet round,
A scroll with Mary's name.
And as they kneel in awe profound,
While high the roofs resound,
The heralds loud proclaim:

"These are thy subjects, gracious Queen,
Wrested from sin and shame
By faithful subjects, who for thee
Have kept their souls from blame,
And bade adieu, for thy sweet sake,
To rank and wealth and fame."

242

APPENDIX.

"But one fair land," the Queen replies,
"Hath yielded me no spoil;
Beneath Columbia's lovely skies
Have I no saints to toil?"

"Alas, fair Queen, no noble band
Hath yet enrolled in that fair land."
"This must not be," the Virgin said;
"Bring hither to my throne
Some chosen spirits from that clime
Which yet my power must own."
Forthwith they came, and, bowing low,
Waited the Queen's behests to know.
"Know ye, my children, in that broad, fair land
Where ye as exiles once did bide a time
Some holy soul, prepared at my command,
A chosen troupe to guard from sin and crime,
To follow Him the thorny way who trod
And lead Columbia's daughters up to God?"
"Fair liege, there is a holy man and just
Living obscure within our country's bounds,
Living in fear of God and humble trust
In thee, whose lofty praise he daily sounds,
A Christlike oblate priest, whose only zeal
Burns for his neighbors' good, his country's weal."

Swift as the lurid lightning flash across the vaulted skies
A winged messenger shoots forth and to Columbia flies.

The courts of heaven again resound with praise,
When back this angelic Mercury cleaves his way,
A new religious order dates its birth,
And Mary's choirs triumphant chant its lay;
The name of "Nerinckx" thrills the proud array,
And on a banner borne by angels bright,
All clad in purest white, fulgent as day,
On burnished silvery scroll, dazzling the sight,
The word "Loretto" flashing shines, a blaze of living light.
O happy band! Saint-nurtured, God-elect!
On this grand feast, this Diamond-tipped bright day,
Memorial of that natural time in Heaven,
All fruit and blessings on your work we pray!
Another patron smiles on you to-day;
For surely when his body prostrate lies,
After long life in years and service gray,
The name of Machebeuf shall with Nerinckx strive,
And both the crown of merit claim, and both divide the prize.

243

APPENDIX.

SEDET MATER GLORIOSA.

"Juxta Thronum sedet Mater ejus."

Sedet Mater Gloriosa
Juxta thronum speciosa
  In quo sedet Filius.
Cujus animam beatam
Super stellas elevatam
  Solis implet radius.

O quam læta et formosa
Est nunc illa luminosa
  Mater Unigeniti.
Quæ lætatur et miratur
Et exultant dum spectatur
  Nati decor inclyti;

Quis est homo qui videret
Christi Matrem, nec gauderet
  Tanto Matris jubilo?
Quis posset non collætari
Piam Matrem contemplari
  Gaudentem cum Filio?

Nati corpus immortale
Supra mortem triumphale
  Videt plenum gloriæ:
Videt suum dulcem natum
Trinitatis collocatum
  Solio Sanctissimæ.

Eja Mater fons amoris
Me sentire vim ardoris
  Fac ut tecum gaudeam:
Fac ut ardeat cor meum
In amando Christum Deum
  Ut ei complaceam.

Sancta Mater! istud agas
Resurgentis fige plagas
  Cordi meo valide
Tui Nati refulgentis
Patris ad dextram sedentis
  Decus mecum divide.

244

APPENDIX.

Fac me tecum exultare
Gloriosum adamare
  Natum donec vixero:
Juxta thronum te videre
Semper juxta te manere
In Cœlis desidero.

Virgo virginum præclara
Mihi dulcis et perchara
  Fiam gratior Tibi!
Fac me Christum cogitare,
Mente juxta thronum stare,
  Vos audire colloqui.

Fac me plagis vulnerari,
Et amore conflagrari
  Qui pellit formidinem:
Sic crematus et accensus
Et per Virginem defensus
  Non timebo judicem:

Fac me sub throno crescere,
Virtute invalescere
  Confoveri gratia:
Quando corpus morietur
Fac ut animæ donetur
  Sedes Tibi proxima.
          Amen.
                  Francis Wuyts.

September 30, 1887.

APPENDIX.

REVEREND CHARLES NERINCKX.

When Revolution smote the face of France
And Peace retired with sad and tearful glance,
Bold Reason by the rabble was enthroned,
Religion could no more be safely owned.
God's ministers were mocked at and reviled,
Sent to the guillotine or hopelessly exiled;
Religious rites foul treason were pronounced,
Godfearing men as traitors were denounced.
Poor France! to turn from God in such an hour,
When most she needed His protecting power!
In such times Nerinckx lived. His Flemish home
With French restrictions hateful had become,
And he, but late anointed, felt his heart
With zeal and indignation rent apart.
His eyes across the trackless ocean turned
To free America—for souls he yearned,
Here souls, he knew, were famishing and sore
And he could give them bread. He sought our shore.

What was Kentucky in that early time?
'Neath Nature's smile indeed a favored clime;
But few were here who worshipped Nature's God,
And asked a blessing on the virgin sod.
Wide spread the oak boughs on the sloping hill,
From springs like crystal trickled many a rill,
Low willow branches drooped o'er glassy streams,
And sweetest wild flowers drank the morning beams.
Gay woodland choirs, untutored, sang God's praise;
Forests more frequent were than fields of maize.
These noble hills stretched upward to the skies,
Silent and sad, tho' crowned with sunset dyes;
For ah! beneath the chestnut's leafy shade
The Indian wigwam frequently was made,
And forth the warrior stole as evening fell
To slay the pale face in the verdant dell.
The poisoned shaft and tomahawk were sent
To those who sought their homes in sweet content.
And men who looked to pass a peaceful night
Awoke ere morn in terror and affright.
Men, from afar, such gloomy prospects found
They called this spot the "Dark and Bloody Ground."

But Nerinckx came, with prayerful love and hope,
To cheer and bless. Scarce other tongue he spoke

246

VIA MATRIS DOLOROSÆ, LORETTO.

APPENDIX.

As yet but those of Fatherland and Church,
So eager he for straying souls to search
He could not linger, and God blessed each word,
Men understood, and felt their bosom stirred.
Were not sweet angel faces hovering near
When that lone horseman slowly did appear,
Weary and travel-stained? Yea, Heaven was glad;
No longer should these hills be dark or sad.
By yon small dwelling, with a heaving breast,
Badin spoke welcome to his holy guest;
And as they prayed, united heart and hand,
A blessing fell upon the darksome land.
Years onward sped, of unexampled toil,
Hearts harder seeming than the rocky soil,
But still this giant labored, waited, prayed,
For God he worked—he would not be dismayed.
And soon the struggling pioneer looked up and smiled
To hear sweet church bells echoing thro' the wild.
Men's hearts were touched; remembering home and youth,
With eager steps they thronged to hear God's truth.
The missionary traveled far and wide,
To seek his flock by stream, on mountain side;
Of all the good accomplished no man knows,
His deeds were those the angel's record shows.
He made no laws; 'twas not for that he came,
Nor founded cities burdened with his name;
But temples rose, while sound of hymn and prayer
Was wafted on the misty, incensed air.
While Europe heard Napoleon's blast of war,
While Nelson laurels won at Trafalgar,
When Austerlitz made France forget her loss,
On Western hills brave Nerinckx reared the cross.
He worked for Heaven, so Heaven is his reward,
Yet left on earth one trophy to his Lord,
Loretto is his monument; but see!
'Tis living—spreading like the mustard tree.
Yonder sweet blossoms nod above his breast,
Fitly upon this spot his relics rest,
Near old St. Stephen's—first Kentucky Home—
Now as Loretto well and widely known.
Fair to his eyes, e'en eyes in Heaven that dwell,
Must be the changing scene, as ringing bell
From labor to some sacred duty calls
The gentle inmates of these humble walls;
To youthful eyes doth science here unfold
Her many vistas; youthful hearts are told
The higher aims of life; taught quick to turn
From Folly's shrine, her gilded prize to spurn.

APPENDIX.

Forth to the world Loretto's daughters go
To fight, with feeble arms, the unseen foe;
And their young charges—each year swells the throng—
Go forth likewise, the good work to prolong.
When ev'ning's length'ning shadows veil the day,
And Pleasure to the world chants syren lay,
Loretto's hymn floats upward clear and sweet
From pure hearts gathered round the Saviour's feet,
"Shield thou from harm, O Mother bright,
Thy children shield till dawning light."
Nerinckx is seated now mid victor throngs,
Unhurt by earthly miseries and wrongs,
His apostolic heart with love still burns
For us, his people, e'en in bliss he yearns.
Marion, thou art happy to have been his choice,
Blest wilderness, where cried the prophet's voice,
"Make straight His paths, be crooked ways made plain;"
O Marion, cried that prophet's voice in vain?

SISTER M. WILFRID LAMOTTE.

APPENDIX.

REVEREND CHARLES NERINCKX.

(On the occasion of Unveiling of His Statue, June 15, 1910, at
Loretto Mother House, Kentucky.)

Long cherished, tho' at first as in a dream,
  To-day we see the noble figure rise,
As if an angel-sculptor, choice of theme,
  Had brought a spotless image from the skies
And placed it here. Loretto hails with joy
  Her Founder, carved in effigy of stone,
And blesses those who means and gifts employ
  So fitly thus true virtue to enthrone.

These same green hills in majesty around
  Once saw a weary pilgrim from the East,
When first his steps, with reverence profound,
  Turned toward Kentucky's lonely mission priest.
Two men, whose hearts no fire owned save zeal,
  Clasped hands, with feeling each had found a friend;
The joy of Badin tears and smiles reveal,
  His work will now continue to the end.

Good Nerinckx came to stay. The savage wild,
  Discomforts, loneliness, ingratitude,
Could not discourage one who, like a child,
  Put trust in Providence for all things good.
Nought but stern persecution could deter,
  This man of God from walking fearless on,
Only when friends turned false did he infer
  The Holy Will decreed he must be gone.

Heart-sick, yet zealous still, he crossed the stream,
  Choosing Missouri for new field of toil,
The Indian missions never left his dream,
  He might soon reach them on some western soil.
But God was satisfied. His course was run;
  Lo! as he journeyed Death a summons spoke,
The labors nineteen years ago begun
  Were ended now; the chain of life now broke.

Forgotten he is not, this morn hath proved;
  Fame born of self-denial does not die;
And Nerinckx' name is honored now and loved
  Where once he labored for reward on high.

APPENDIX.

It may be in that Heaven of blissful peace
  This scene he is permitted to review;
And make petition for a rich increase
  Of blessings on Loretto old and new.

All those who call him father do rejoice
  With that deep inward thrill hearts rarely know,
That speaking countenance needs but a voice,
  Loretto understands and feels the glow
Of tidings from the past. Like star of night
  Came Nerinckx to the clouded skies of yore,
Religious atmosphere, long softly bright,
  Grows brilliant with his figure at the door.

Sister M. Wilfrid LaMotte.

CONVENT CEMETERY, LORETTO.

FATHER WUYTS AND JOHN MORGAN.

Founded on Fact.

Of old war stories there are not few,
But we shall try to offer something new;
Back to the sixties let us go again,
For some event that was soul-stirring then.
The scene at Holy Cross now shall be laid,
Where quiet dramas sometimes have been played;
A local interest thus may catch your ear,
If other merit none my tale shall wear.
Well, it was sixties, as I said before,
A time when our great Nation's heart was sore.
At Holy Cross had been a mission preached,
As if no war news that calm nook had reached.
There Wuyts and Smarius bravely held the fort
And battled foes of quite a different sort
From gallant blue and gray clad soldier boys,
Who filled the outside world with martial noise.
They fought for souls, and the good country folk
Of that sequestered parish scarcely spoke
Of war at all; while on the mission ran
Its holy way through full a week's round span.
One night, when all was sweetly calm and still,
A sound rose faintly o'er the nearest hill—
A sound of horsemen with a wearied tread,
At such a time awakening general dread.
The parsonage soon filled with a fierce band,
A motley crowd, with sword and gun in hand,
While he called leader—Morgan was his name—
Came boldly forth a lodging place to claim.
The priest and captain matched undaunted eyes,
In gaze of each upleaped a faint surprise,
Then, with a chuckling laugh that always won,
Good Father Wuyts said softly, "Hello, John!"
John Morgan for a moment could not speak,
The cleric's coolness made the raider weak,
Tho' weak indeed was he from lack of rest,
Which wakened pity in the churchman's breast.
"I *am* John Morgan, howsoe'er *you* know,
And, with my men, am fleeing from the foe.
In hot pursuit were they till darkness fell,
And mind, Sir Priest, if you but dare to tell
We're lodging here, I'll—" "Tut, tut, man, threats to me
Are shust like water—thrown away, you see,

251

APPENDIX.

Now eat your supper, then you sleep till dawn,
I'll tell you've lodged here ven I'm sure you're gone."
Hard Morgan's mouth relaxed, and with a smile
He bade his comrades eat, then sleep awhile;
Not e'en Loretto saw more calm a night,
Till eastern skies showed bars of rosy light.
The raider and his men prepared with haste
To leave a spot where soon they must be traced;
To Wuyts low bowed the dreaded bandit chief
In thanks most earnest, tho' his words were brief.
"Some here among my men are of your faith,
And believe both soul and body free from scathe
If they the Virgin's medal do but wear.
Now have you any? We should like to share."
"I've plenty, sir, you're welcome to all these,"
The priest replied, "I'm glad your men to please."
While from his heart went up a fervent prayer
That Mary would of their wild lives have care.
The medals with the image we all know,
In mantle draped and peerless brow of snow,
Were handed round, and these grim warriors smiled
To hold a badge of Heaven's Lady mild,
Whose name, perchance, learned at a mother's knee,
Aroused their souls from dangerous lethargy.
Off rode the band; its fate few men can tell,
Yet do we hope most in the end fared well,
For none who wear our Mother's badge with love
Will fail in life or death her power to prove.
A few hours later people knelt in prayer,
Nor dreamed whose footsteps lately halted there.

SISTER M. WILFRID LaMOTTE.

THE MEANY PRINTING CO., NEW YORK